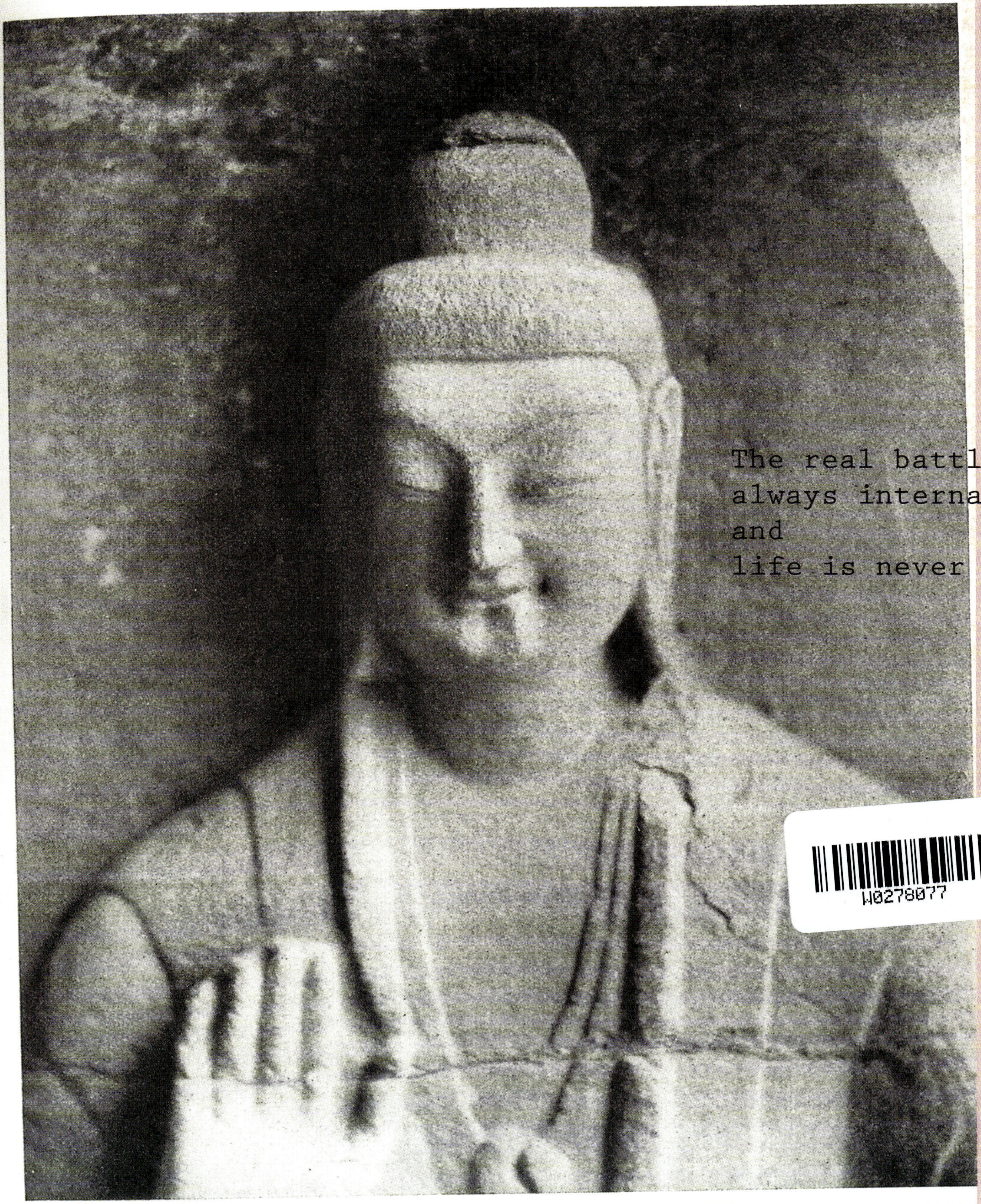

The real battle is
always internal
and
life is never that easy

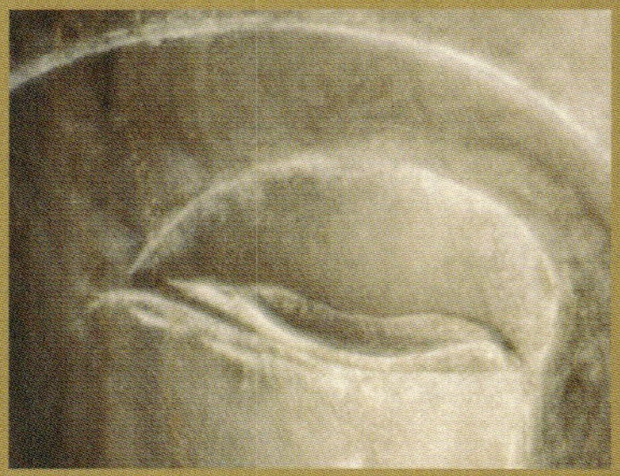

AND IS NOT TIME EVEN AS LOVE IS,
UNDIVIDED AND PACELESS ?

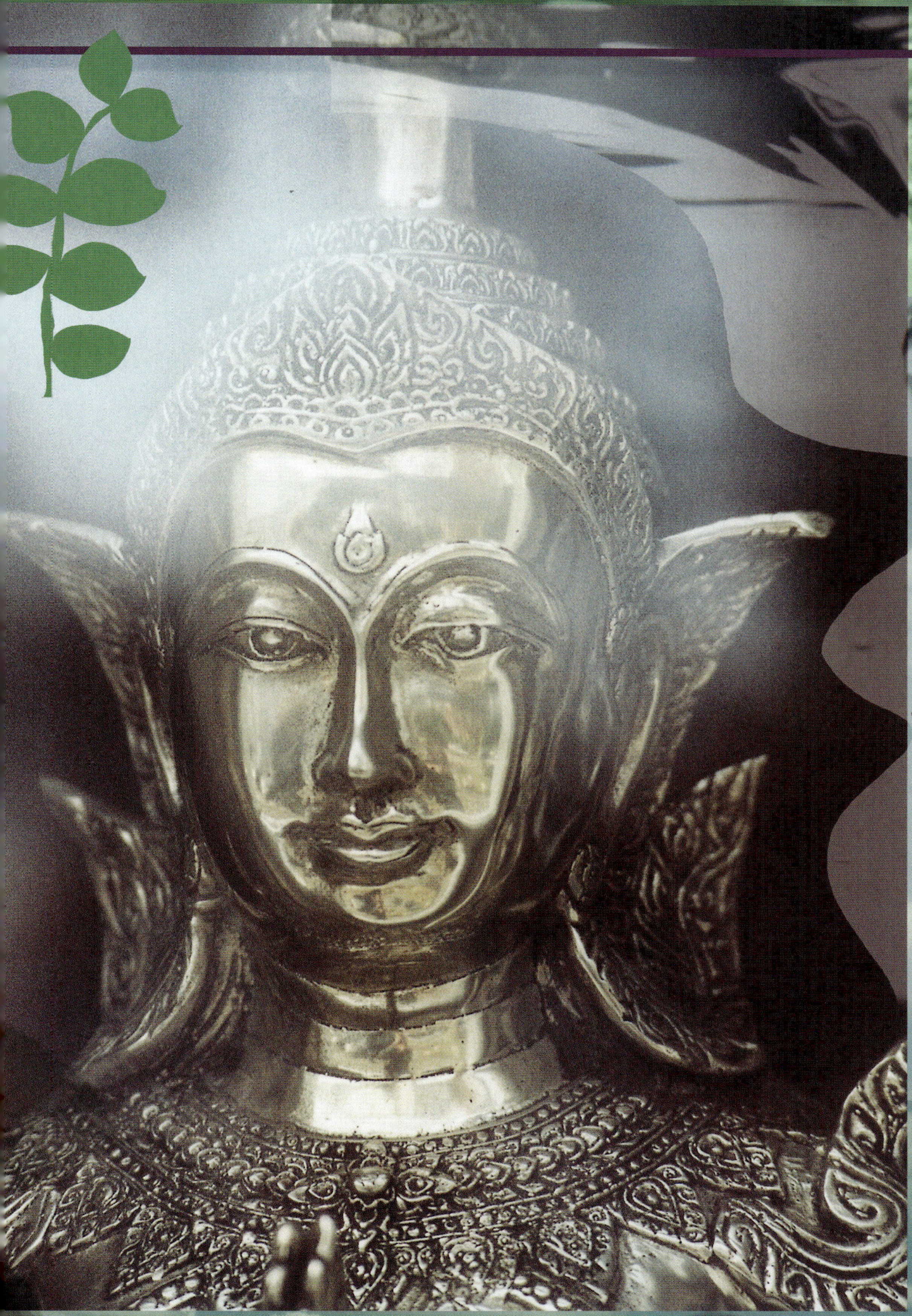

This is an invitation to
make a journey into a
dream world:
limitless, timeless and
without boundaries.
The music makes
the travellers
ease their minds
and wander
through a kaleidoscope
of images and
words.

Text freely cited from the BAHAVAD GITA with the exception of „Children“ by Khalil Gibran

ISBN 3-937406-14-X

Concept, Art Direction and Design by marlo
For more information contact info@marlo-arts.de

Produced by optimal MEDIA PRODUCTION Röbel/Germany

Printed and manufactured in Germany

EarBooks is a project of edel CLASSICS

For more information please visit our website **www.earbooks.net**

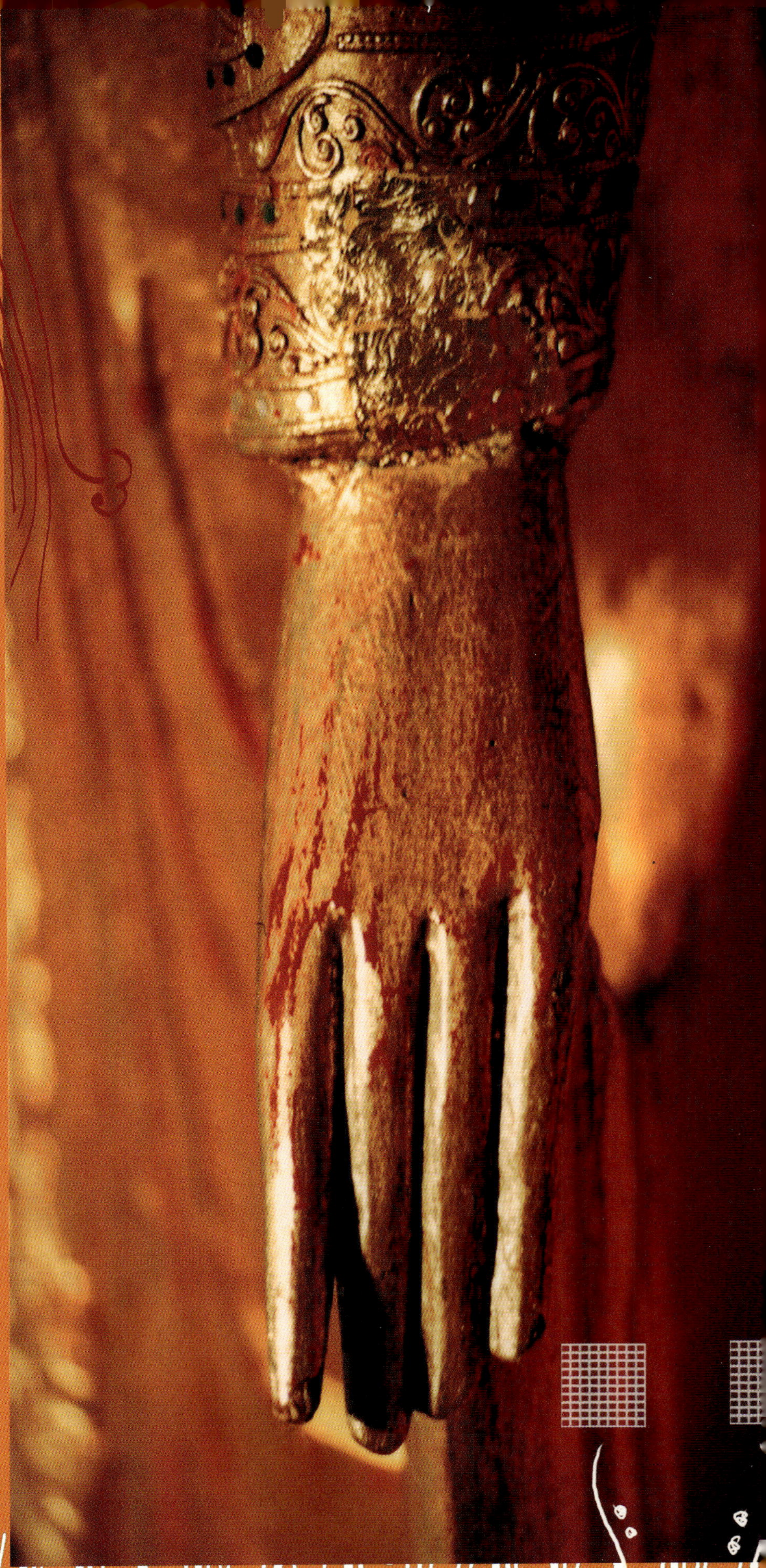

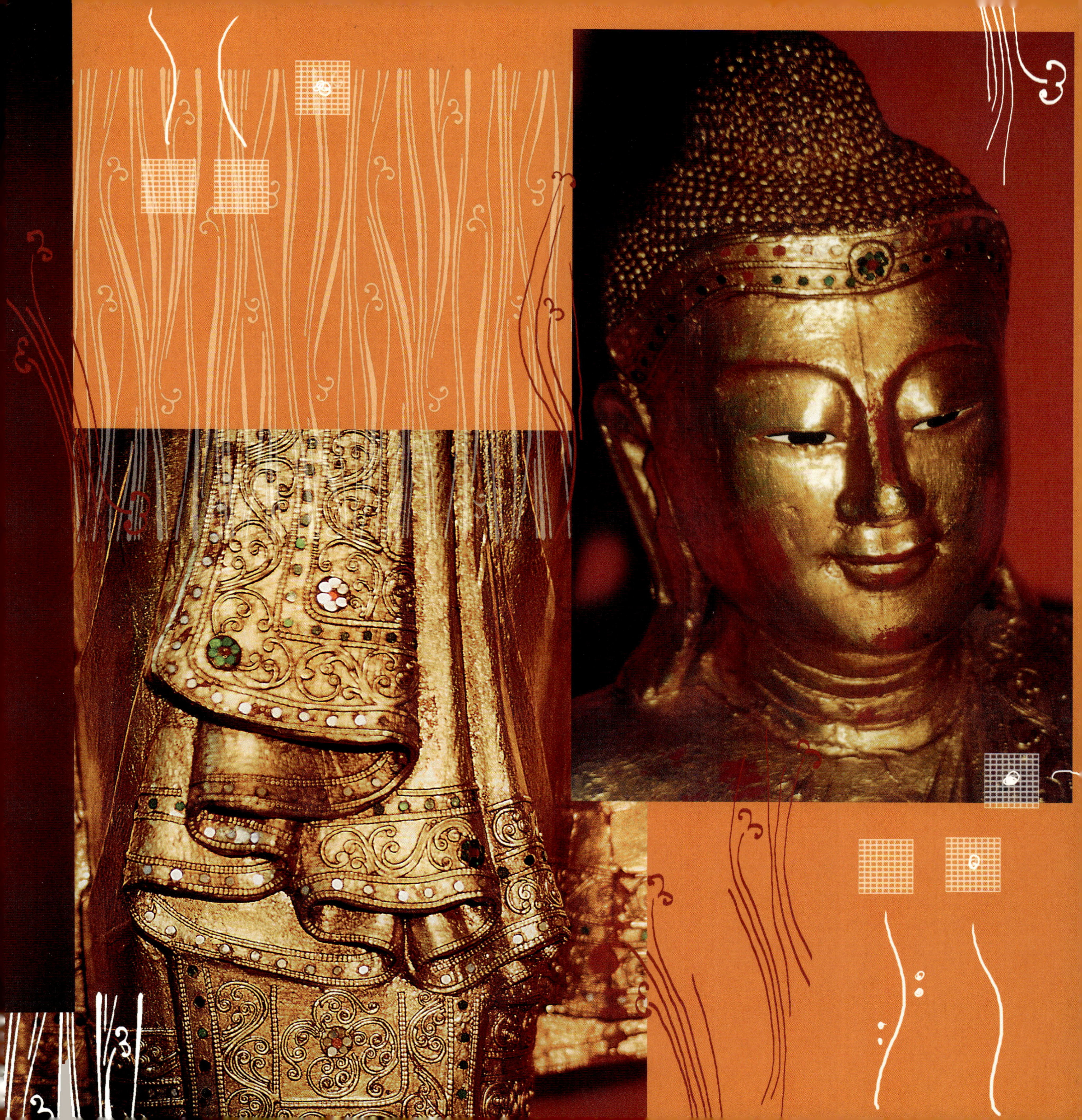

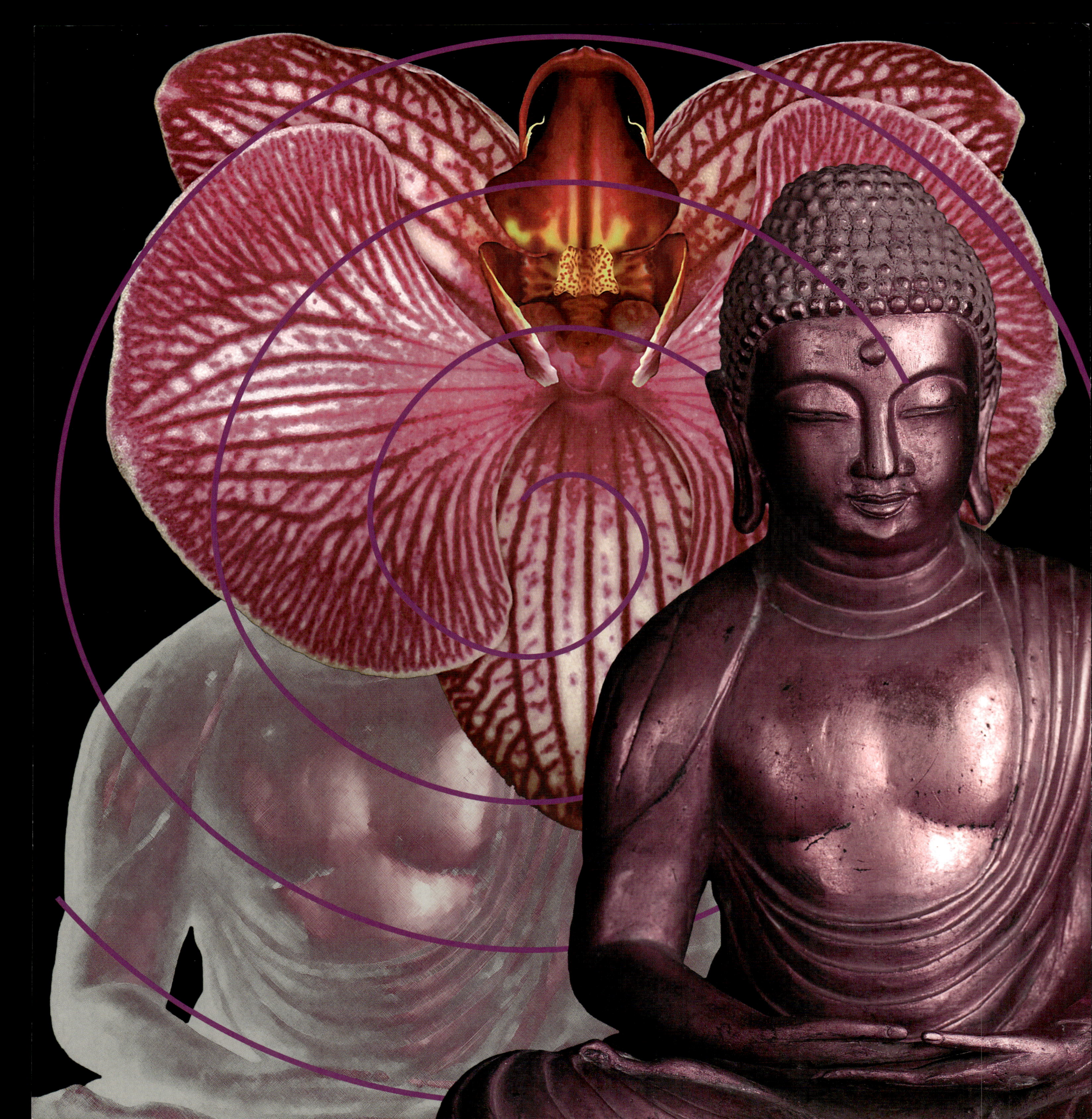

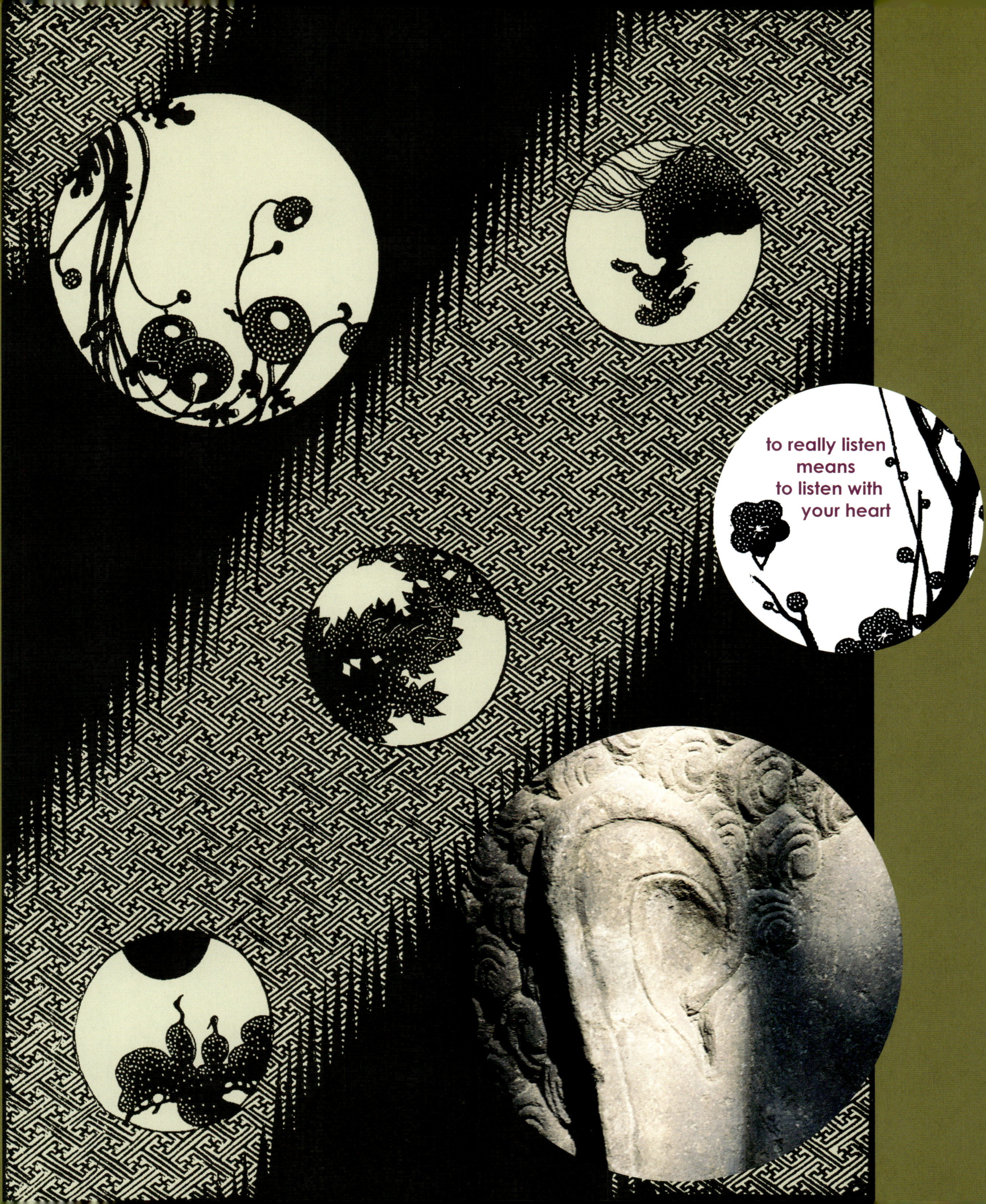
to really listen
means
to listen with
your heart

instead of looking for immediate happiness

have confidence in your own nature

your courage will grow wit

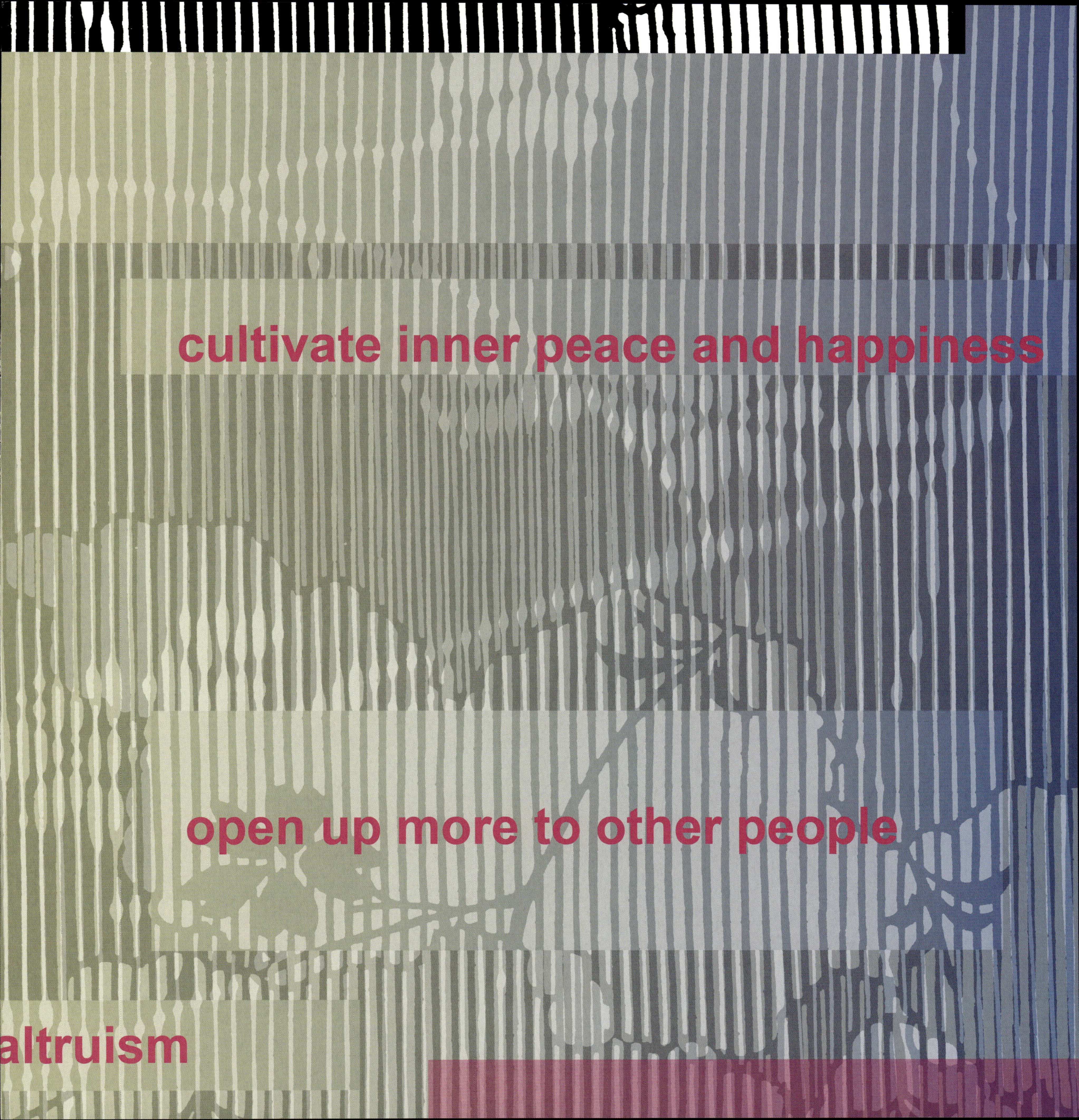
cultivate inner peace and happiness
open up more to other people
altruism

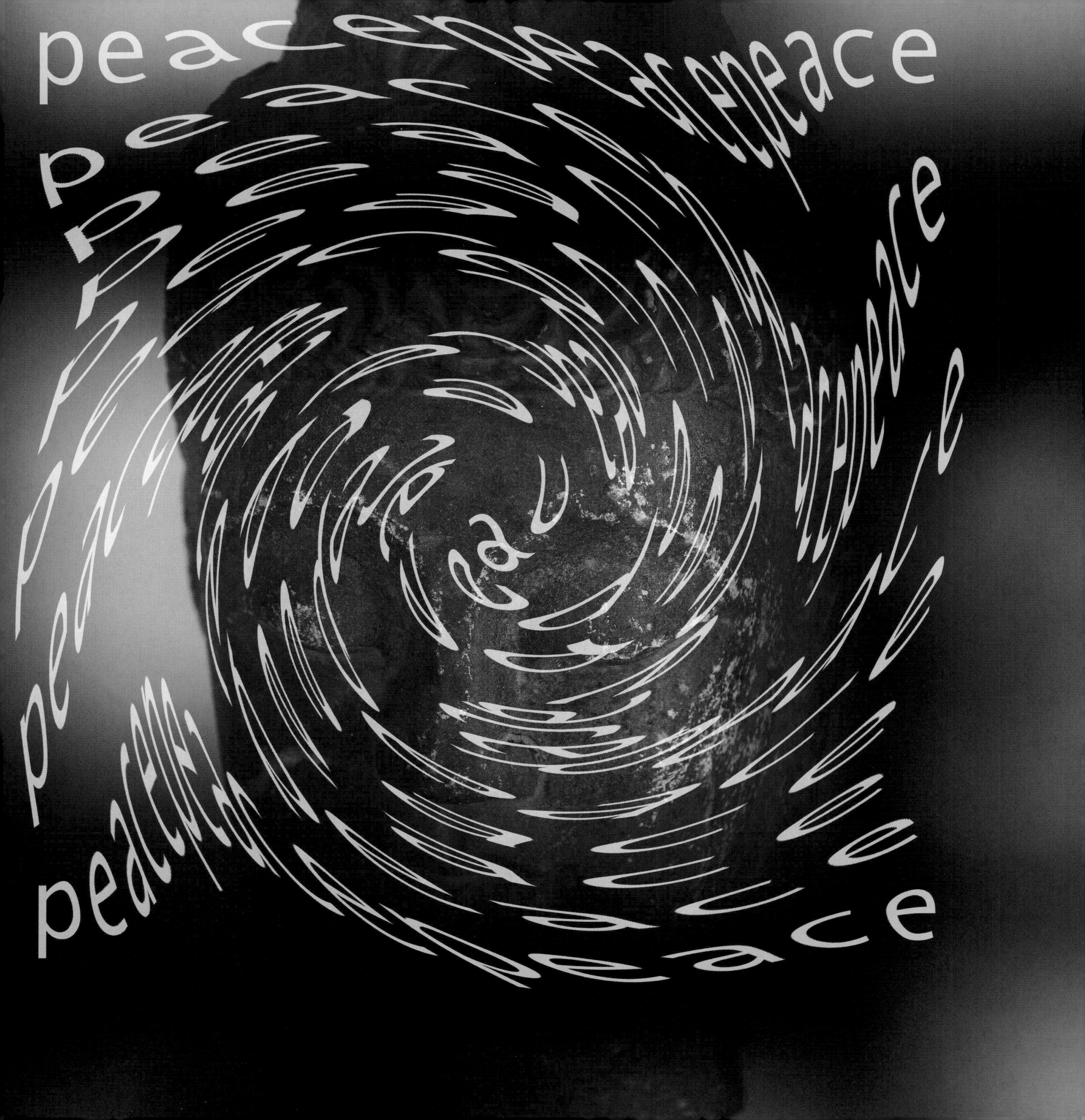
peace
peace
peace
peace

children
give them your love but not your thoughts

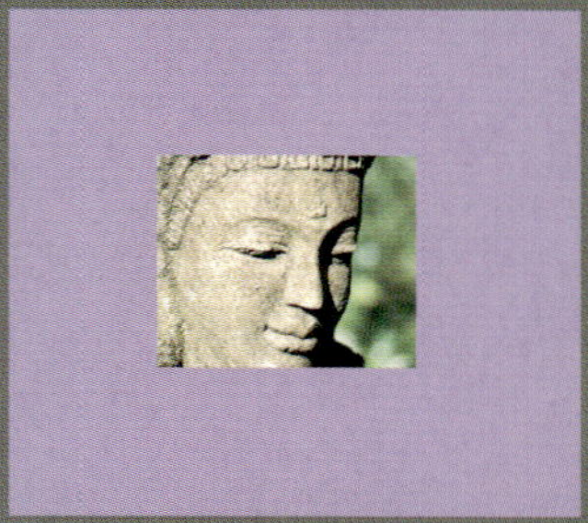

for they have their own thoughts
you may house their bodies
but not their souls
you may strive to be like them
but do not try to make them like you

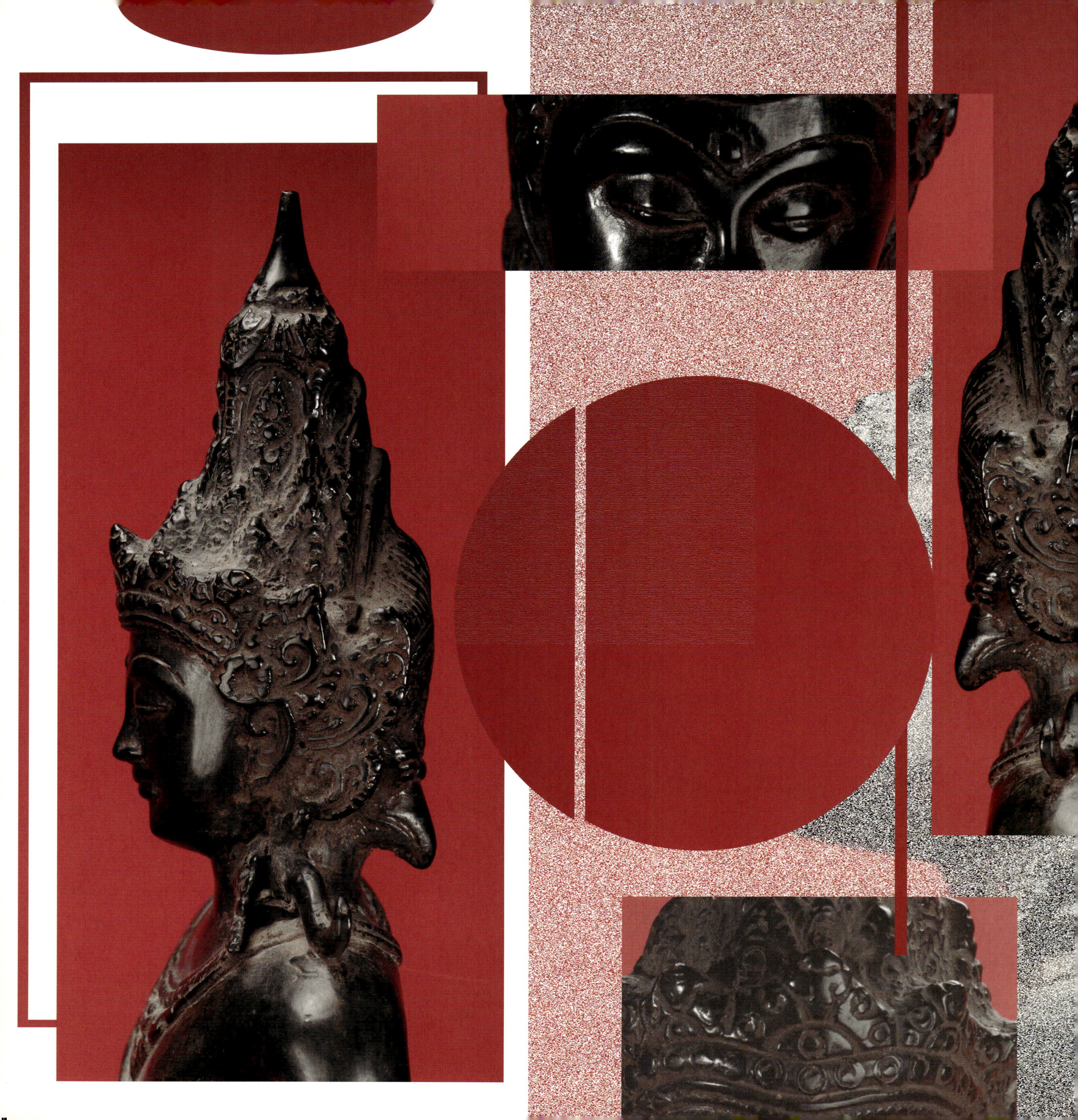

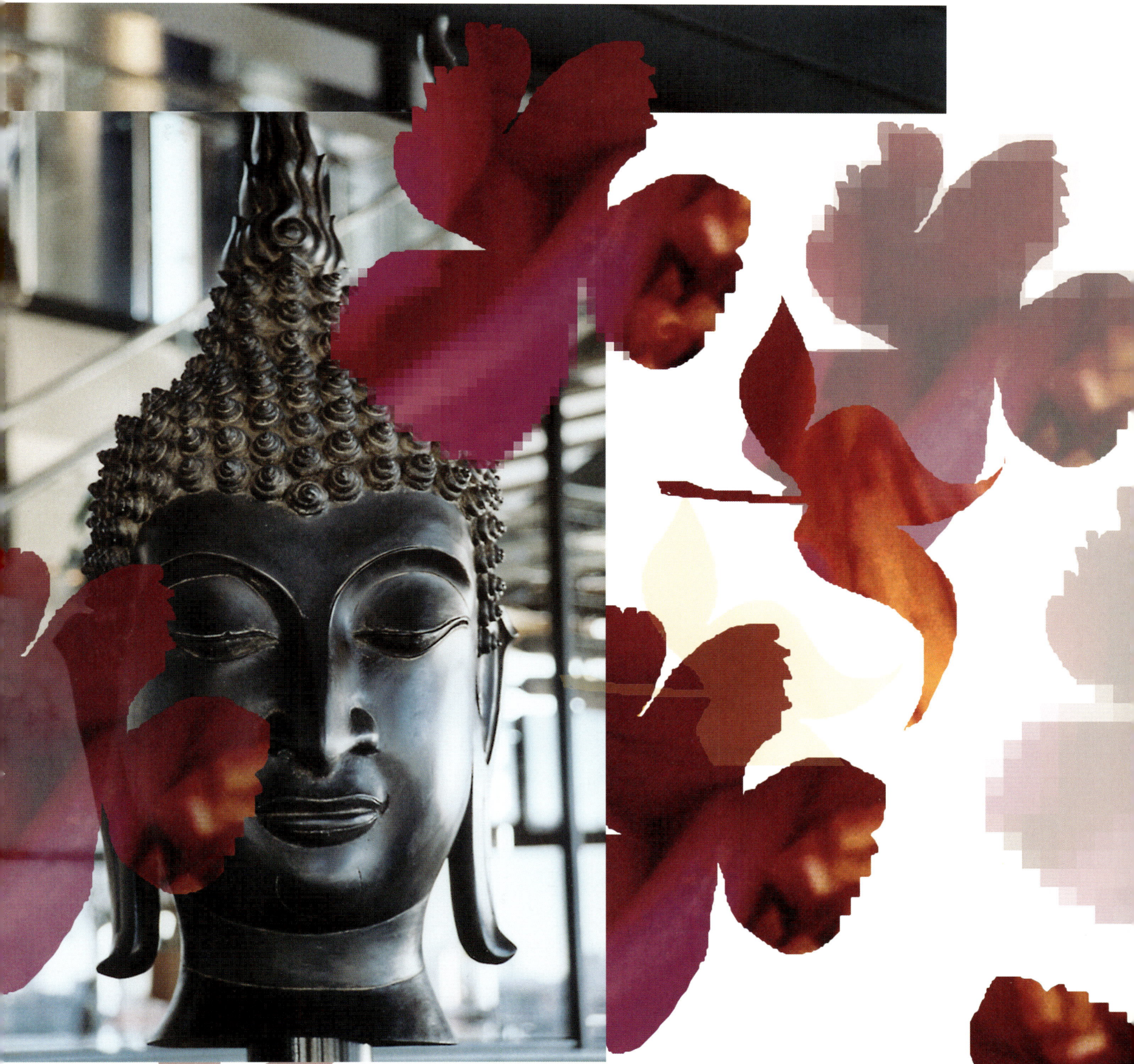

BE PURE OF MIND

ESCAPE THE DELUGE OF MENTAL POLLUTION

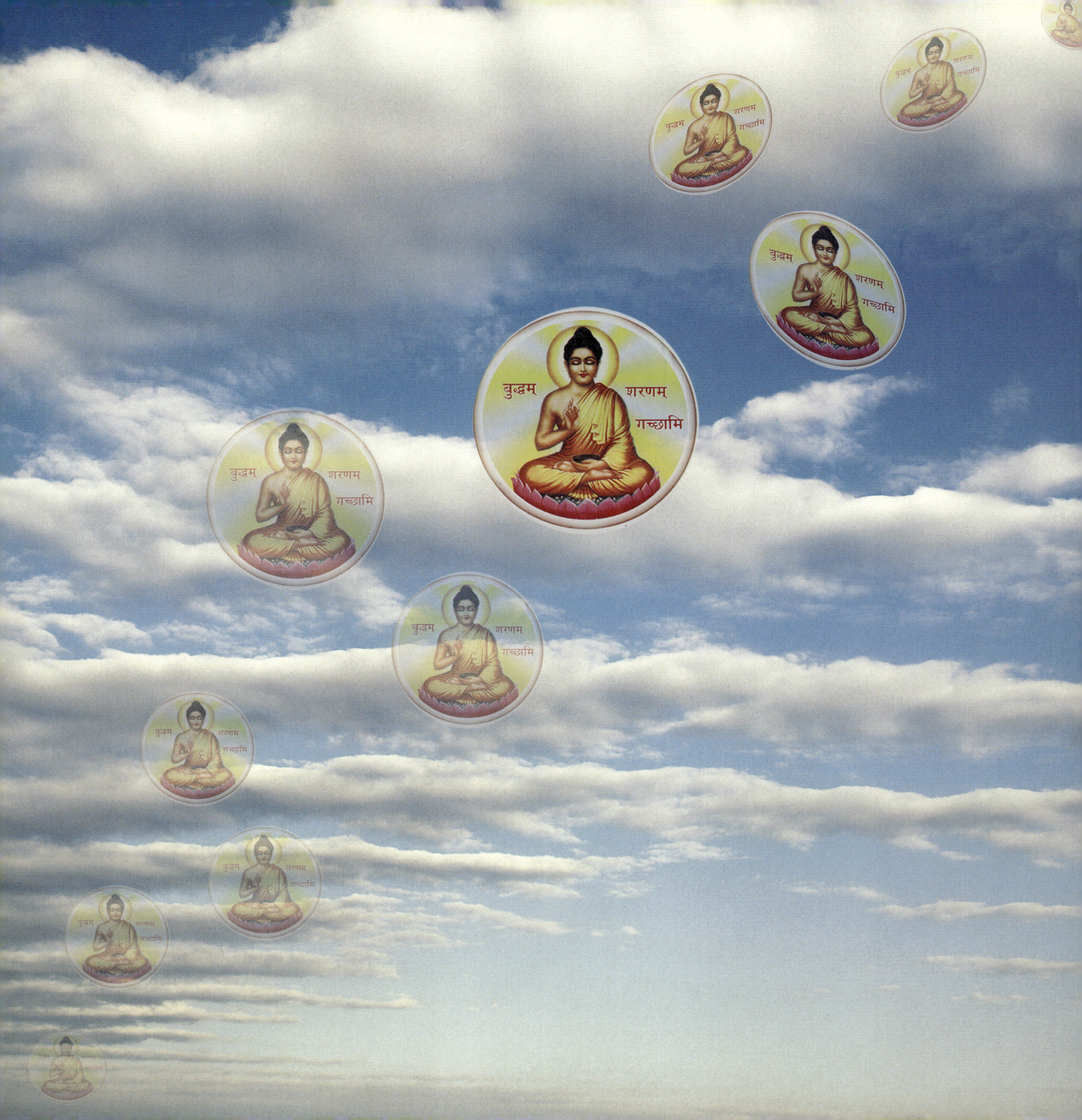
बुद्धम्
शरणम्
गच्छामि

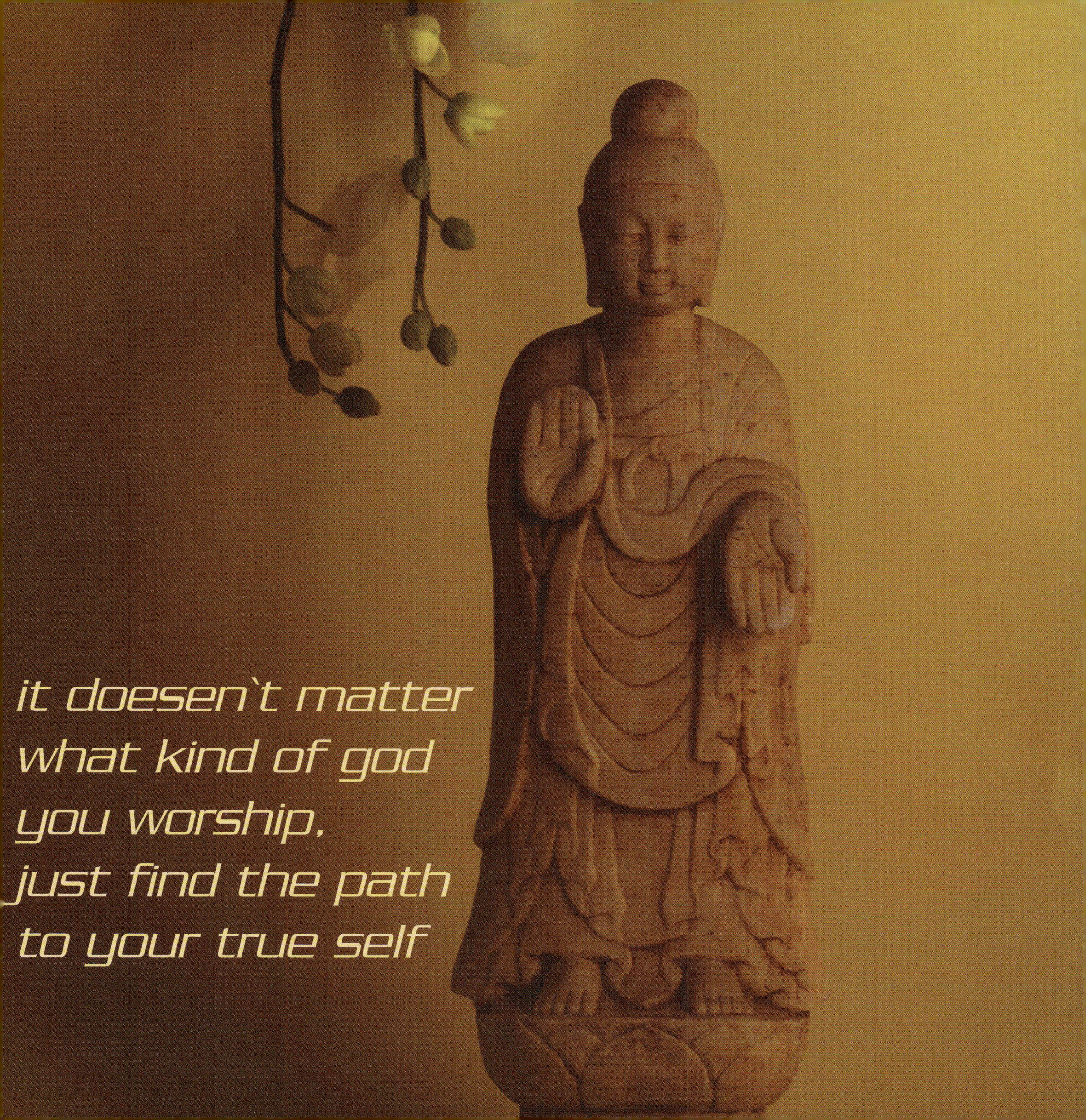
it doesen`t matter
what kind of god
you worship,
just find the path
to your true self

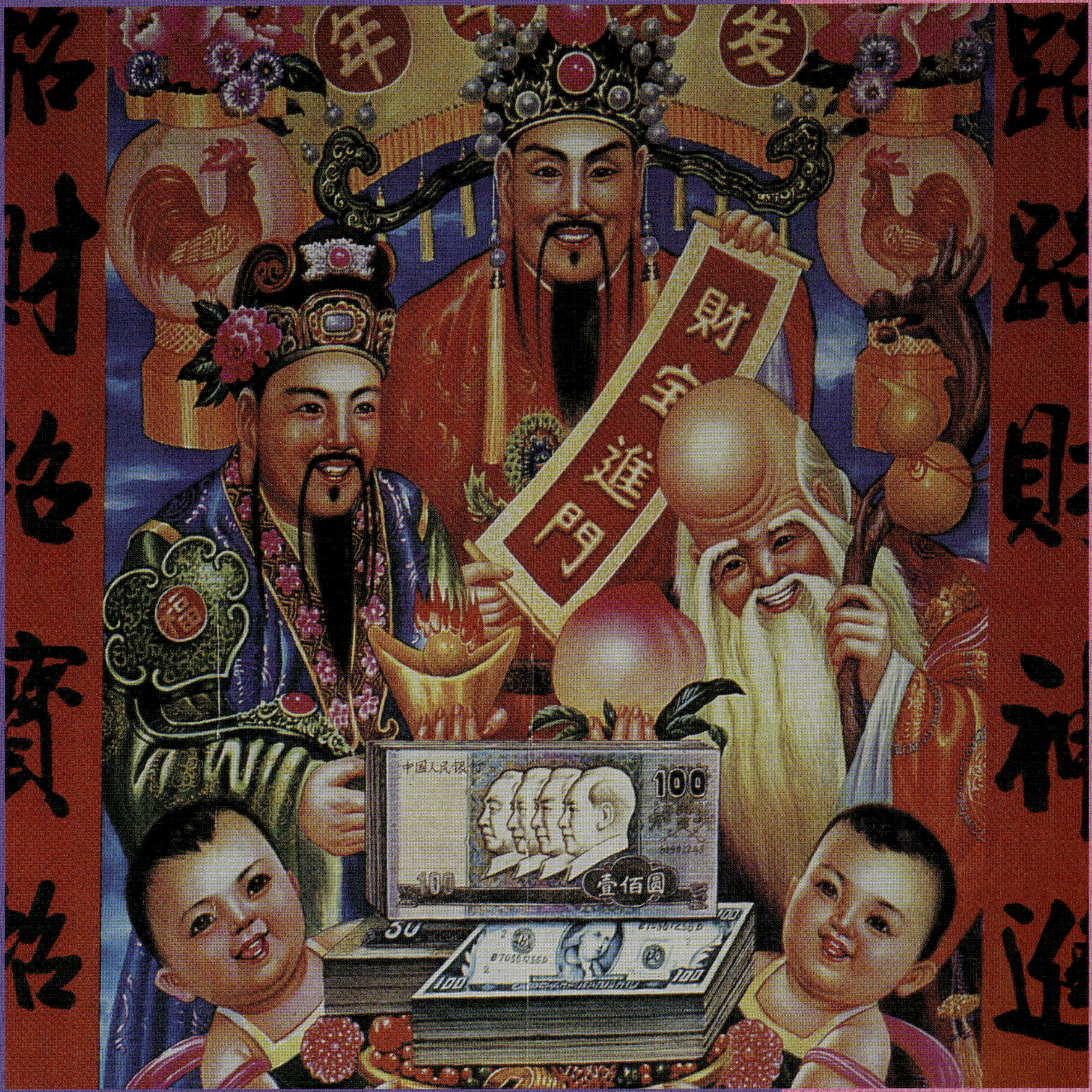

GODS OF PROSPERITY

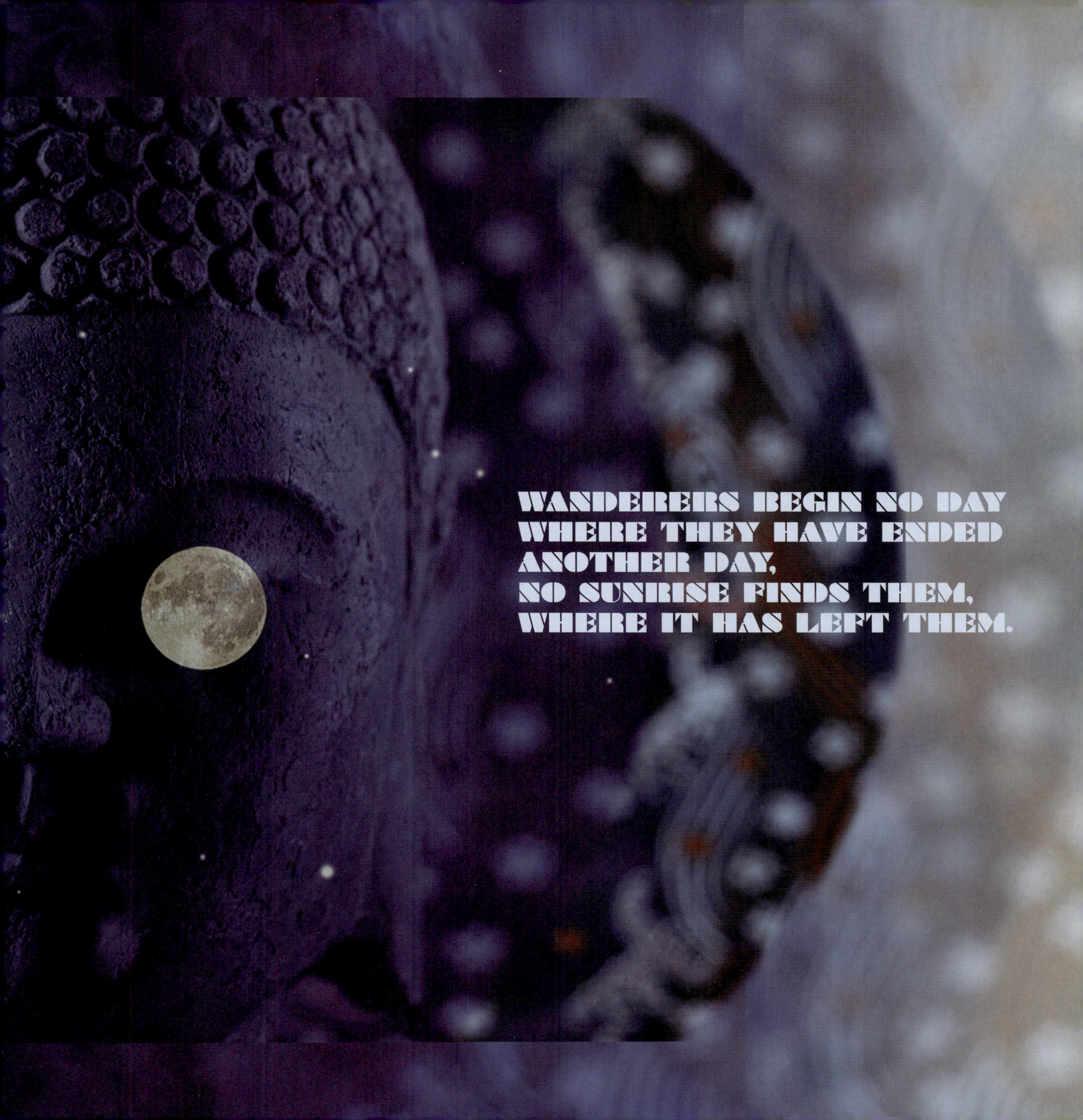
WANDERERS BEGIN NO DAY
WHERE THEY HAVE ENDED
ANOTHER DAY,
NO SUNRISE FINDS THEM,
WHERE IT HAS LEFT THEM.

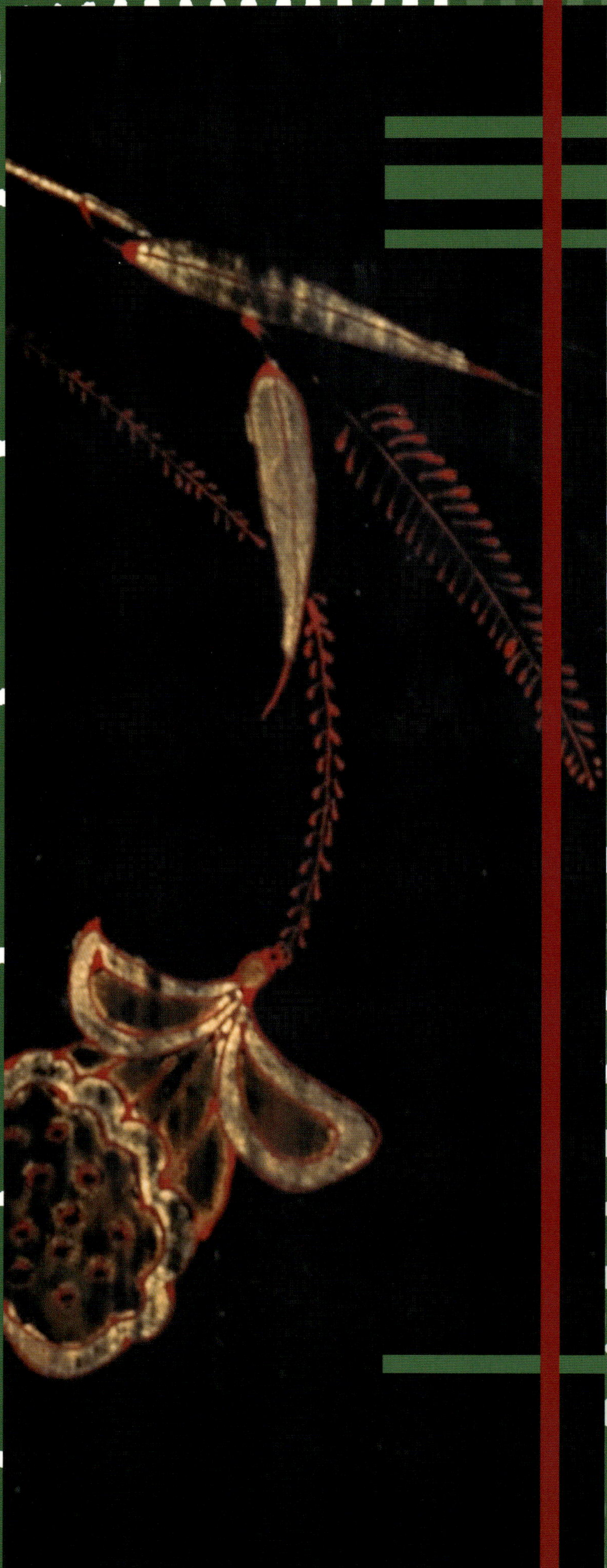

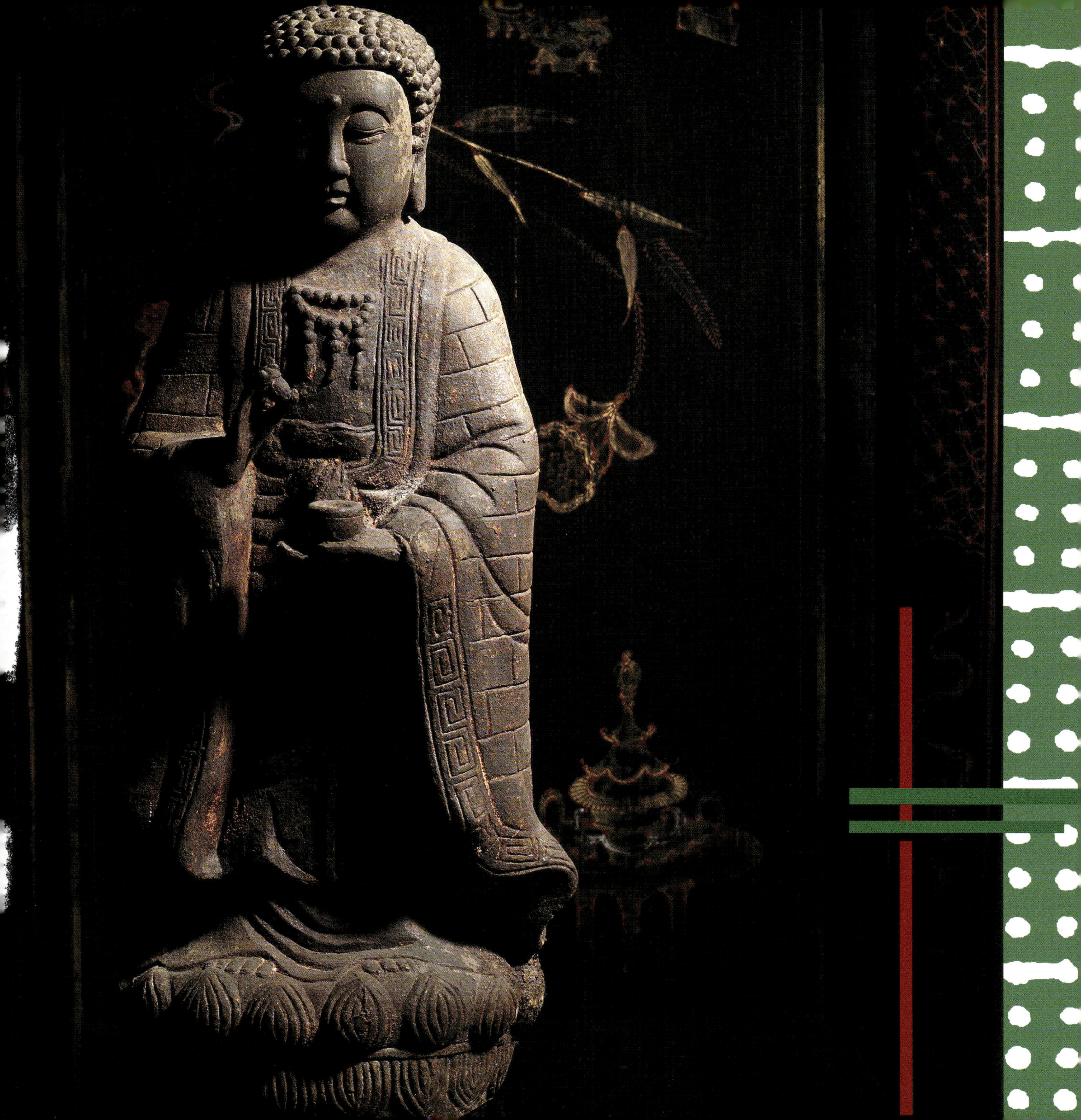

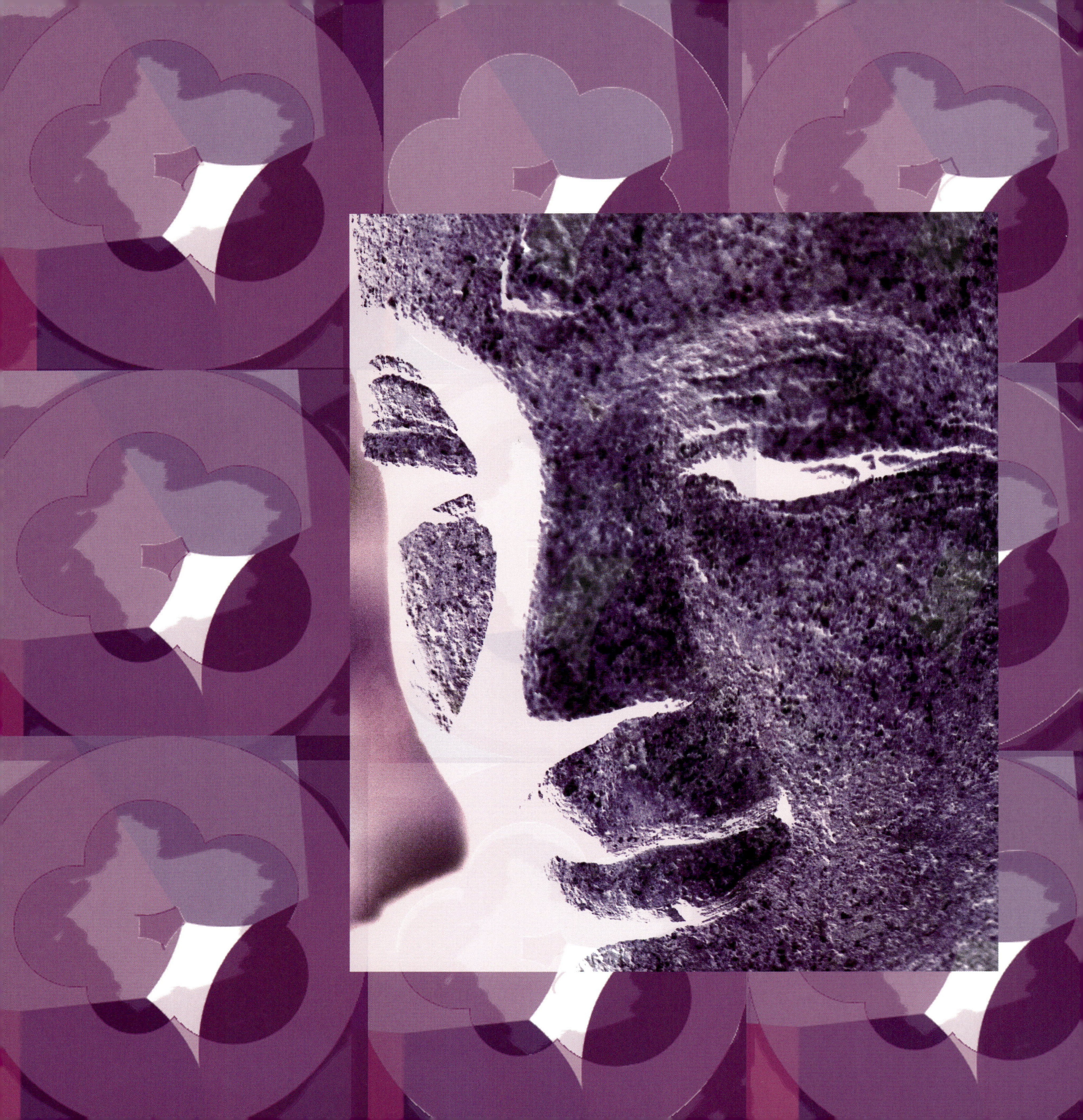

the true
self
is
the ally
the ego mind
self
is
the enemy

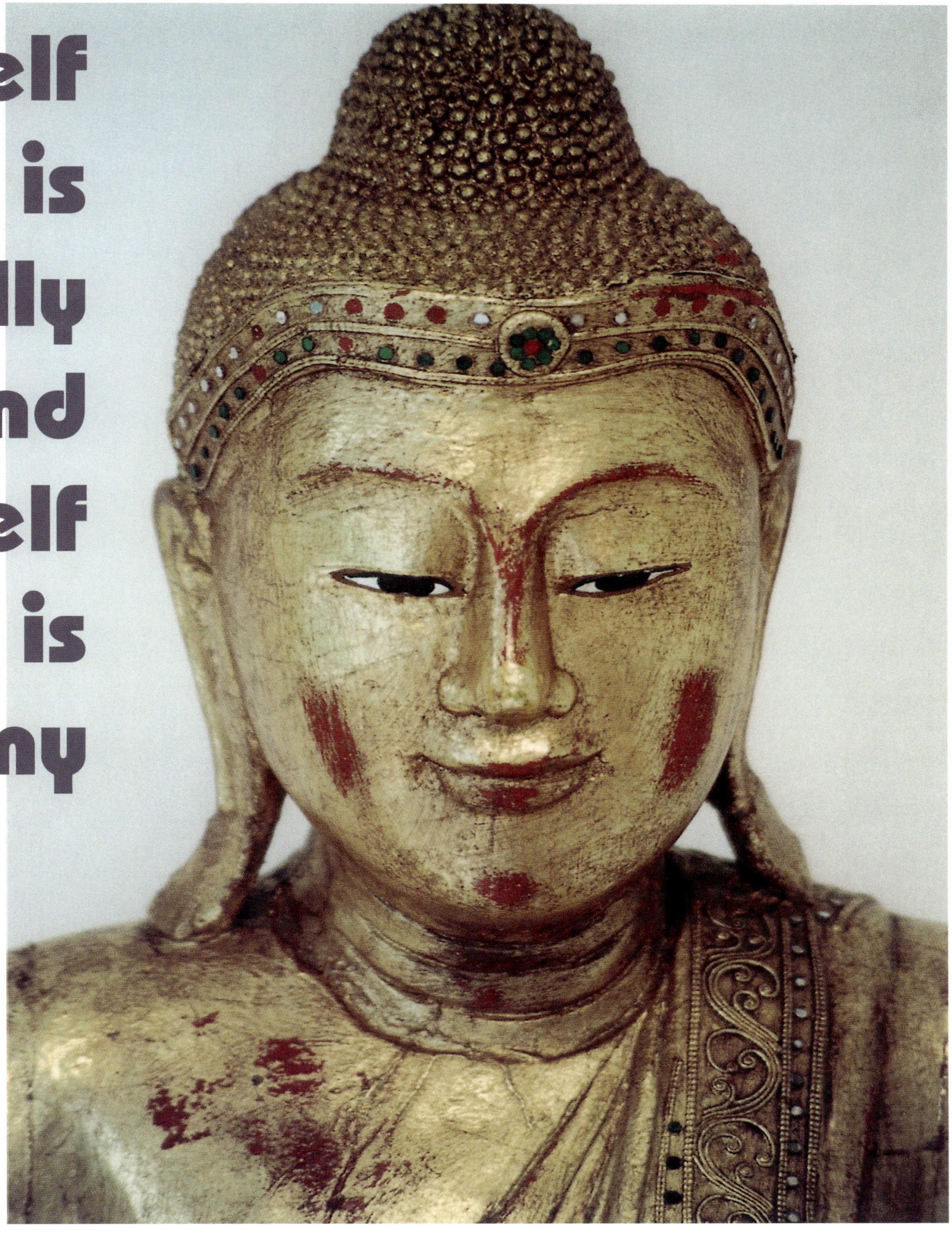

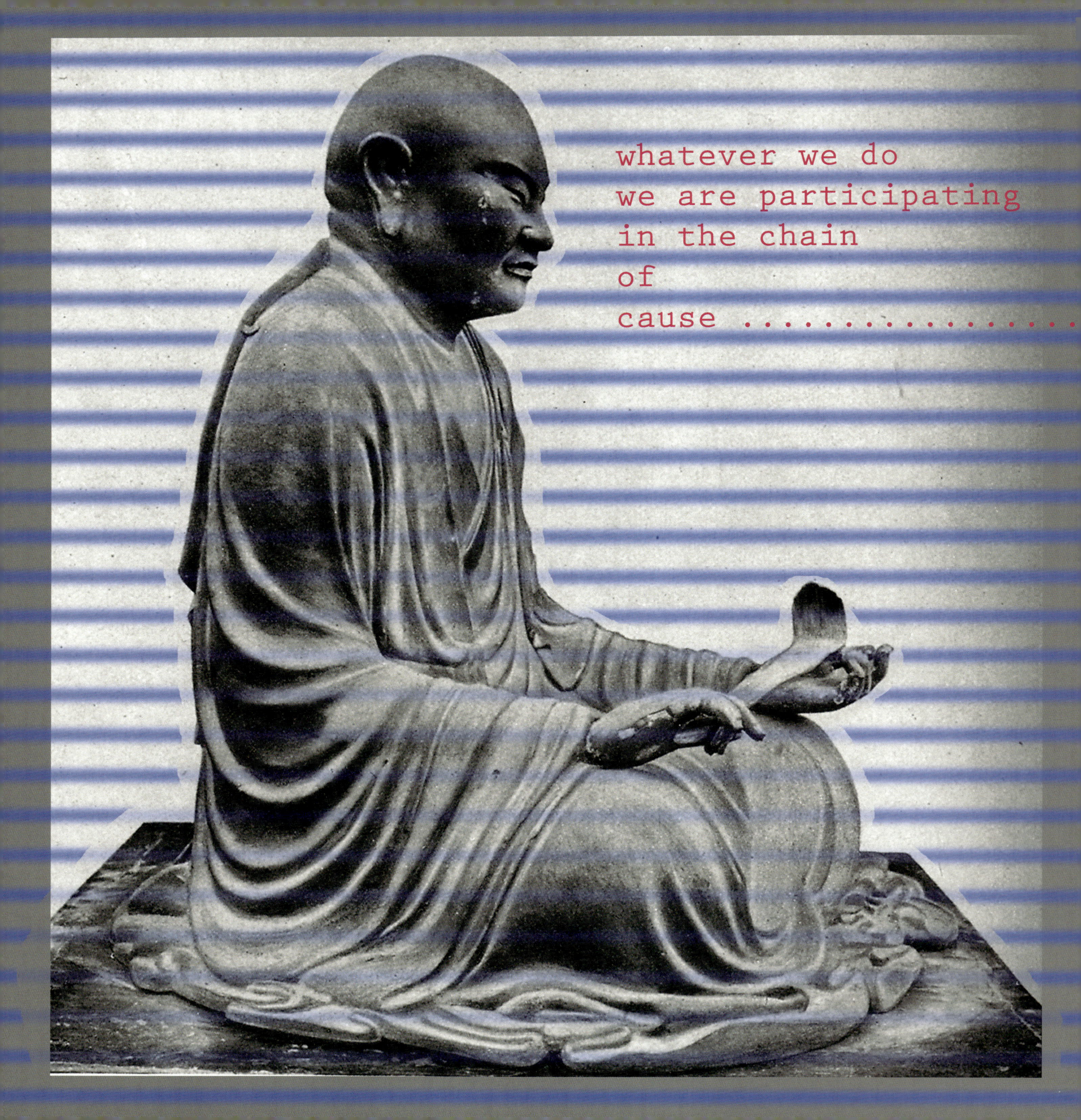
whatever we do
we are participating
in the chain
of
cause ....

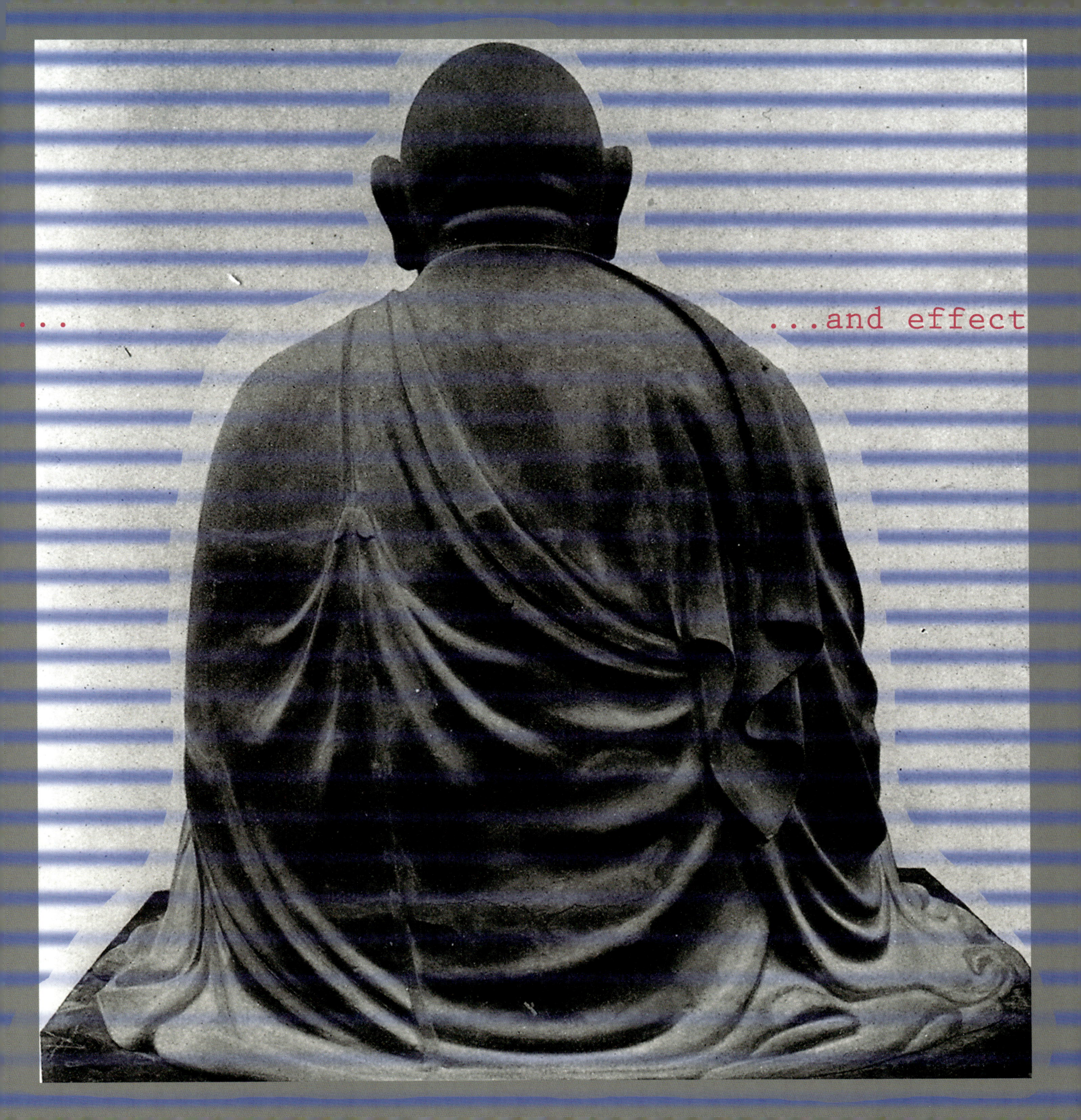
...
...and effect

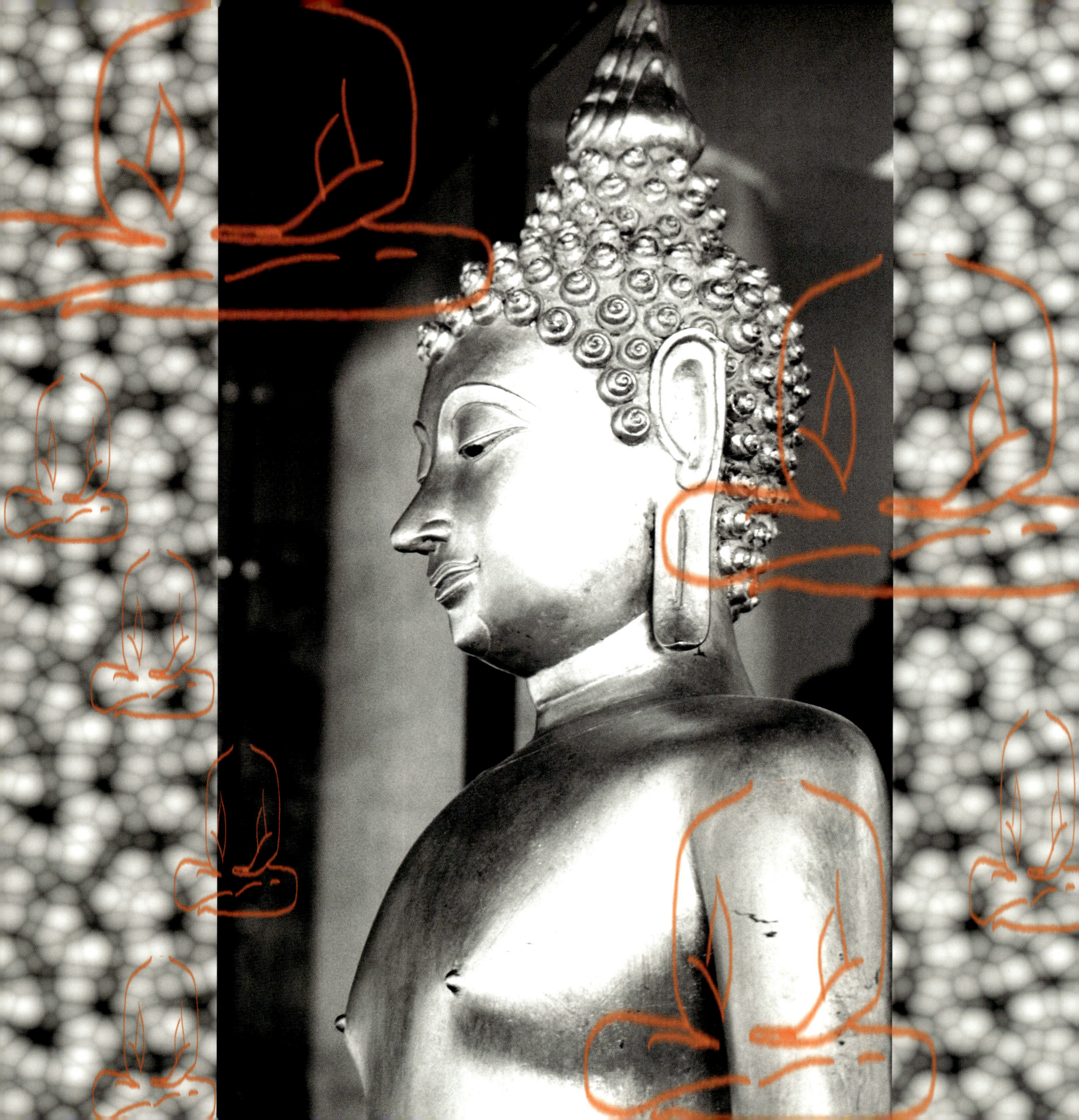

IN TIBET THEY SAY
THE ONLY WAY TO UNBLOCK A CONCH SHELL

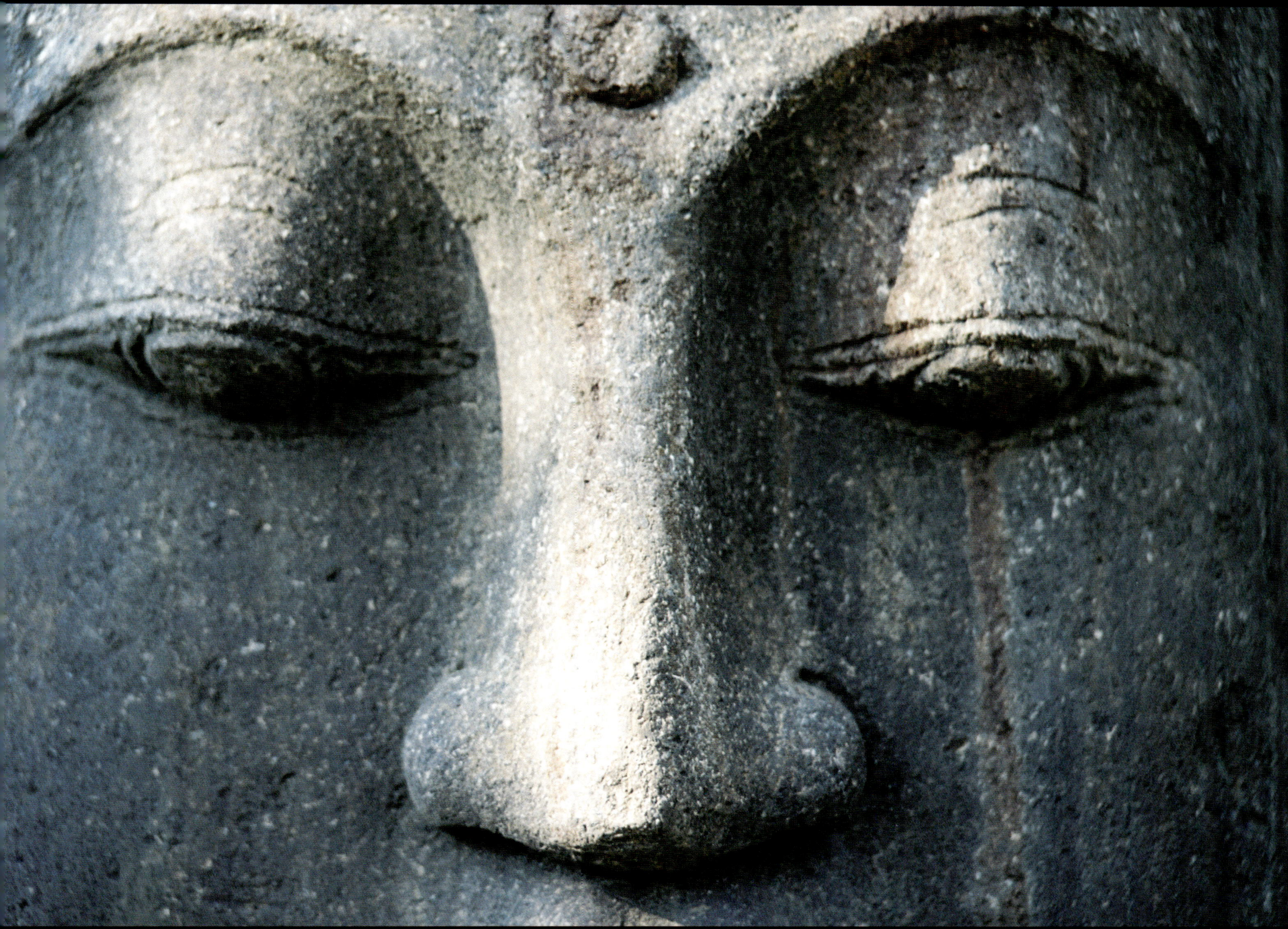

IS BY BLOWING INTO IT

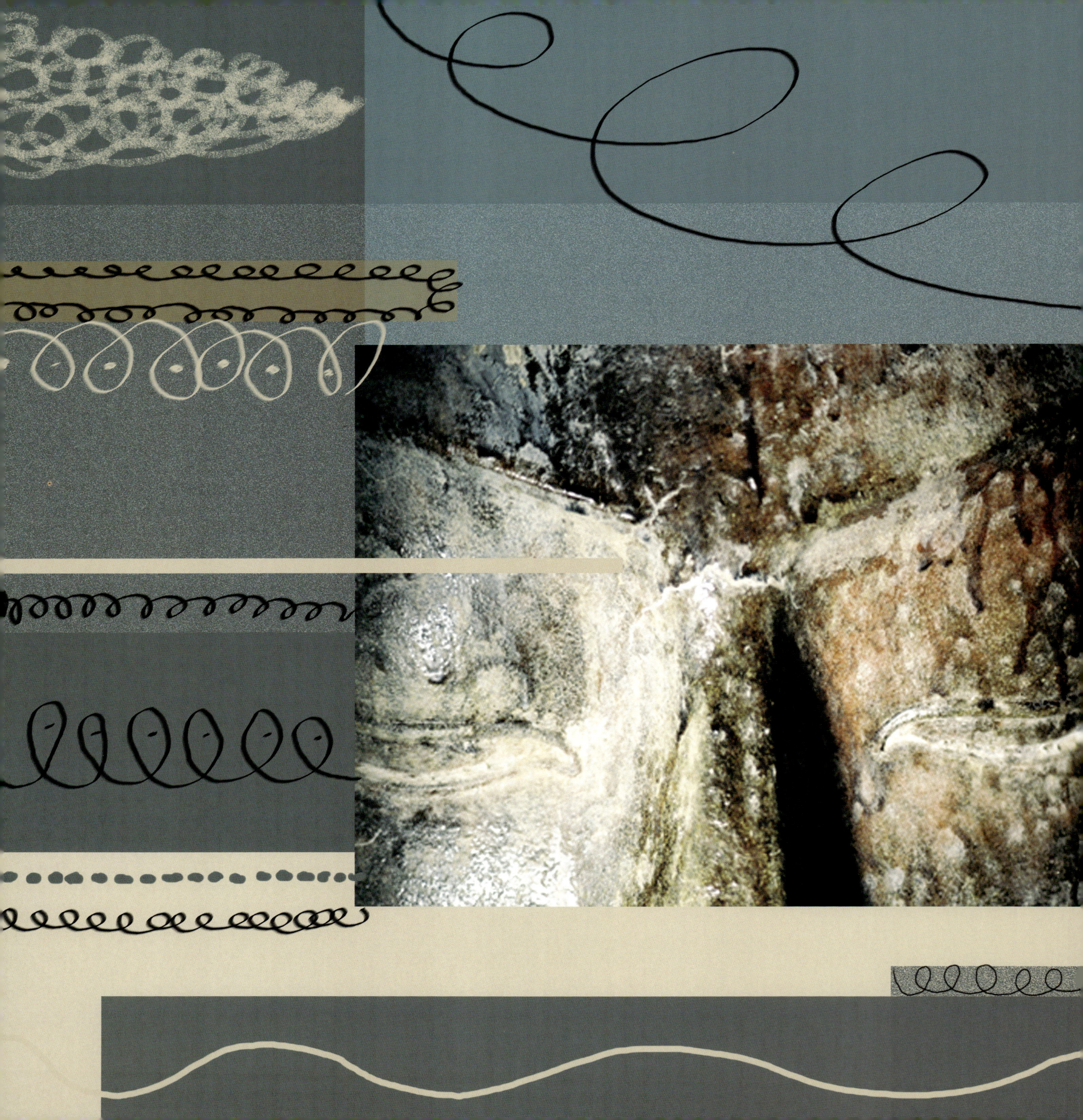

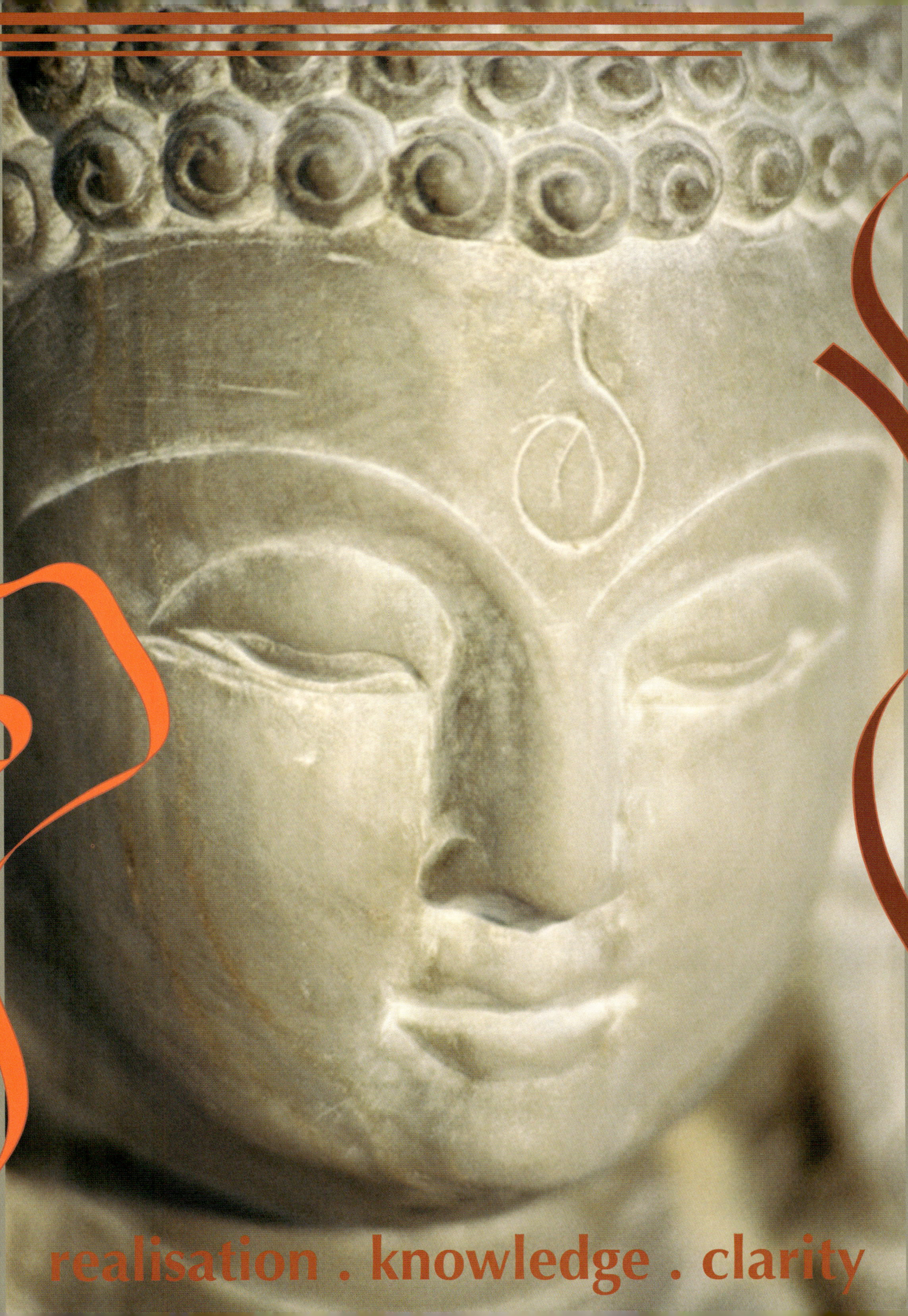
realisation . knowledge . clarity

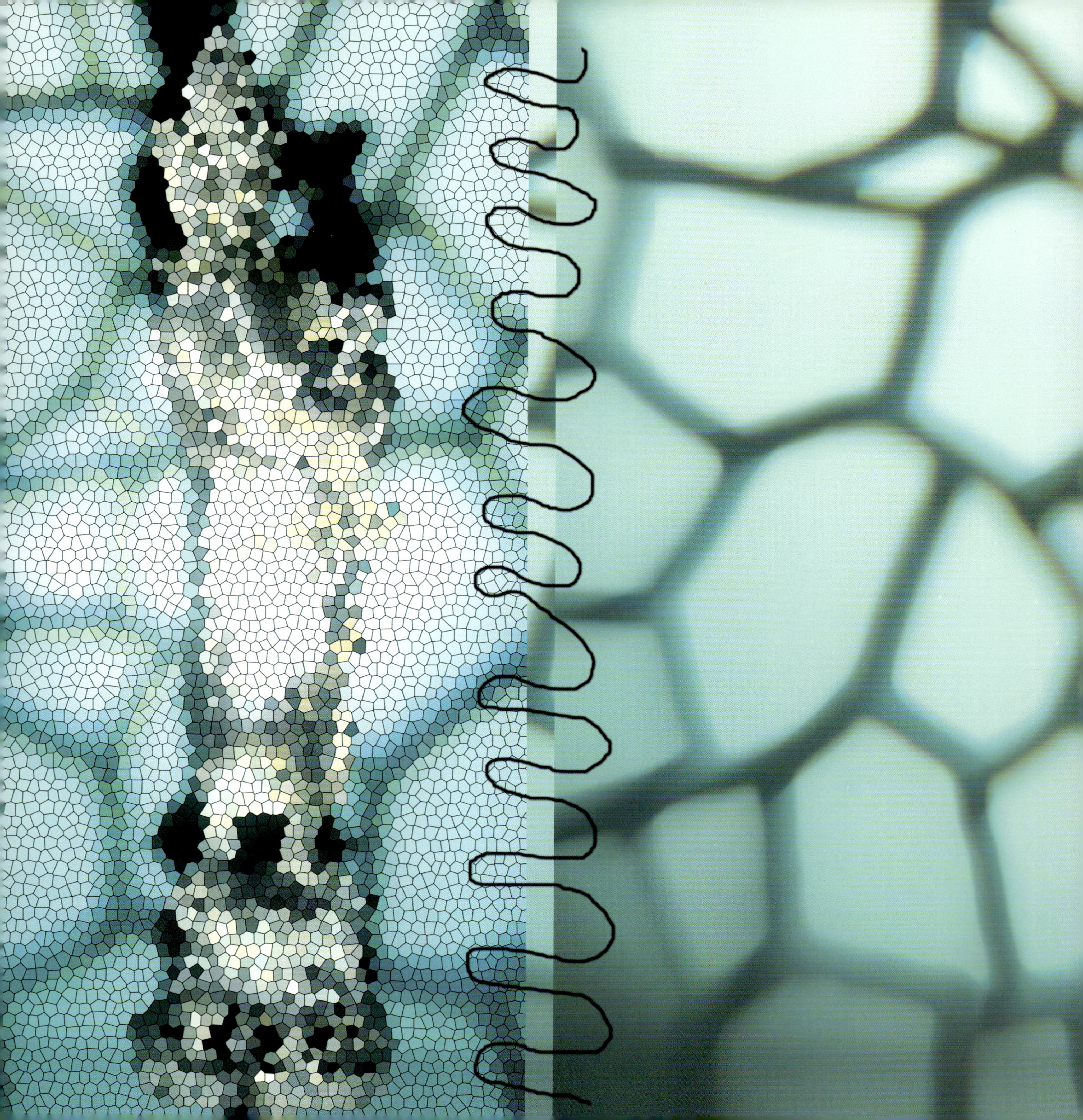

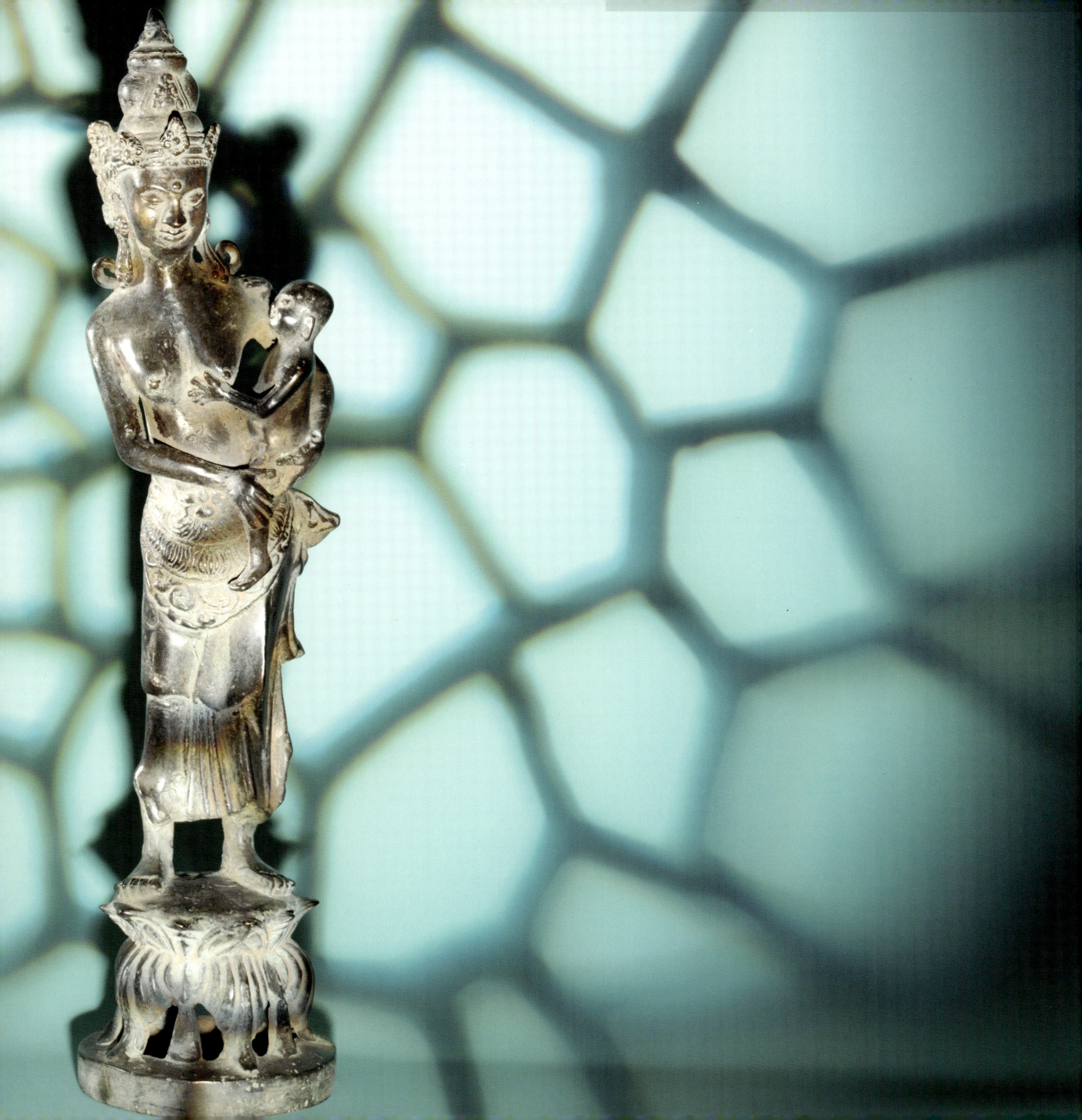

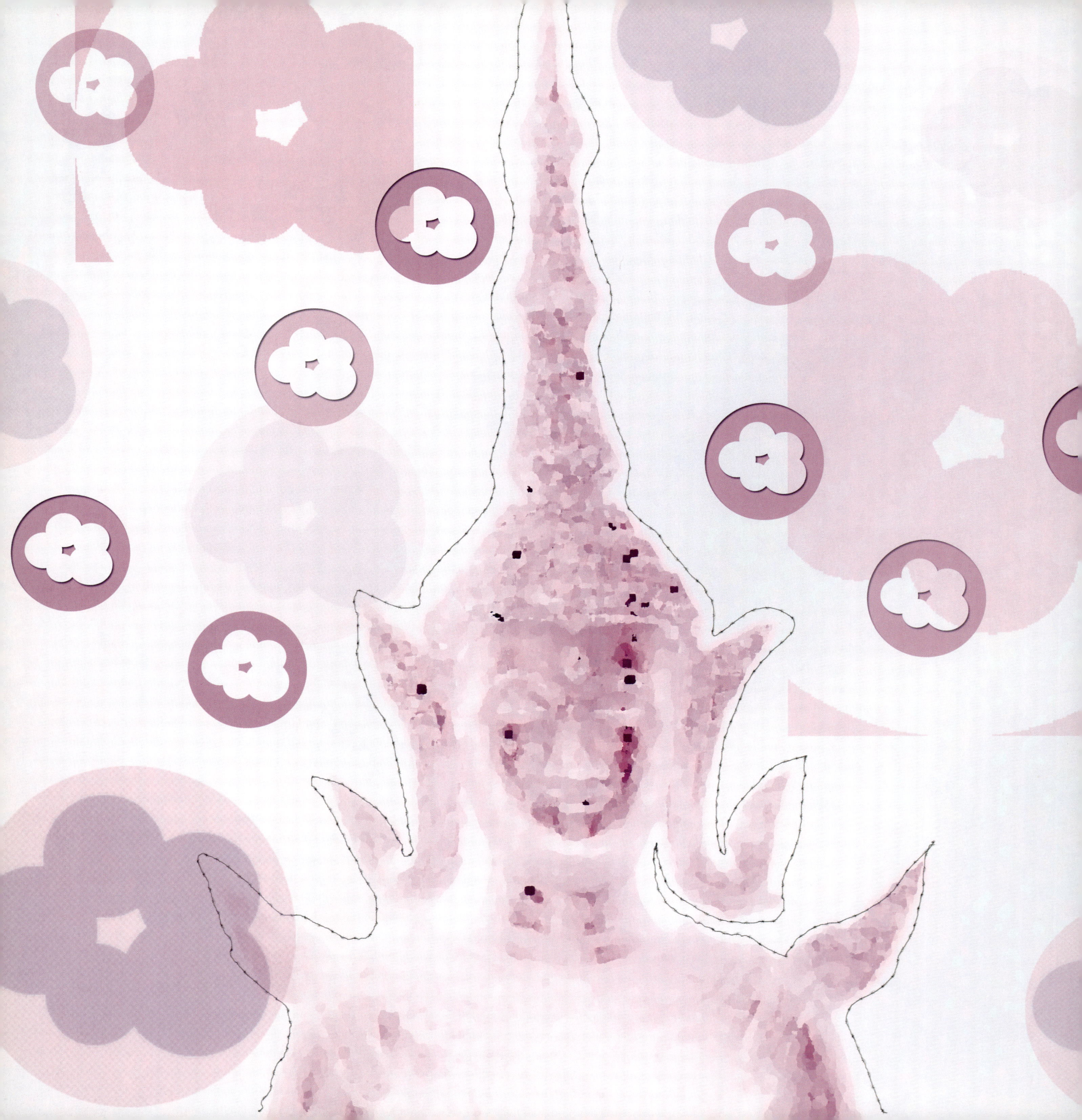

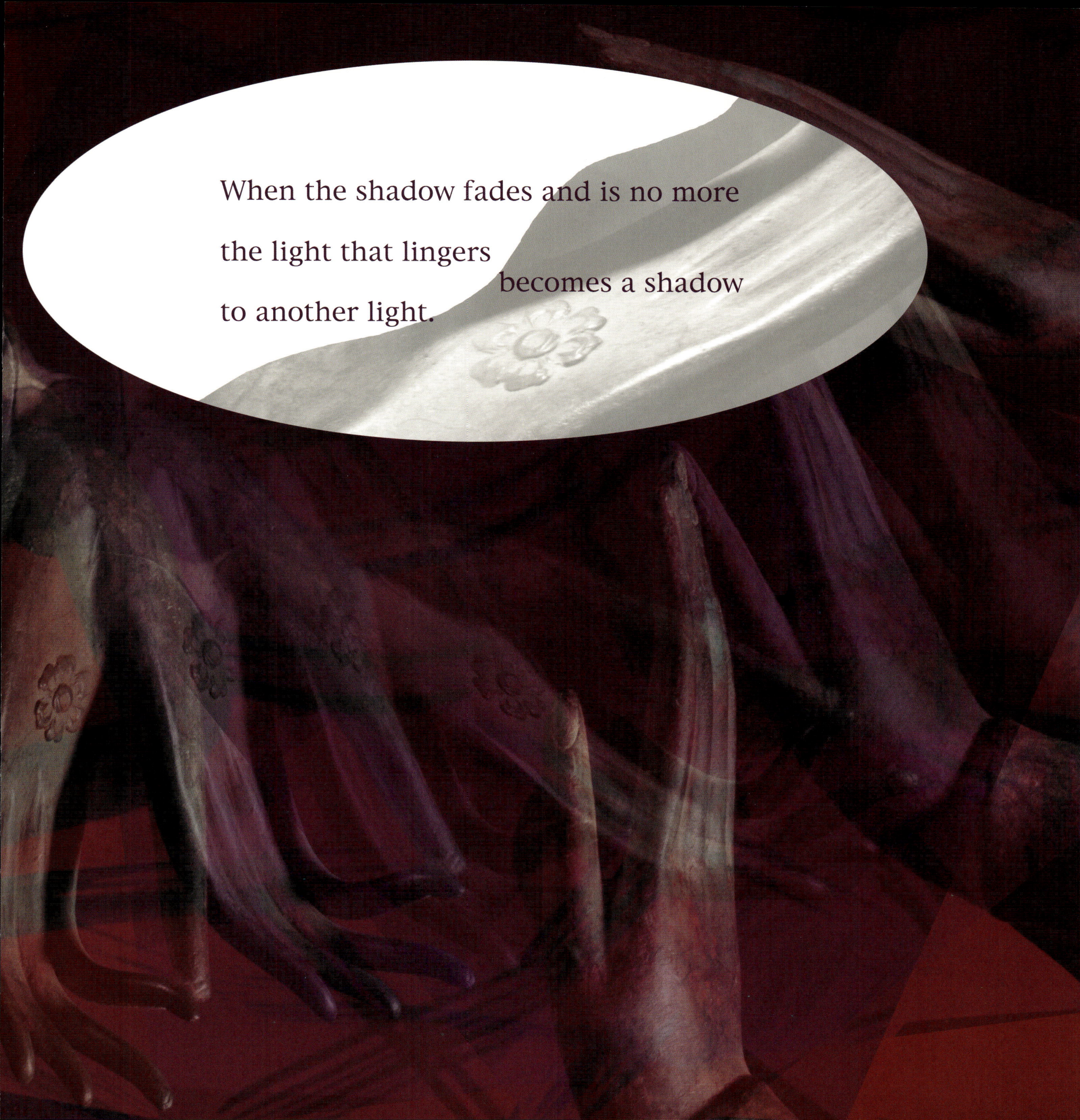

When the shadow fades and is no more

the light that lingers
becomes a shadow
to another light.

Sometimes you do not know
where to turn,
either way
you are afraid to lose

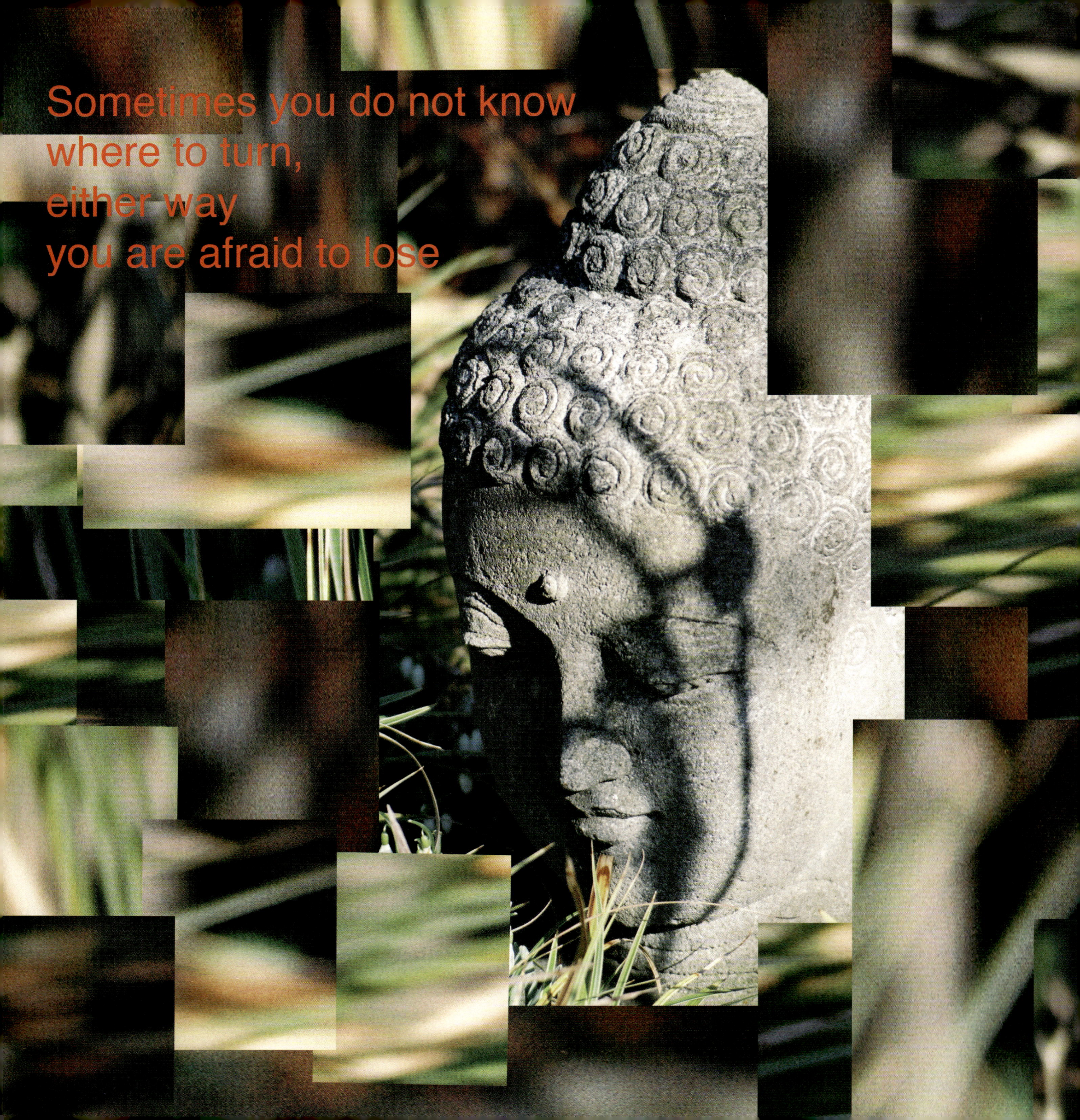

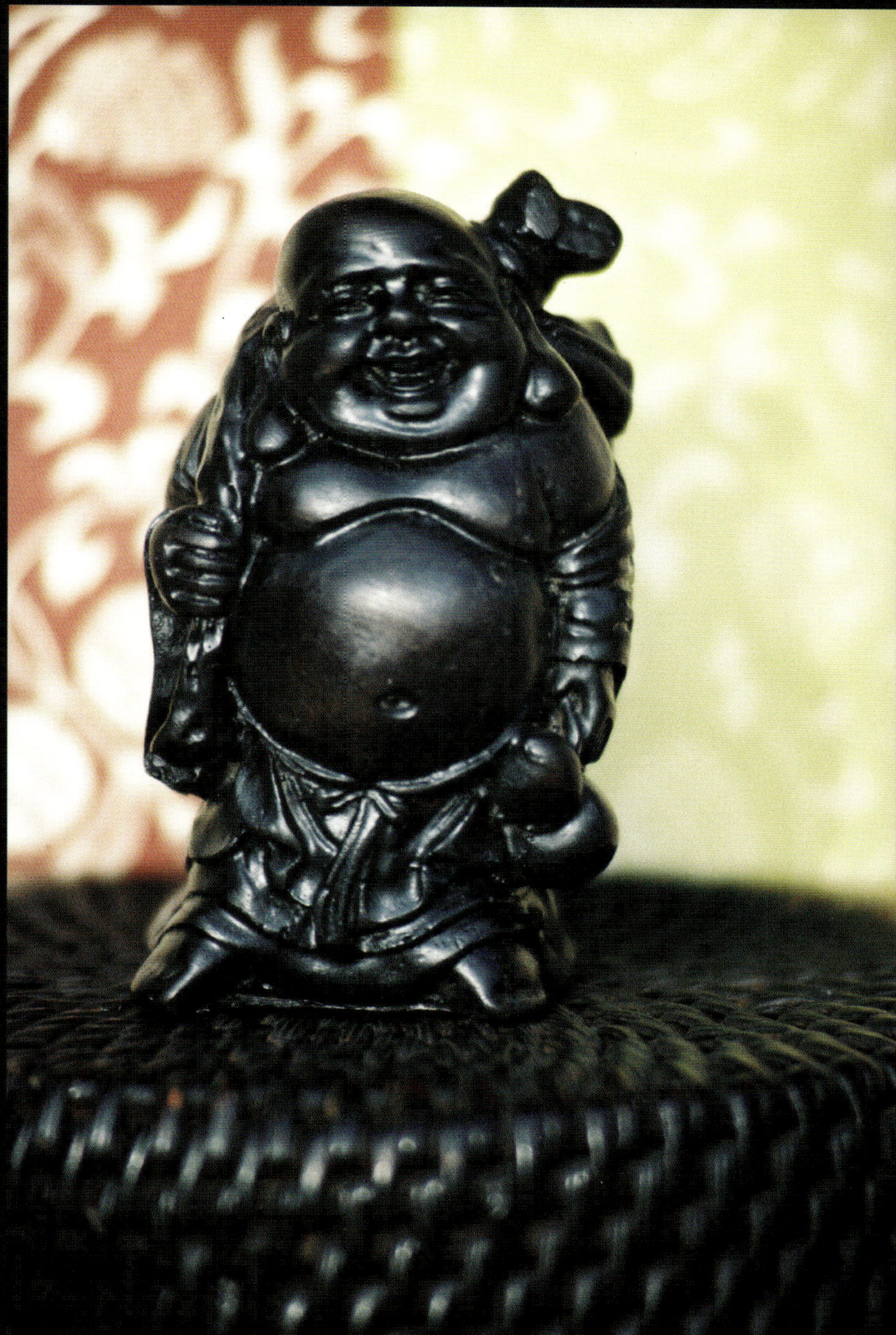

BUDDHA, SINGAPORE
JULY '79

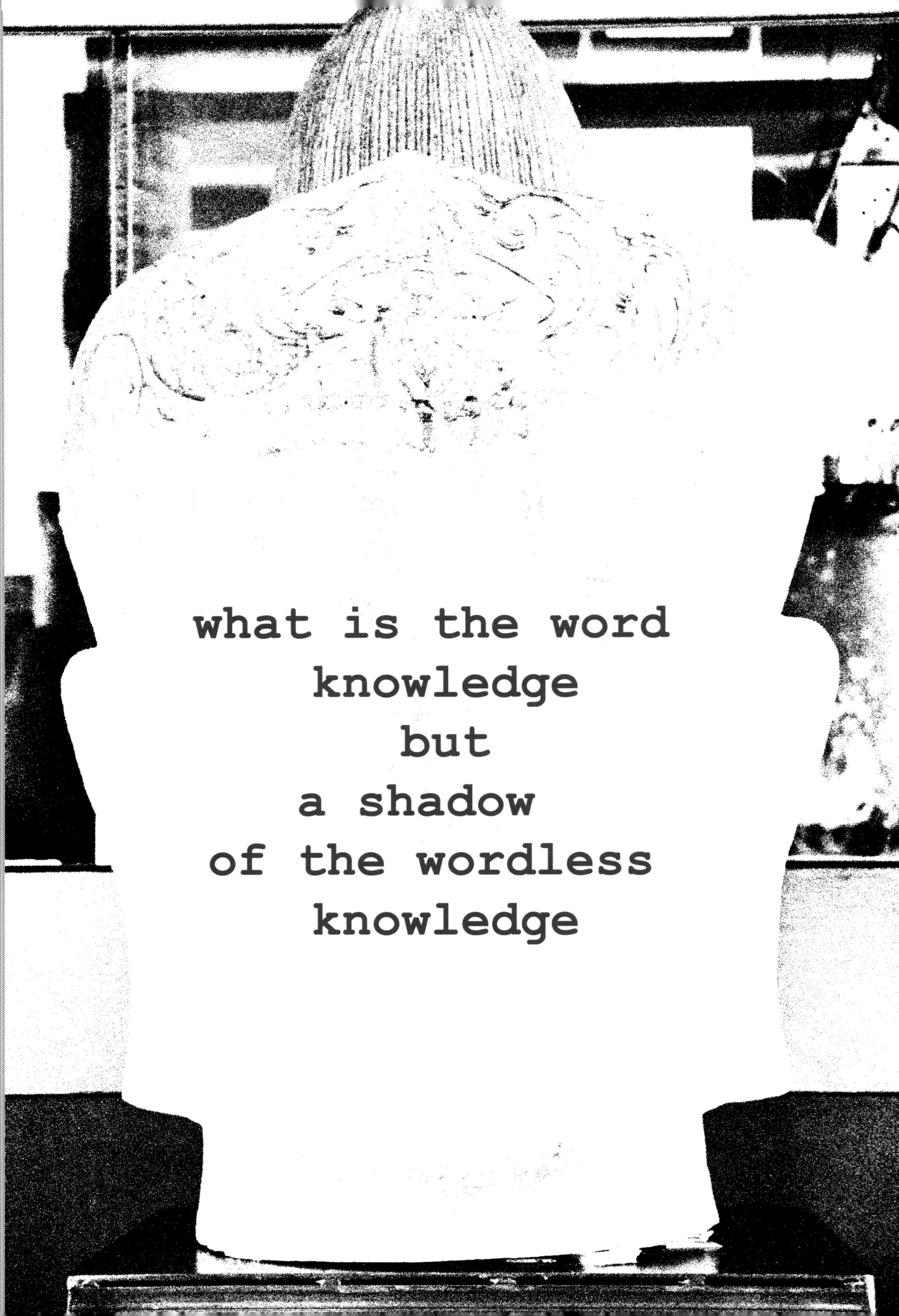
what is the word
knowledge
but
a shadow
of the wordless
knowledge

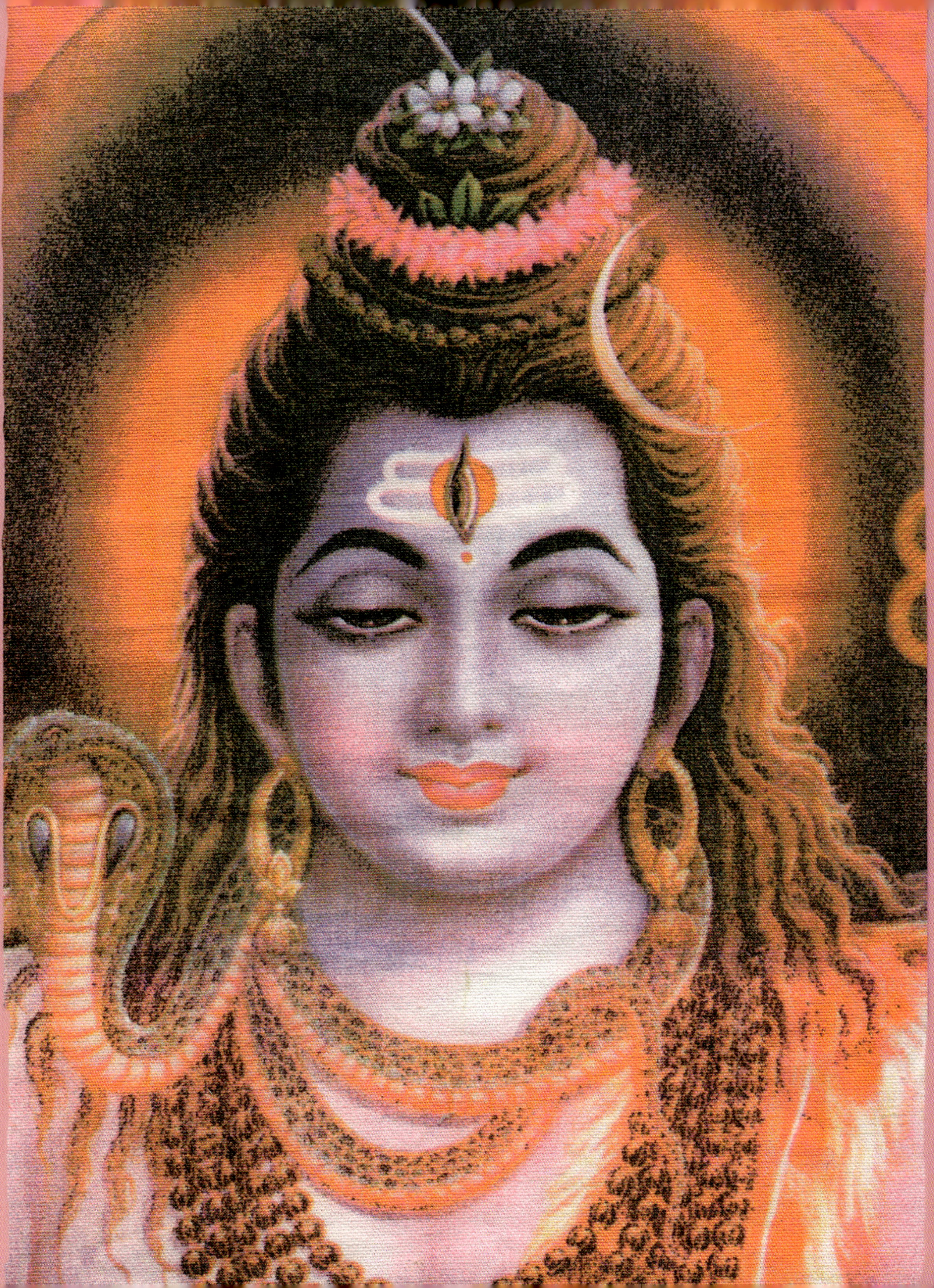

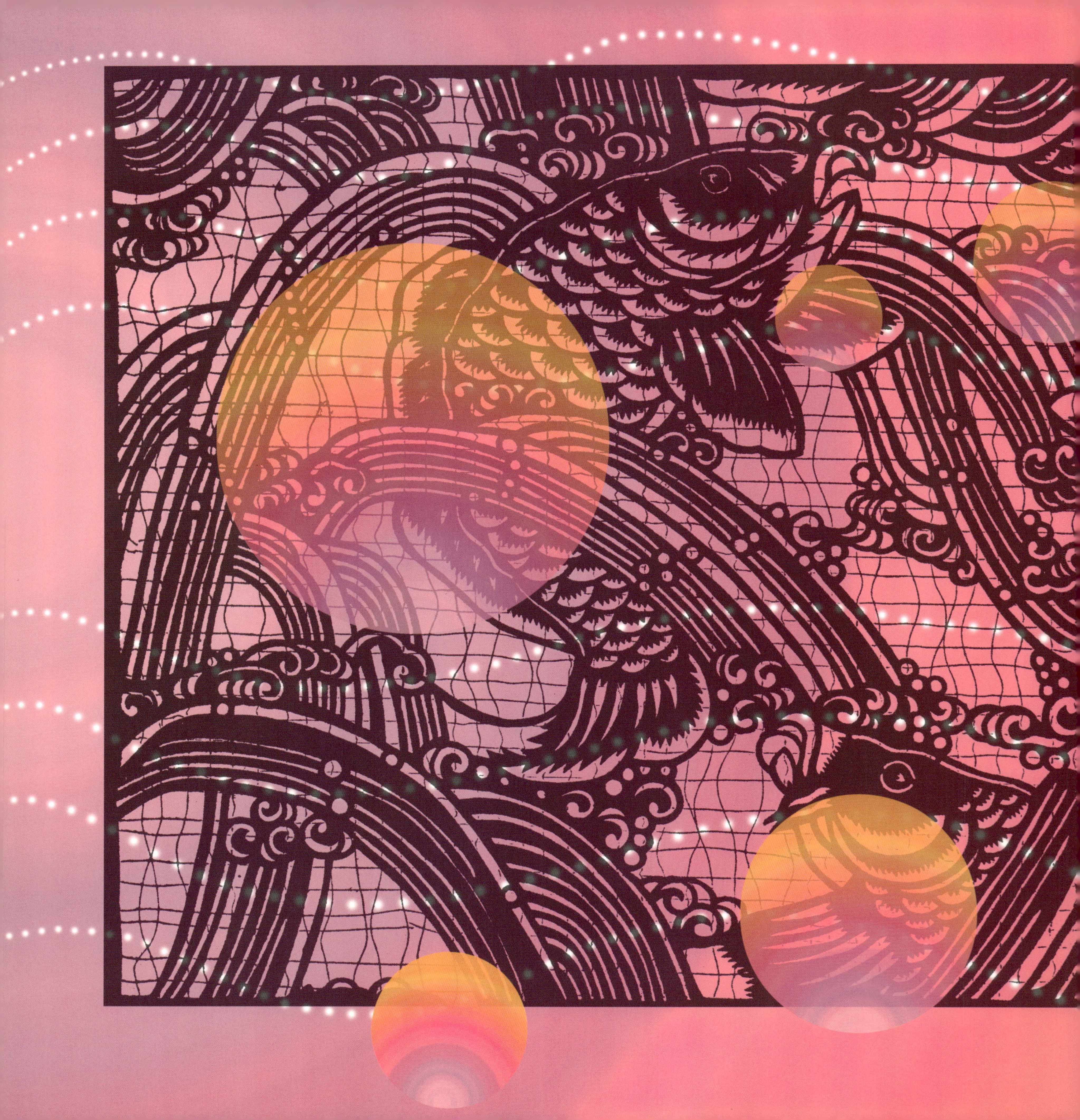

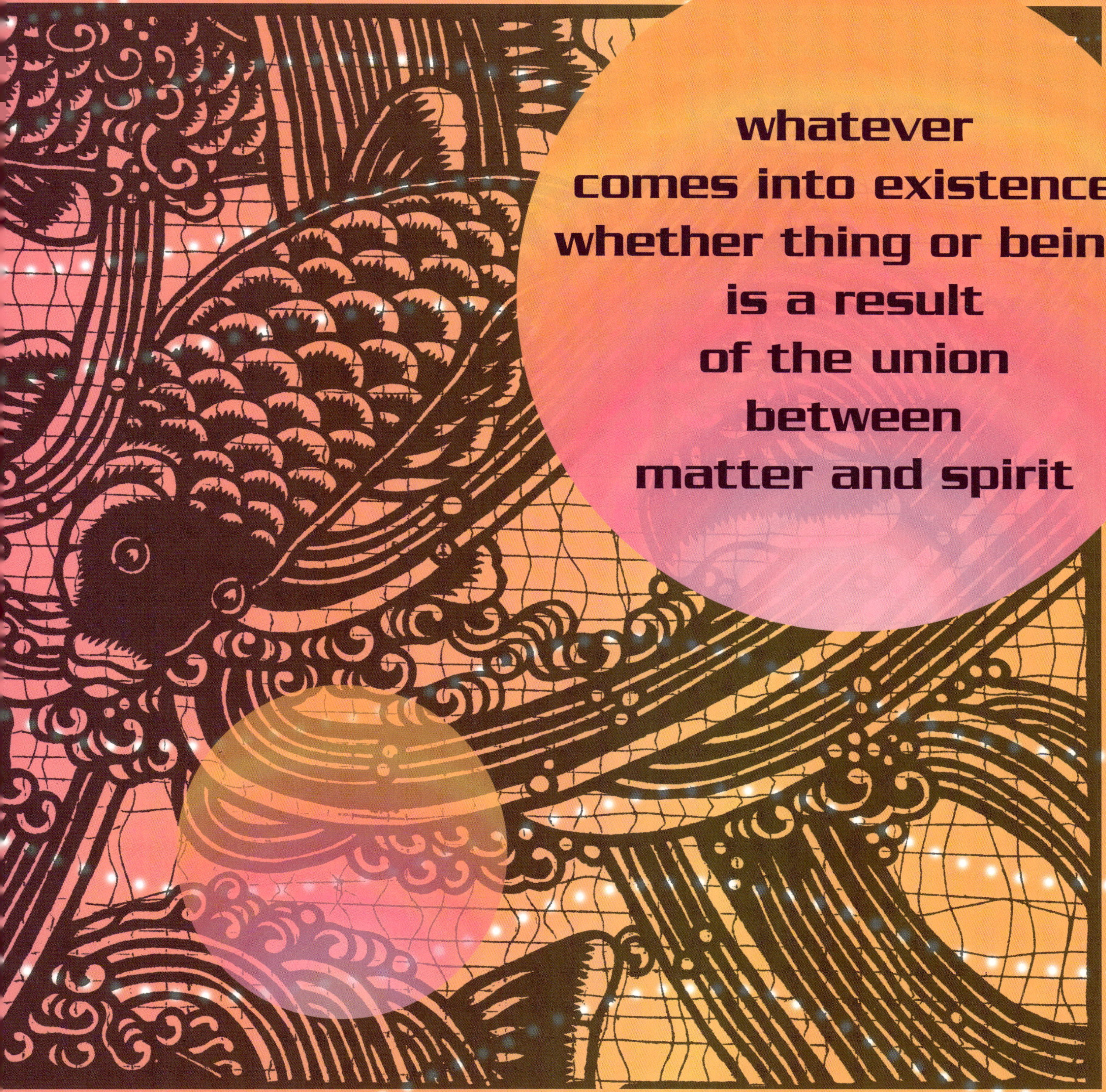

whatever
comes into existence,
whether thing or being,
is a result
of the union
between
matter and spirit

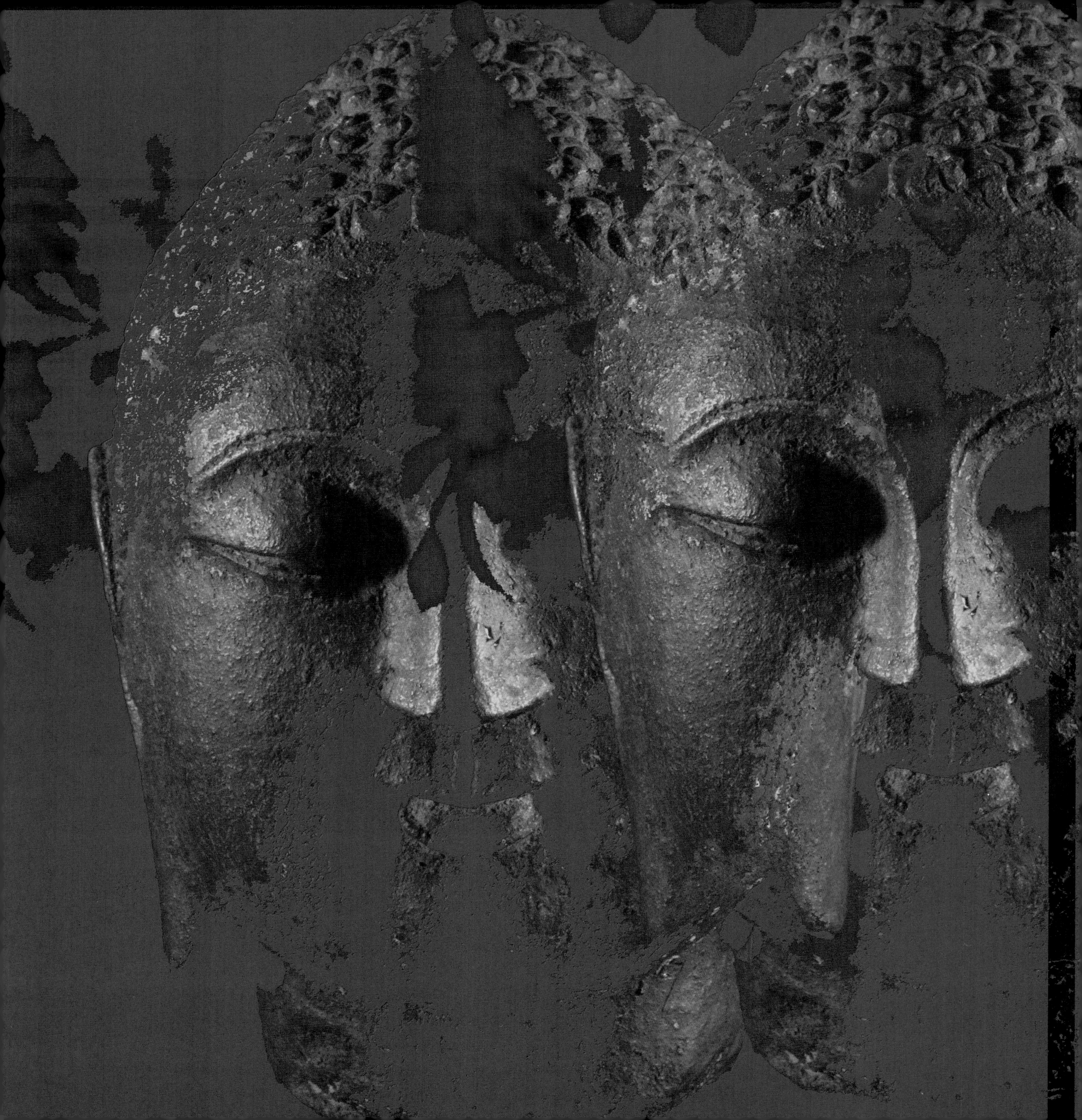

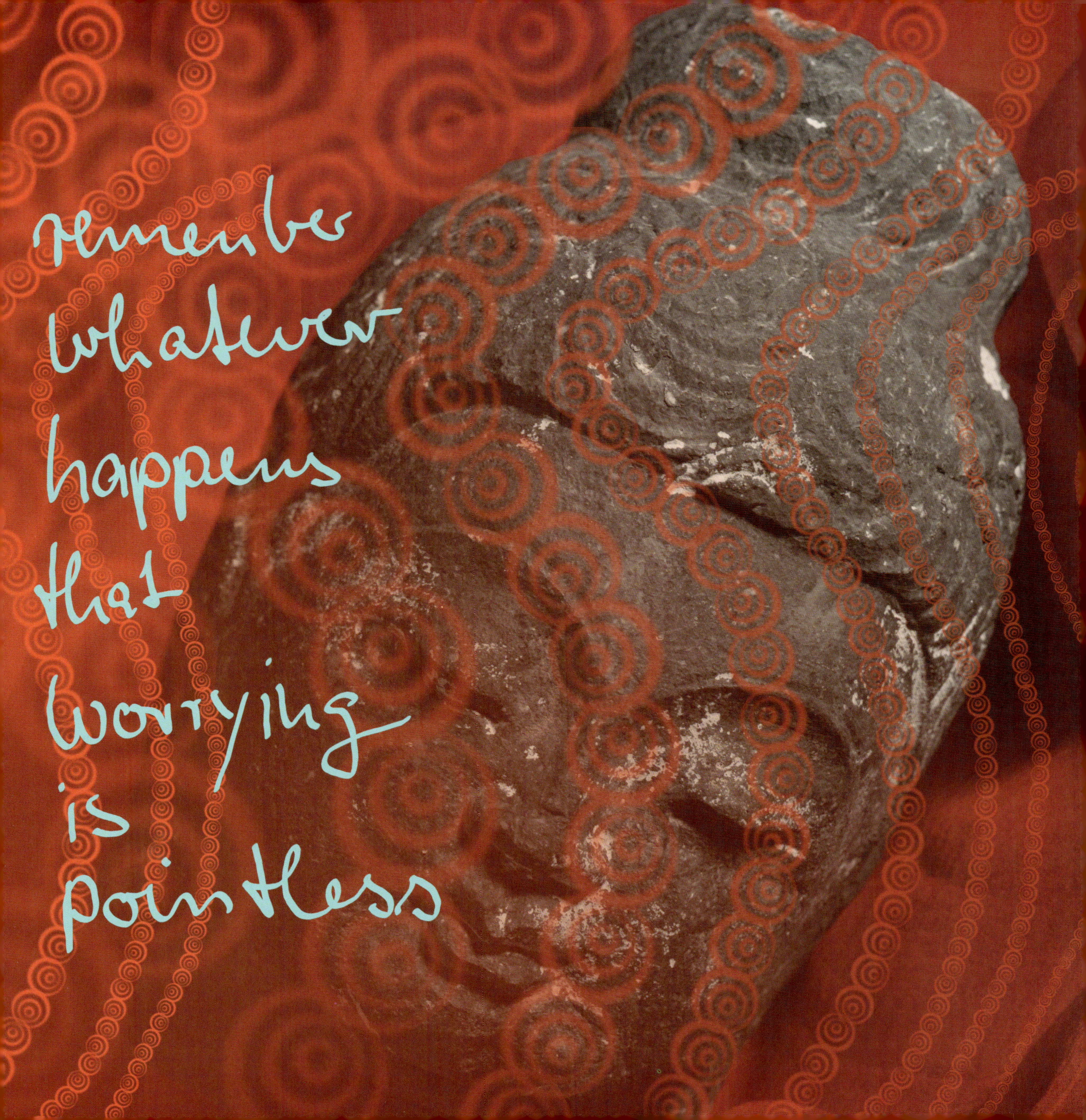
remember
whatever
happens
that
worrying
is
pointless

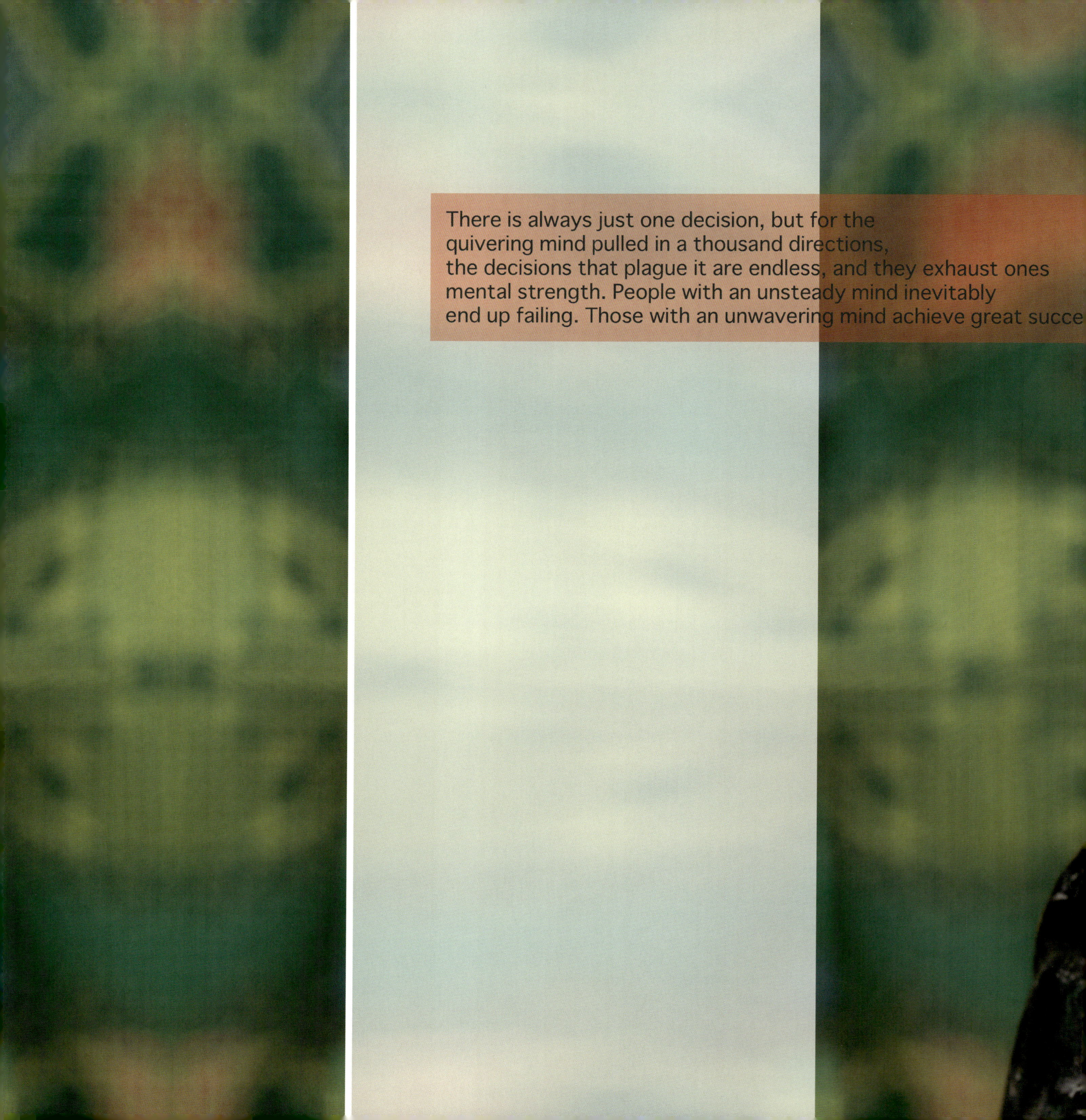

There is always just one decision, but for the quivering mind pulled in a thousand directions, the decisions that plague it are endless, and they exhaust ones mental strength. People with an unsteady mind inevitably end up failing. Those with an unwavering mind achieve great succe

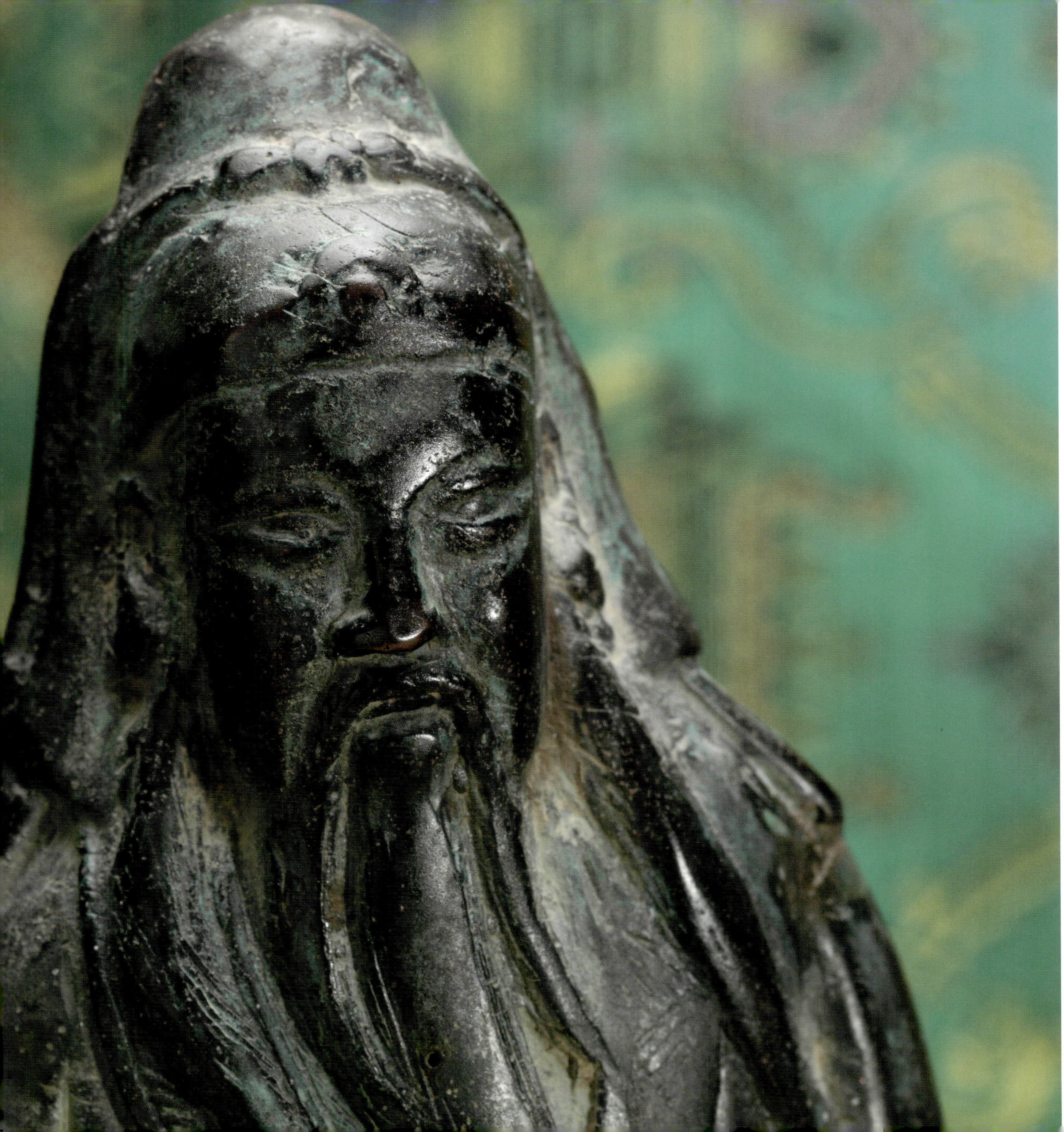

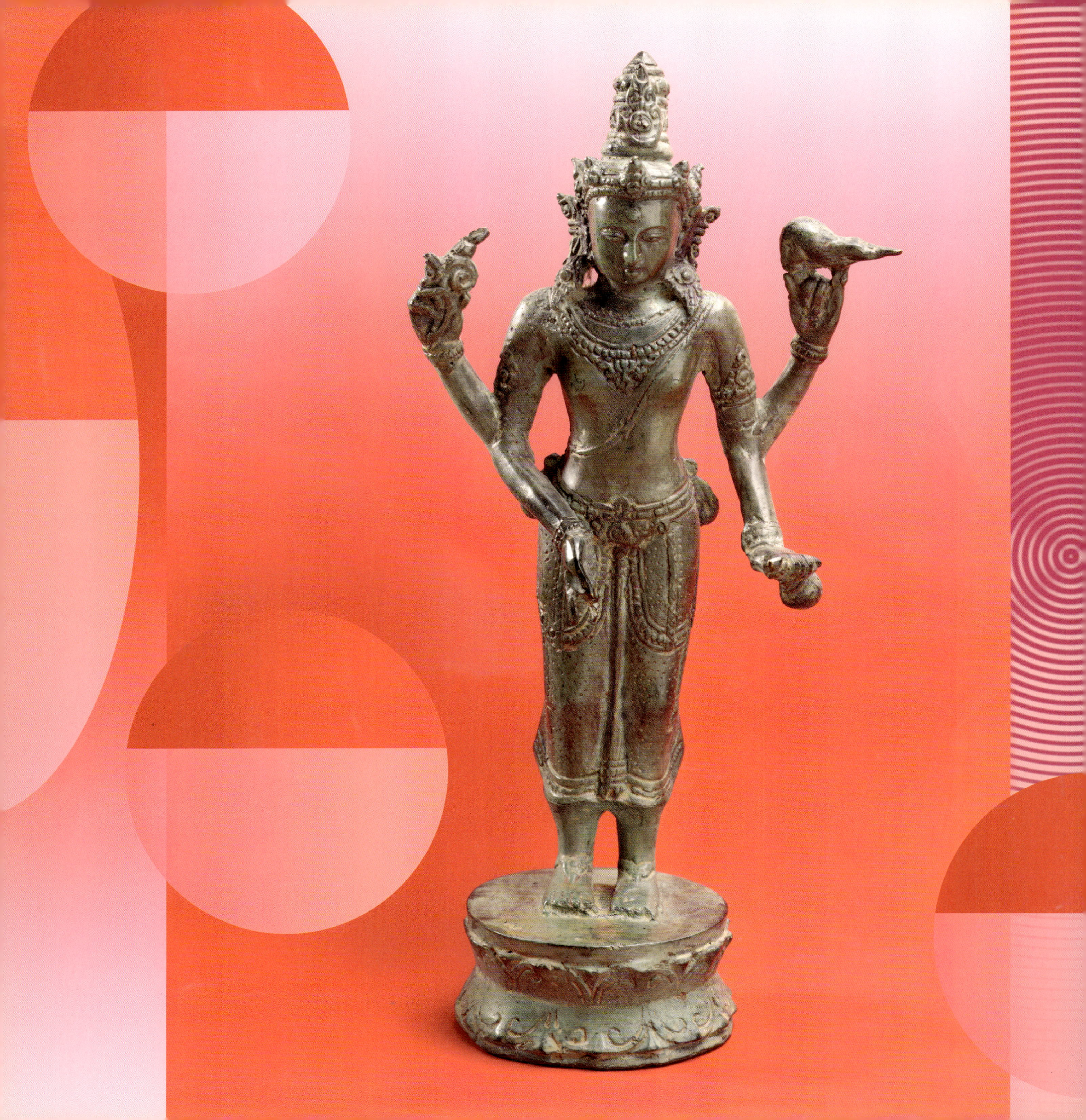

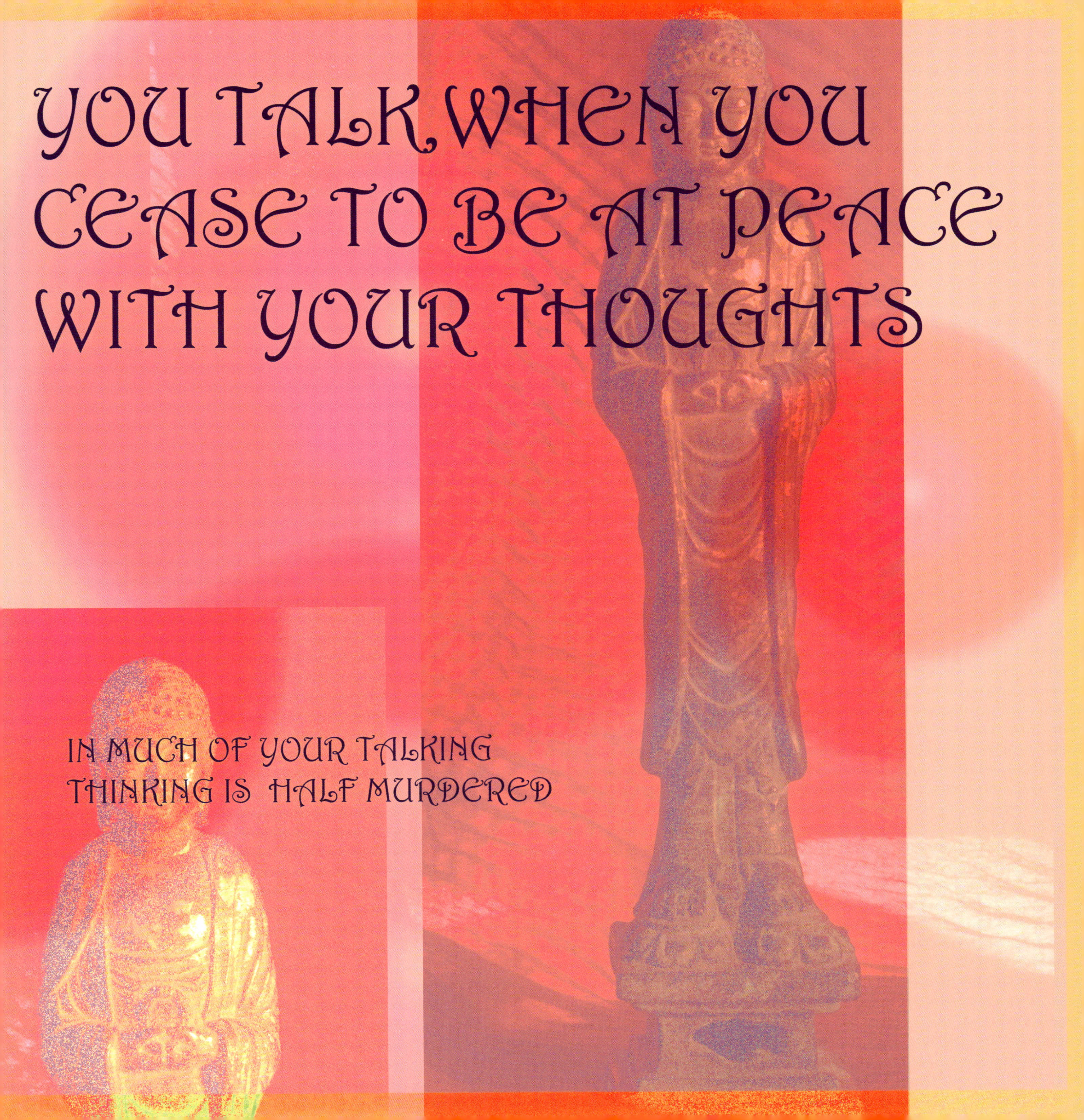

YOU TALK WHEN YOU CEASE TO BE AT PEACE WITH YOUR THOUGHTS

IN MUCH OF YOUR TALKING
THINKING IS HALF MURDERED

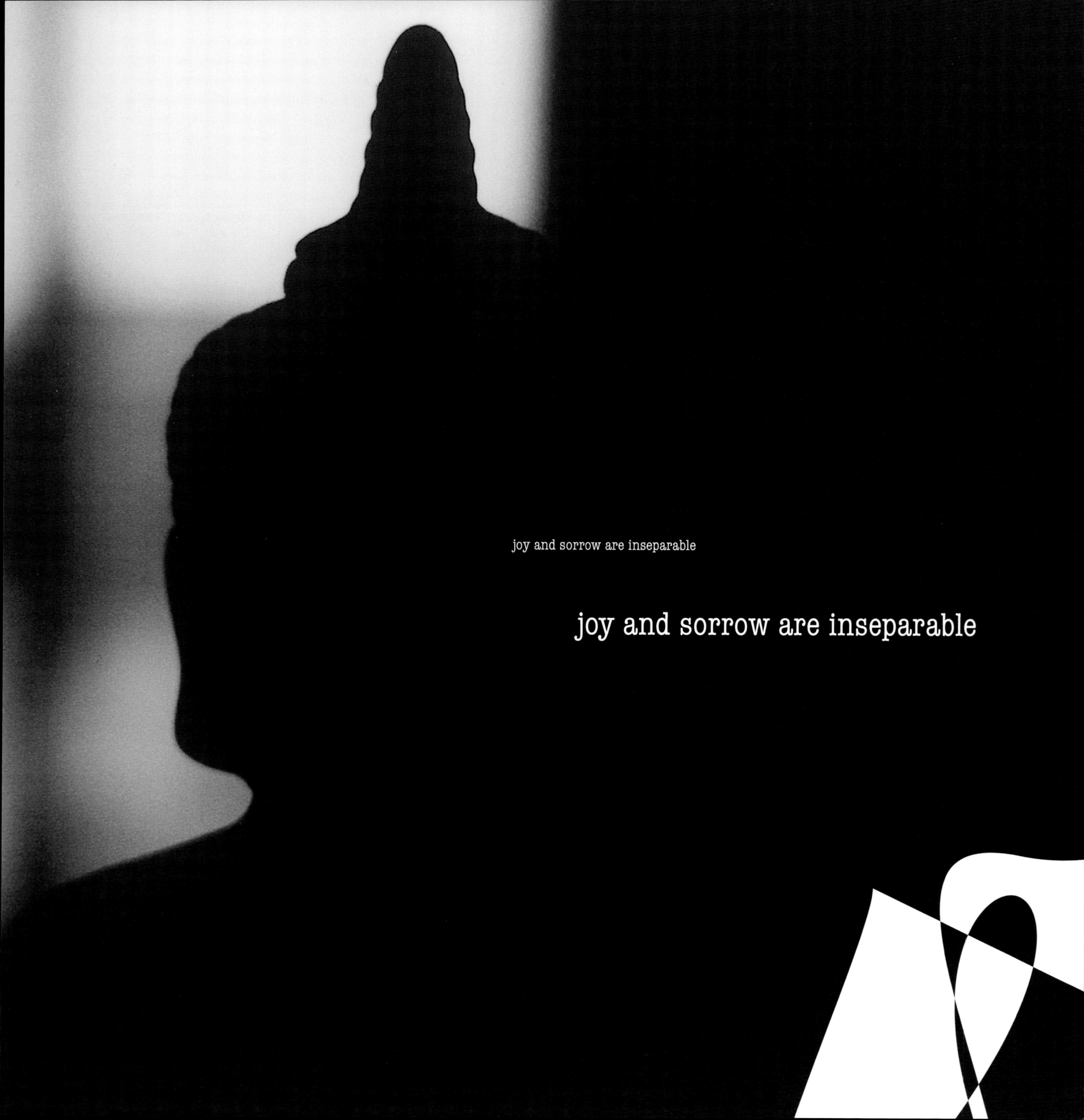
joy and sorrow are inseparable
joy and sorrow are inseparable

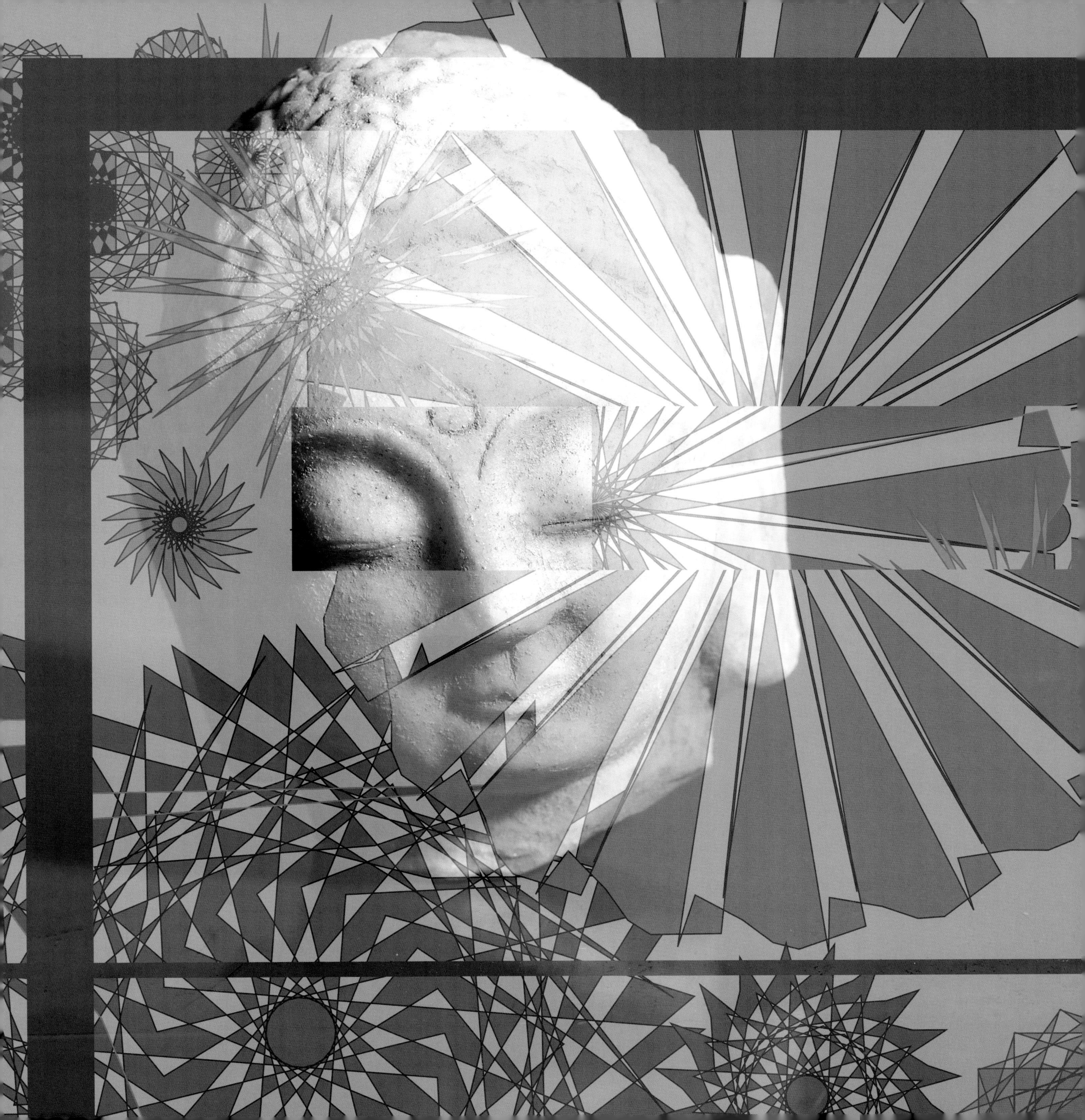

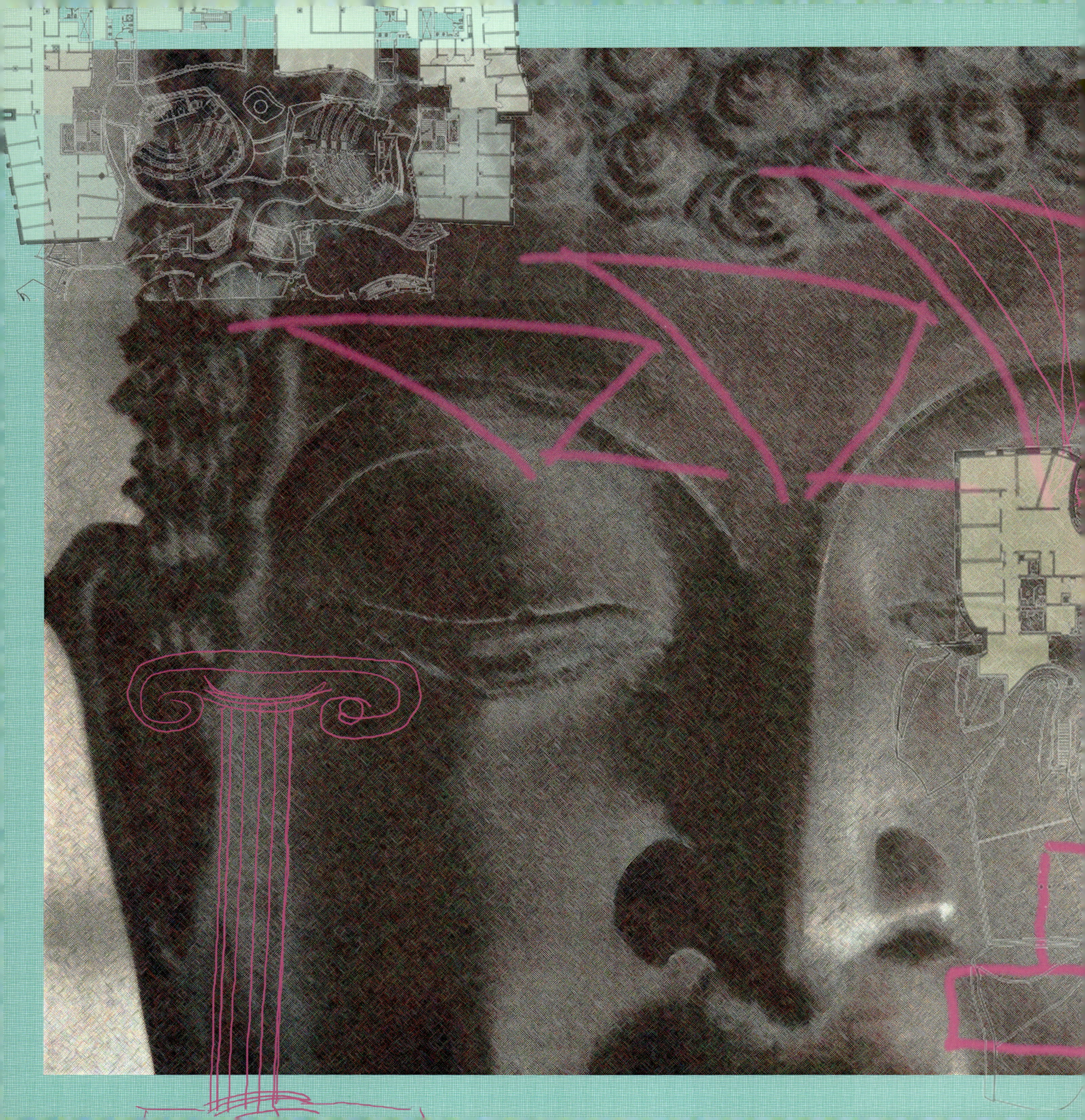

YOUR HOUSE IS YOUR LARGER BODY
IT GROWS IN THE SUN AND IT
SLEEPS IN THE STILLNESS OF THE NIGHT
IT IS NOT DREAMLESS

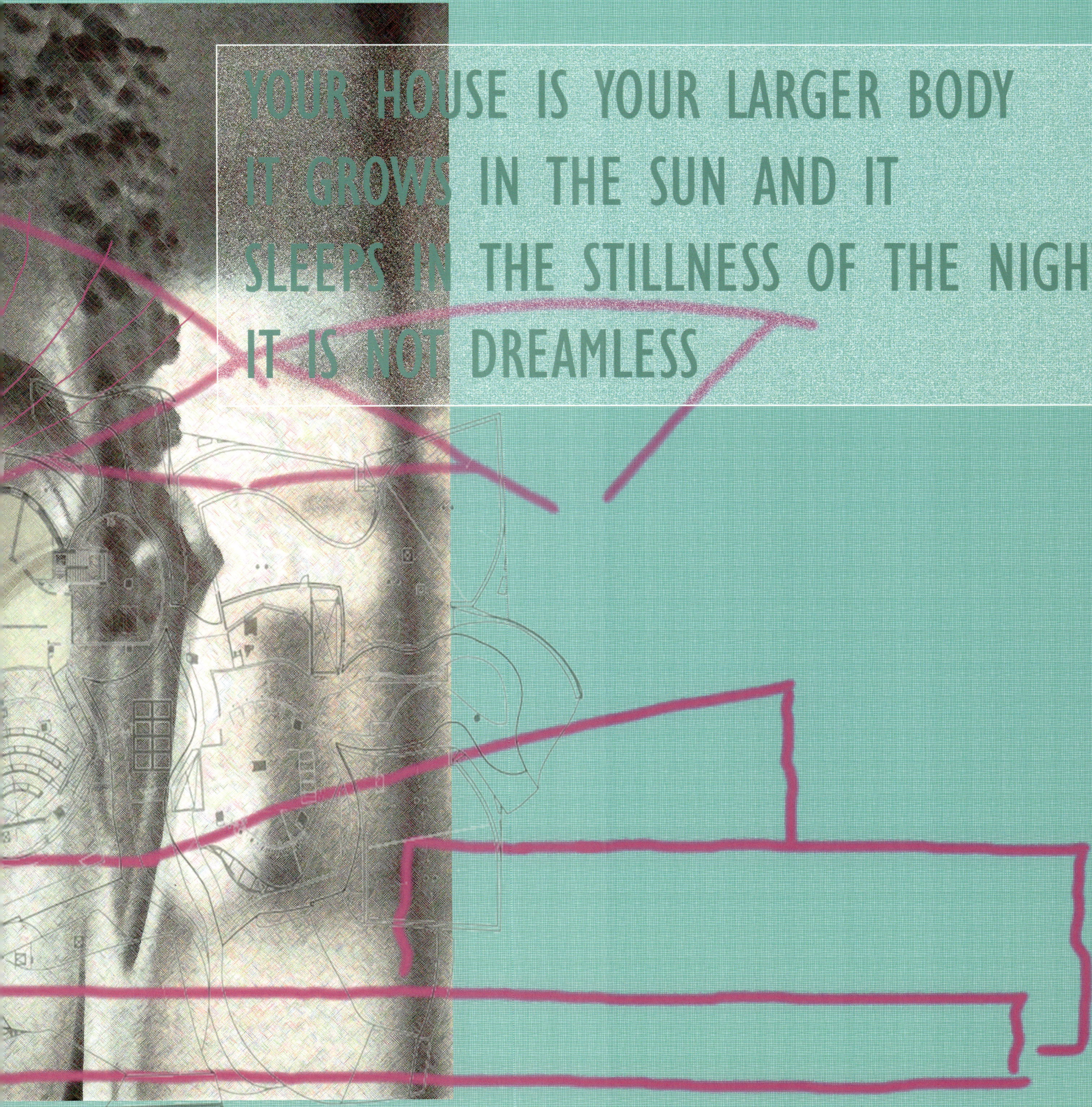

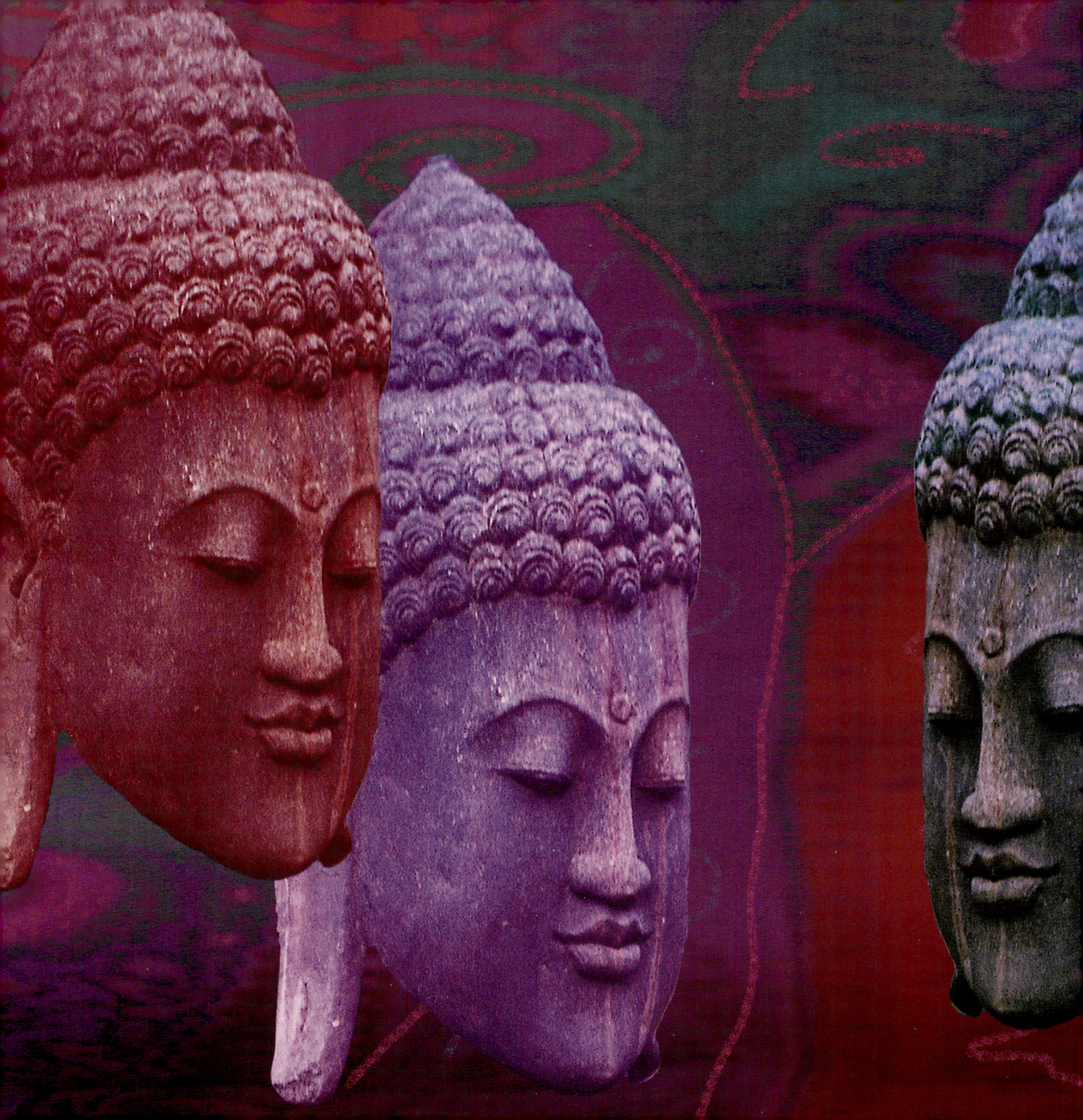

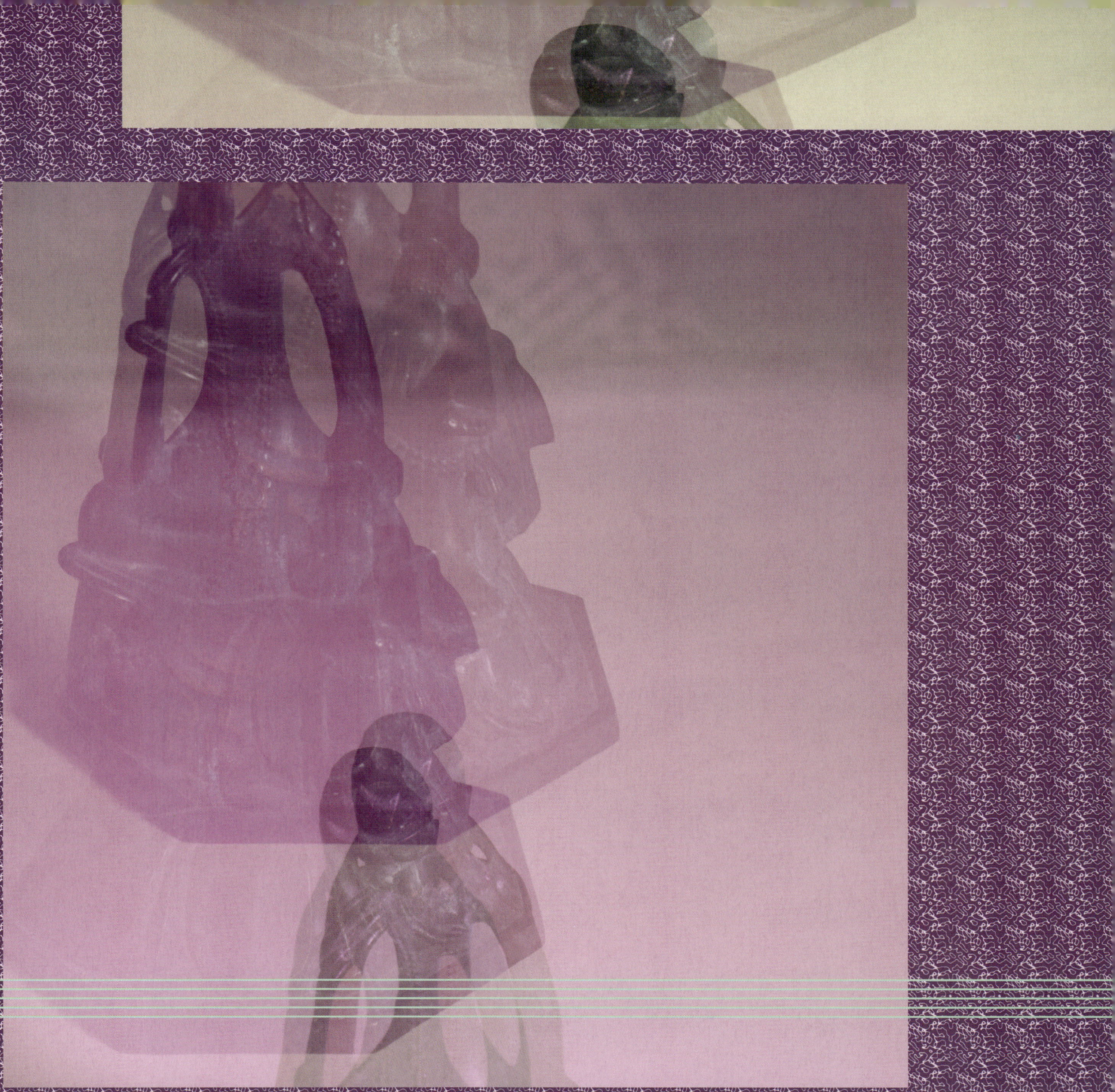

YOUR PAIN IS THE BREAKING OF THE SHELL
THAT ENCLOSES YOUR UNDERSTANDING

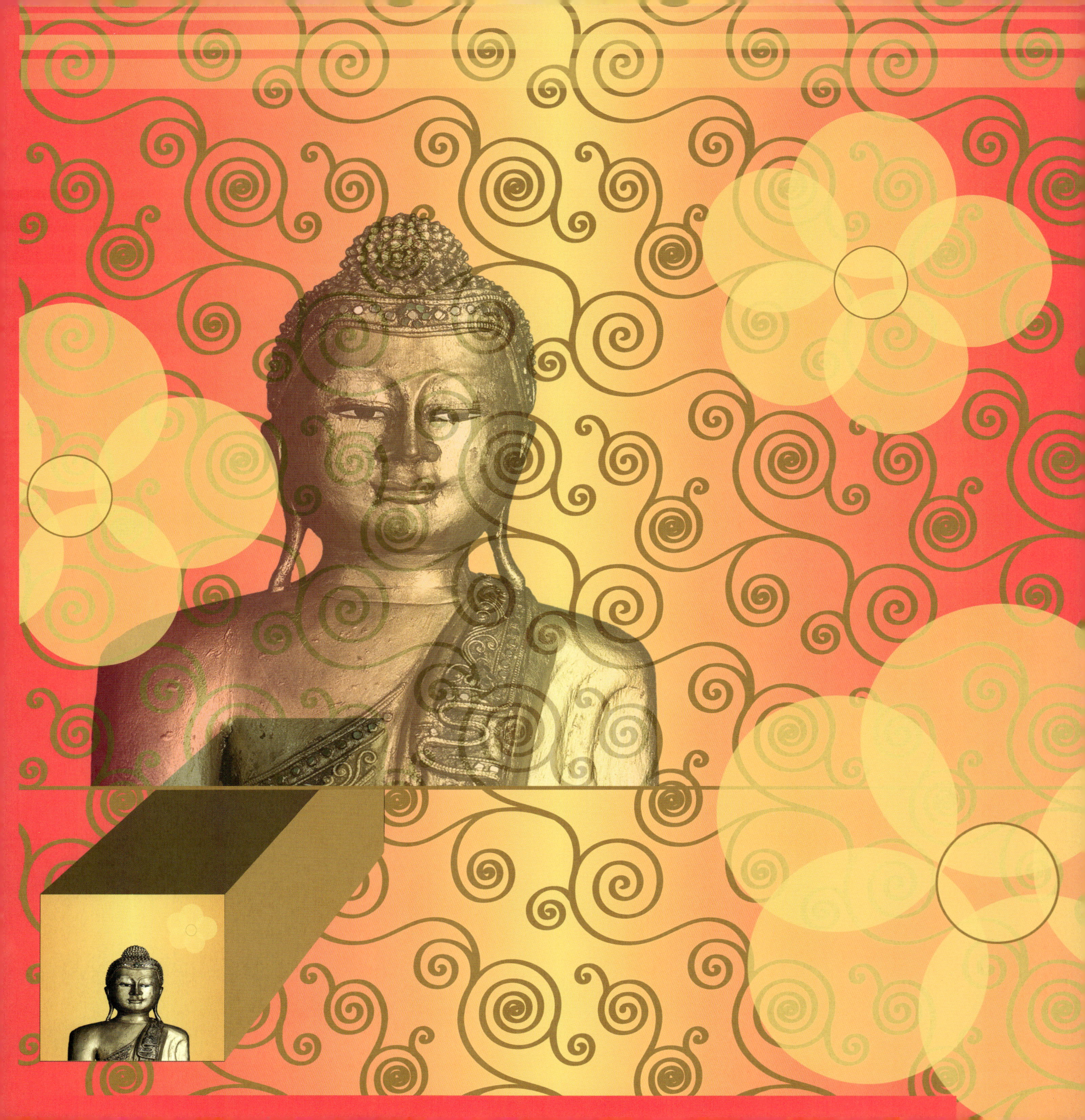

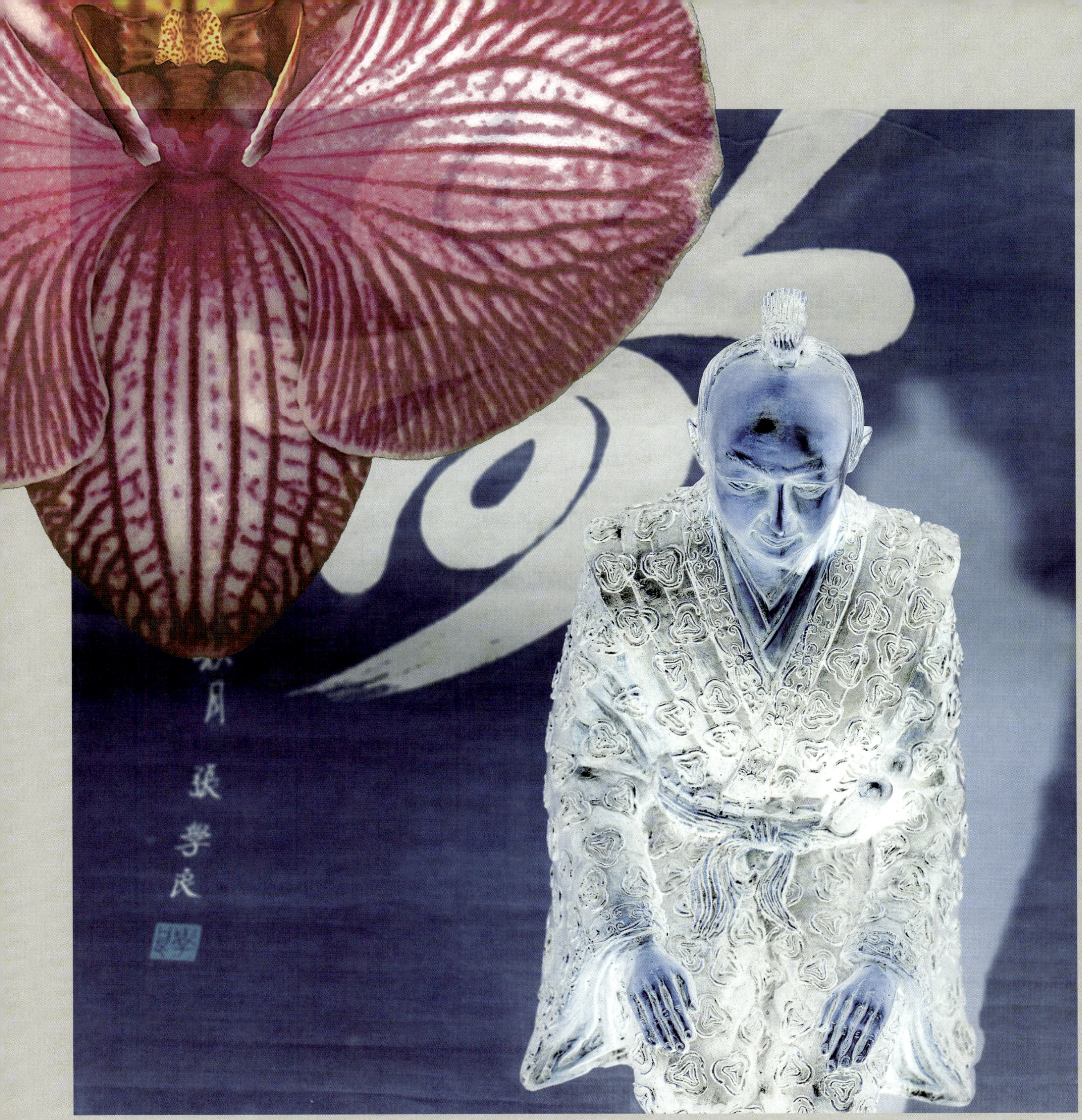
月 張学良

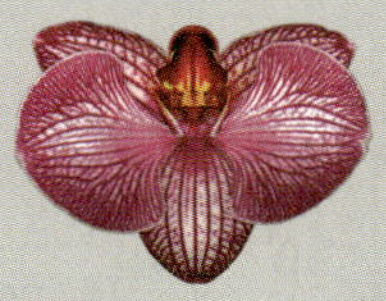

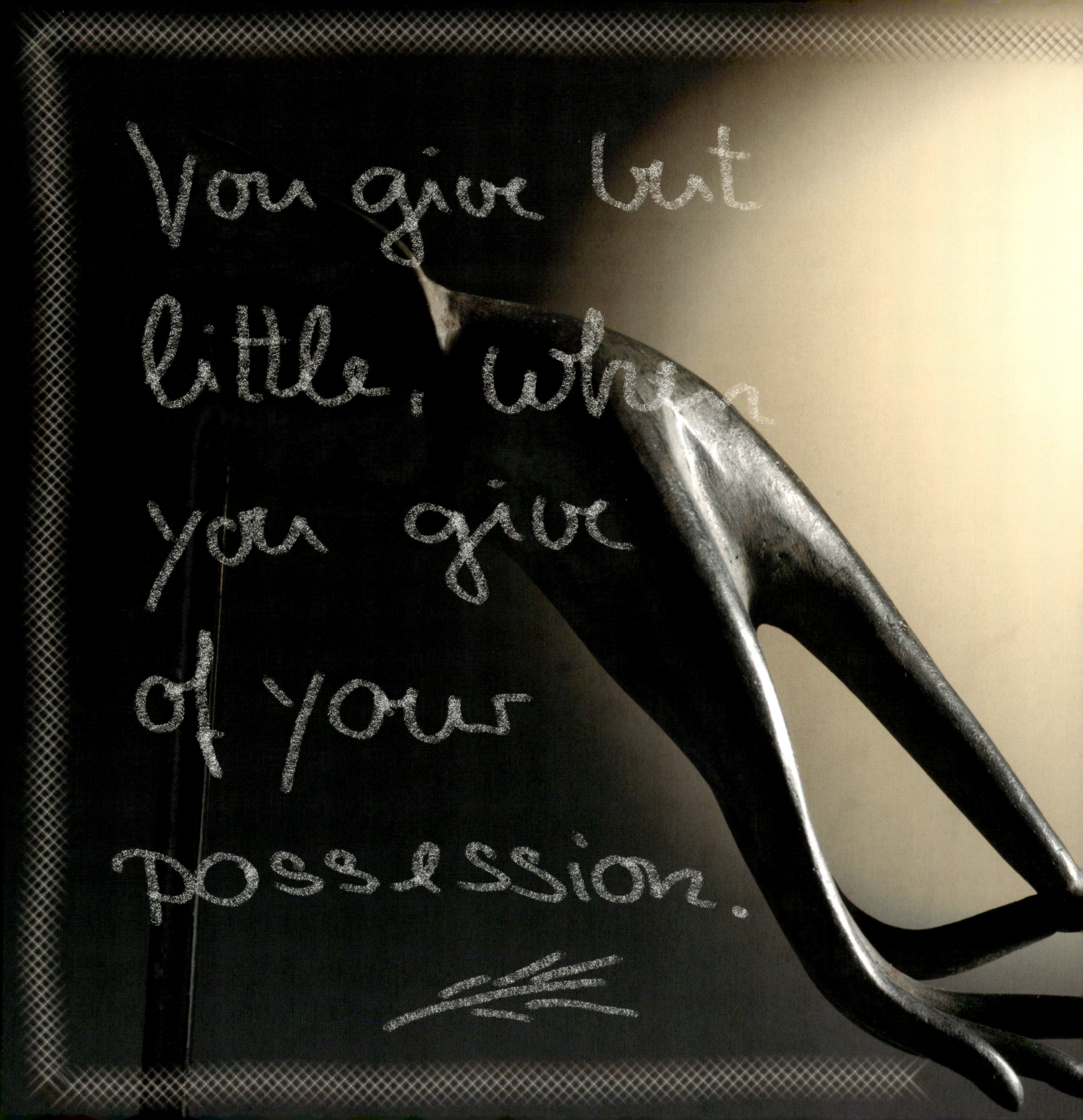
You give but
little. when
you give
of your
possession.

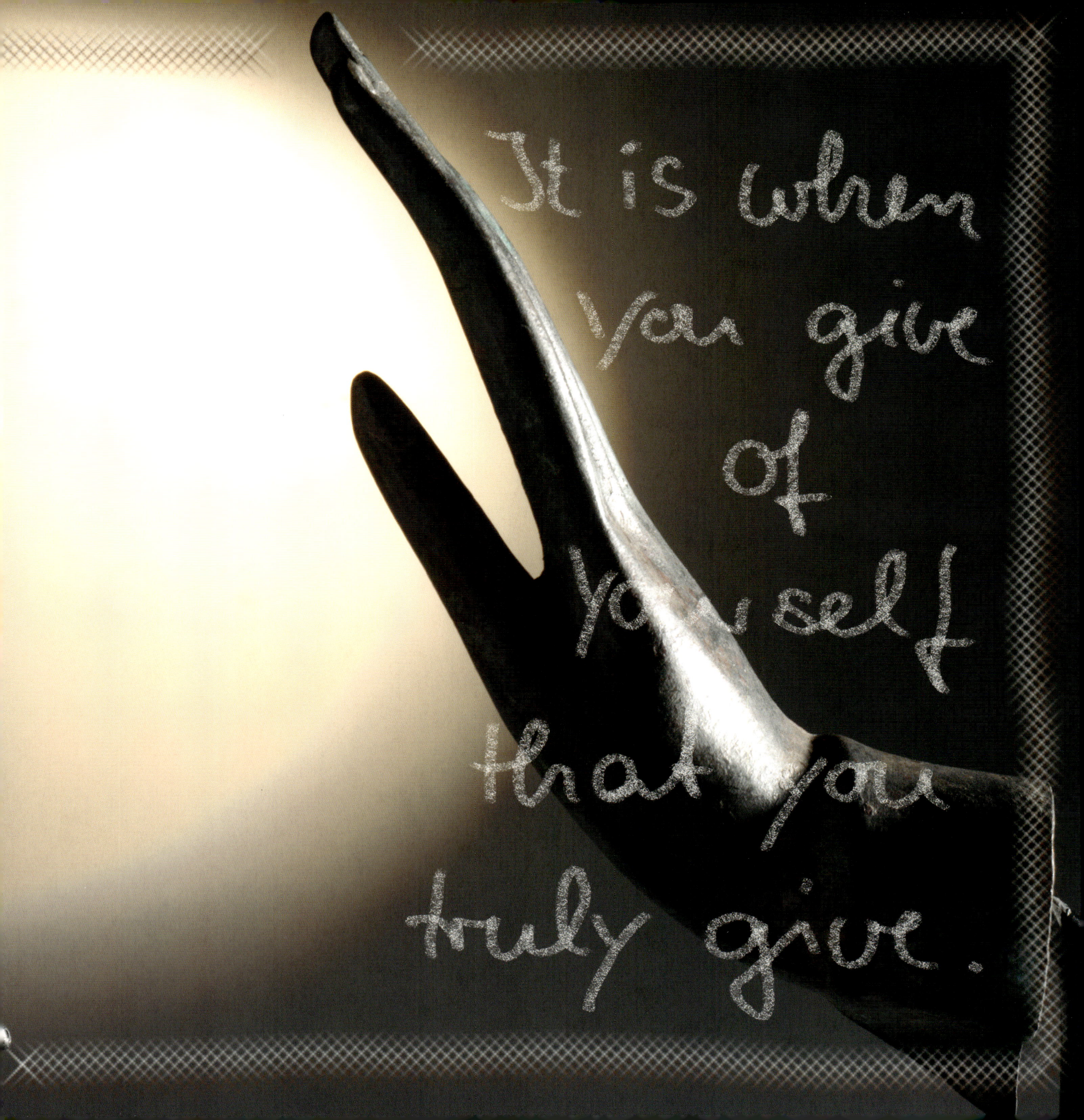
It is when
you give
of
yourself
that you
truly give.

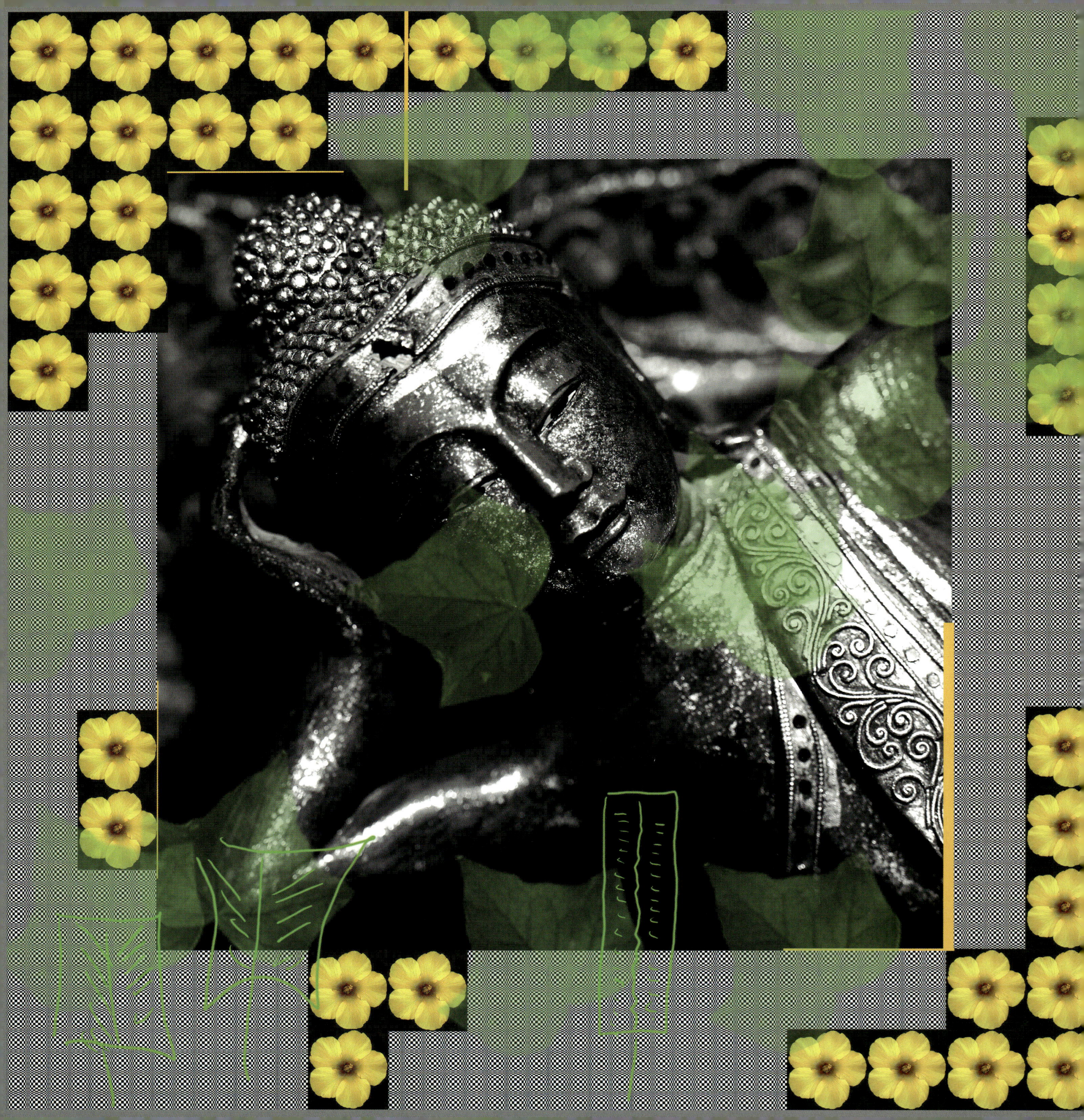

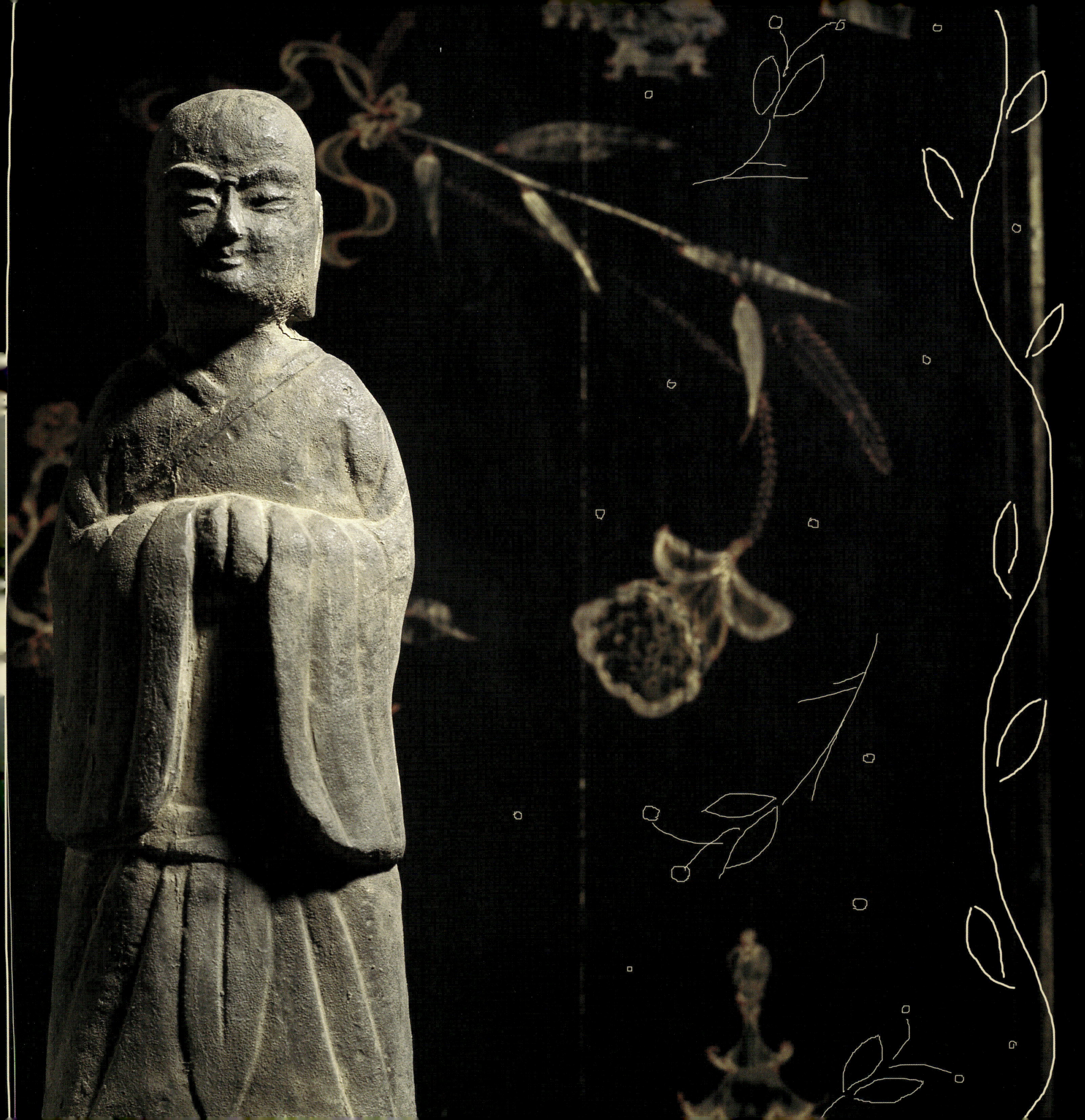

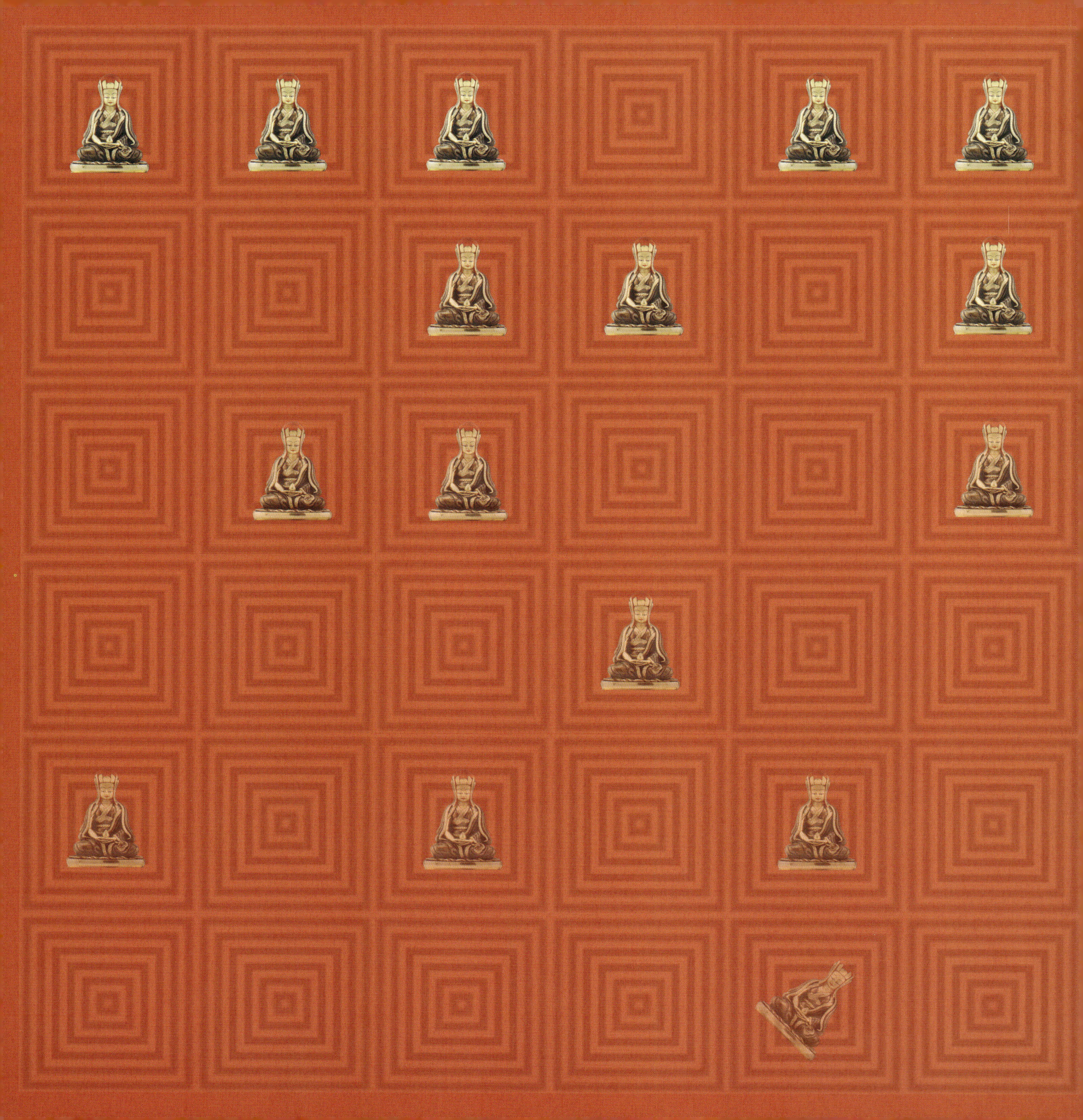

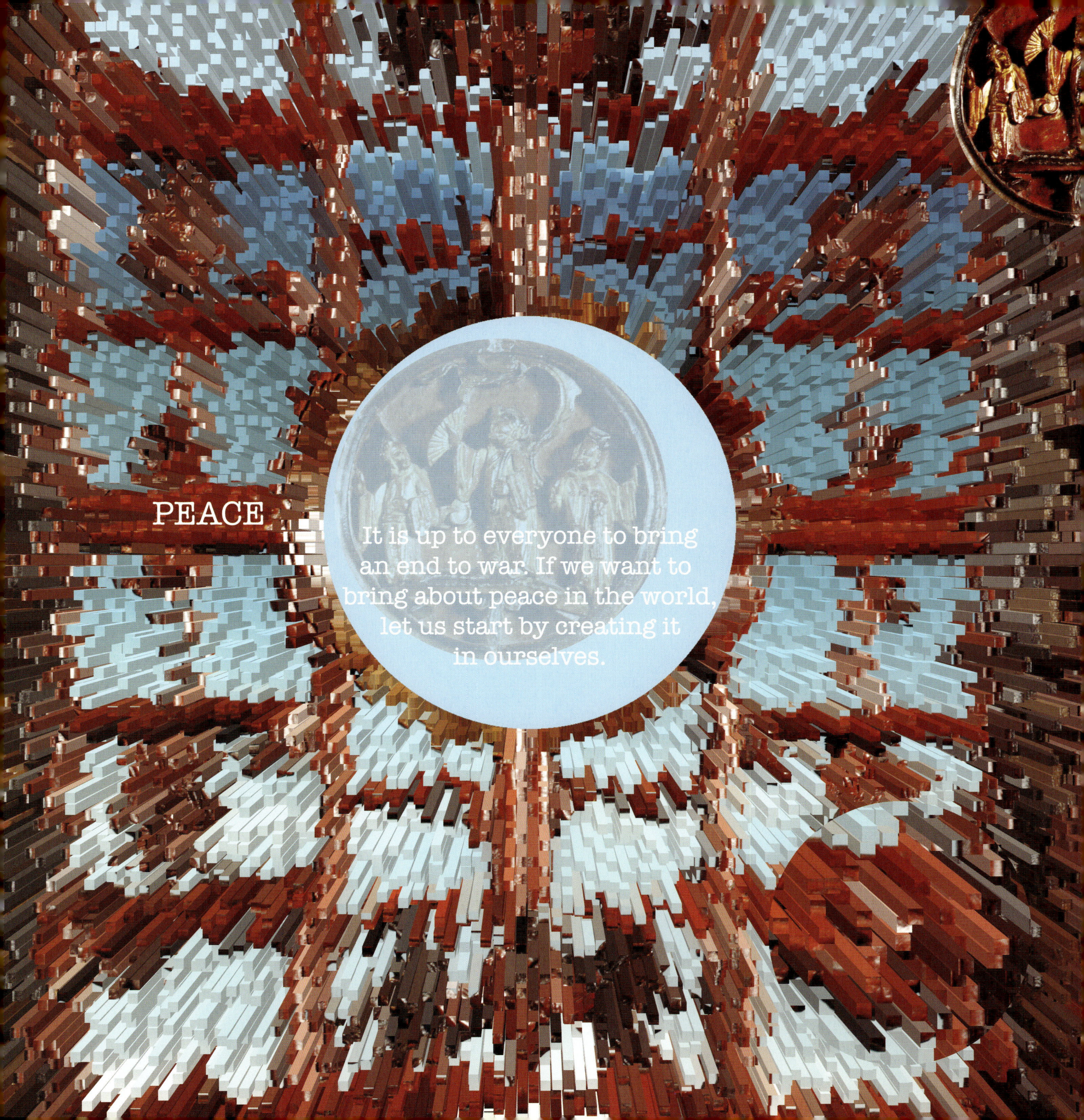

PEACE

It is up to everyone to bring an end to war. If we want to bring about peace in the world, let us start by creating it in ourselves.

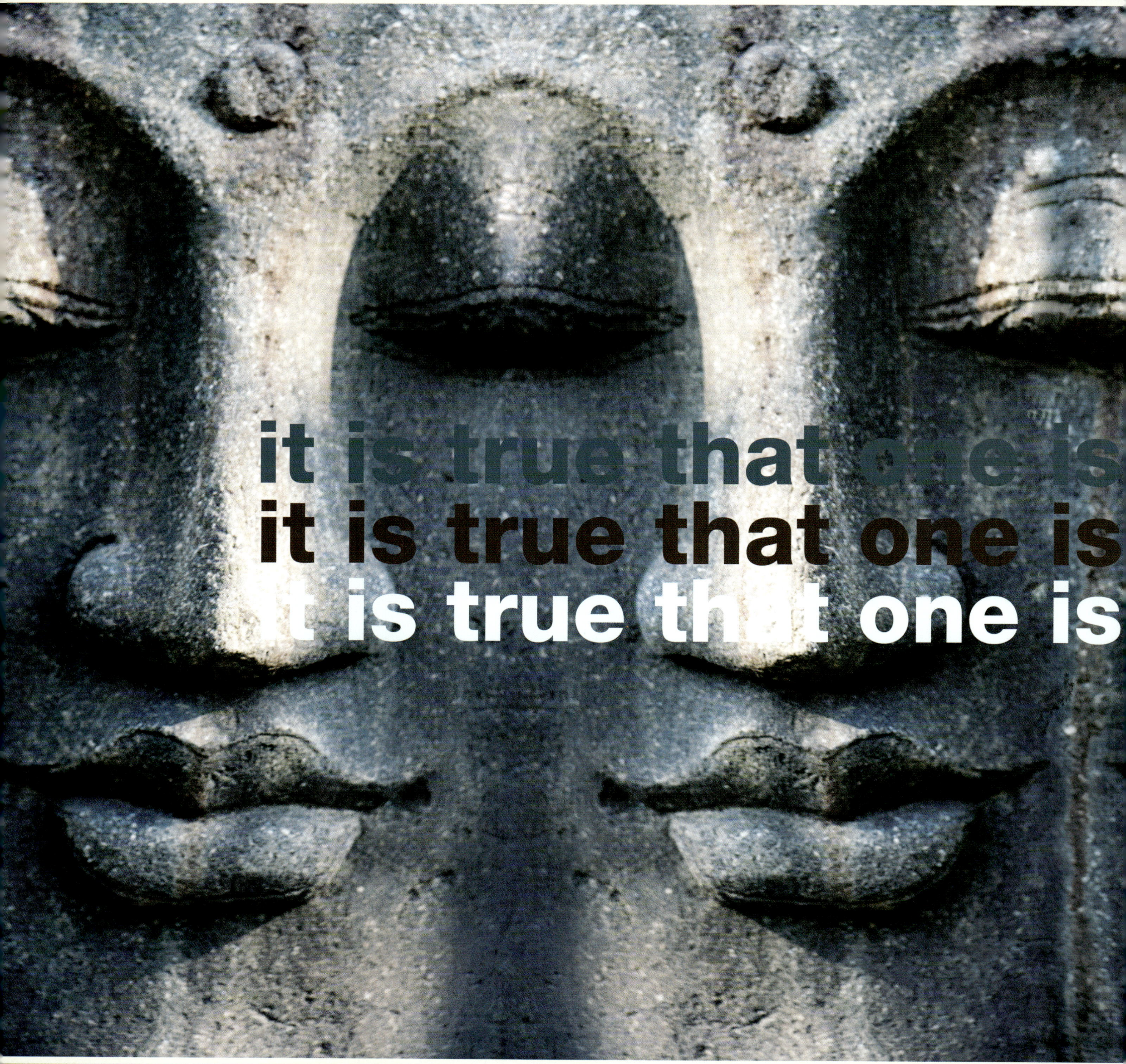
it is true that one is
it is true that one is
it is true that one is

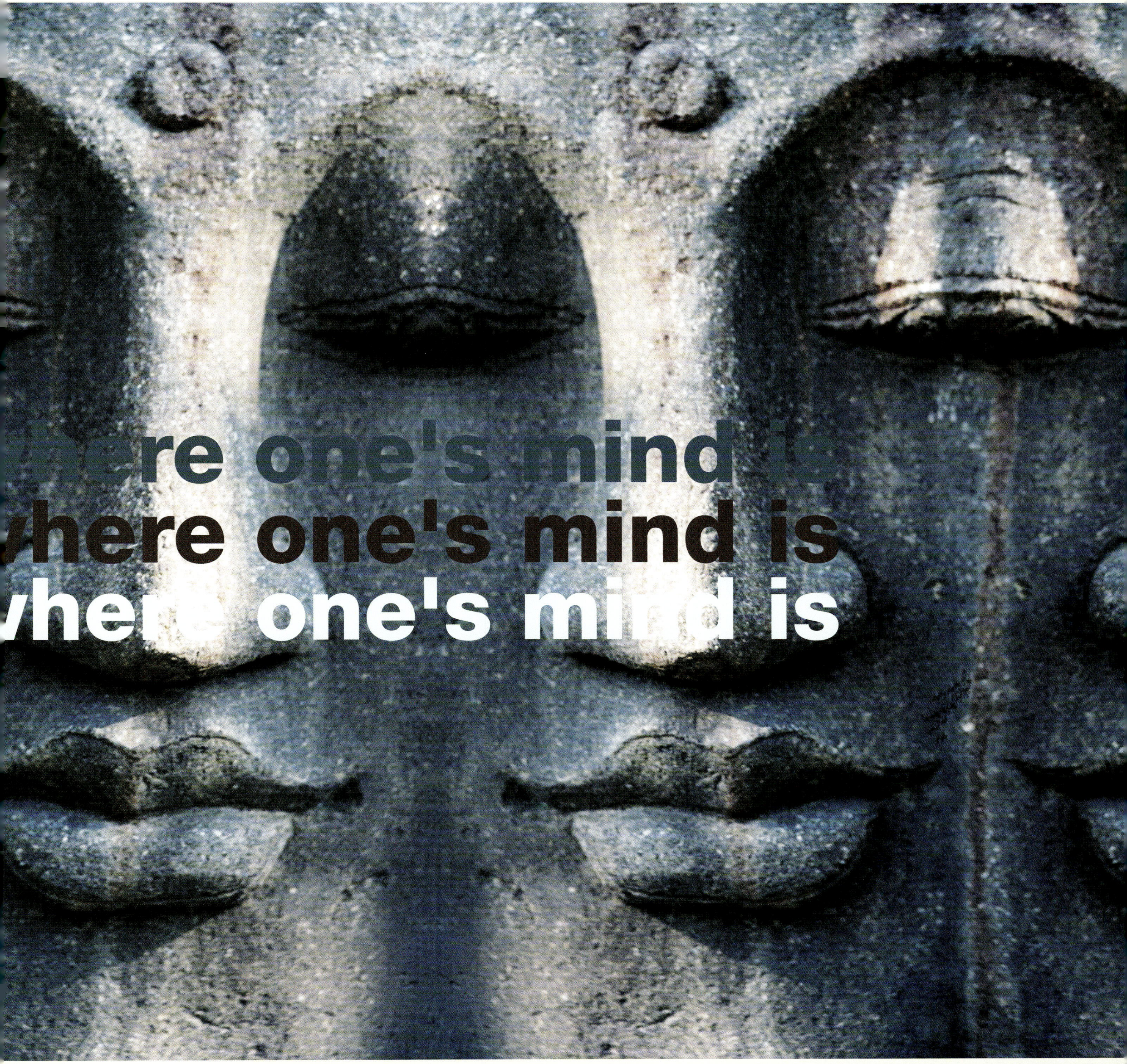
here one's mind is
here one's mind is
here one's mind is

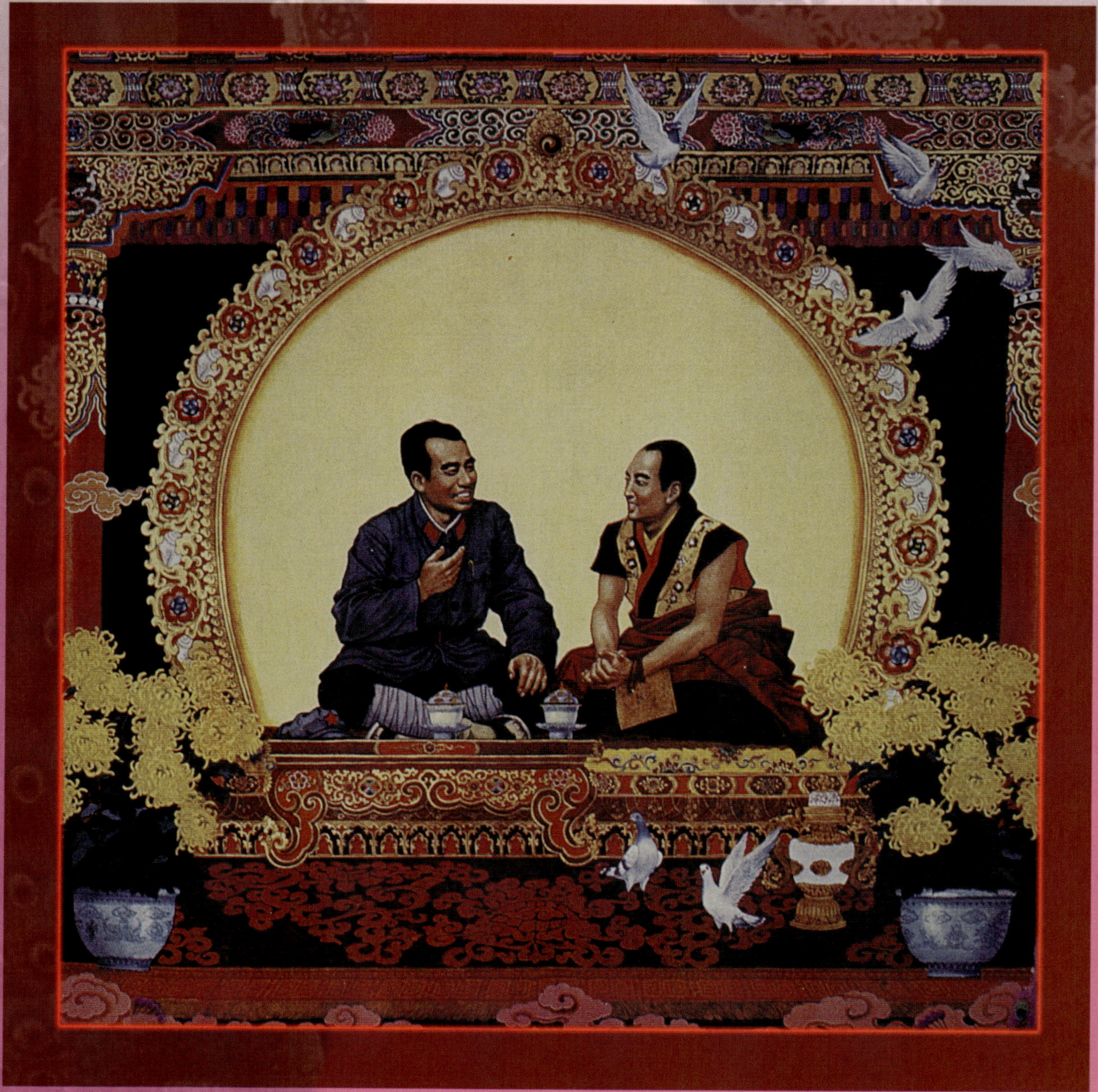

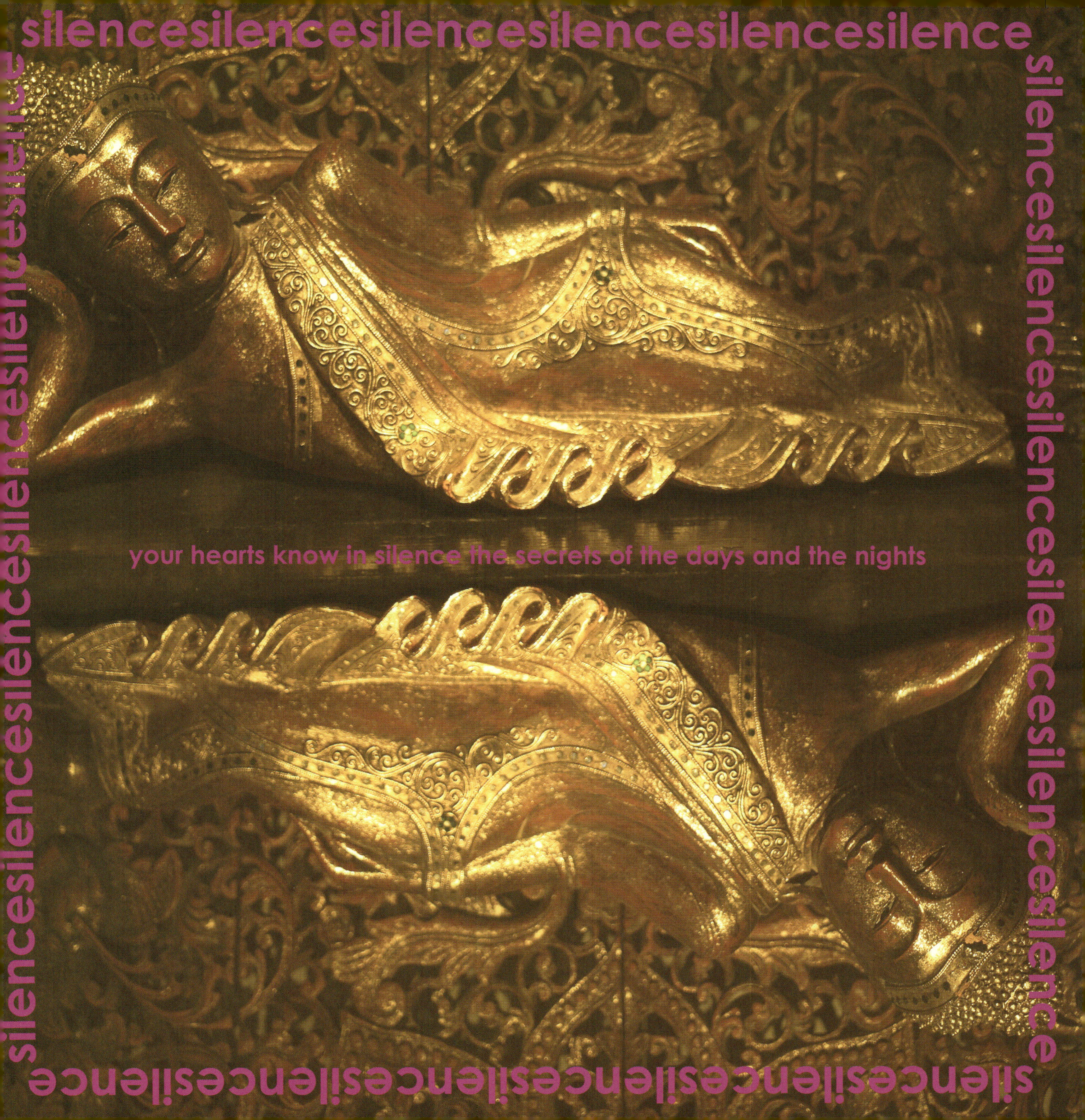
silencesilencesilencesilencesilencesilence
your hearts know in silence the secrets of the days and the nights

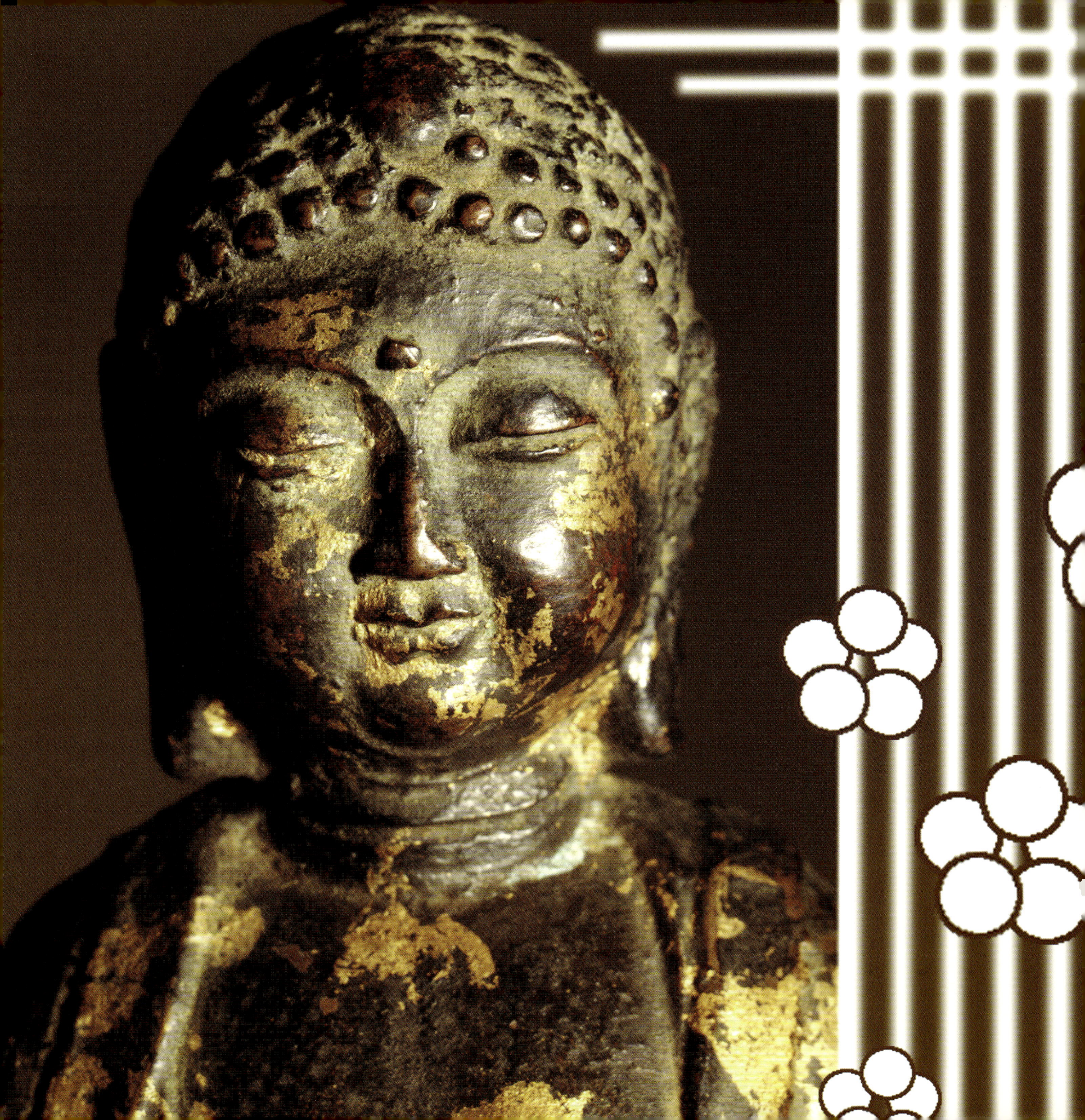

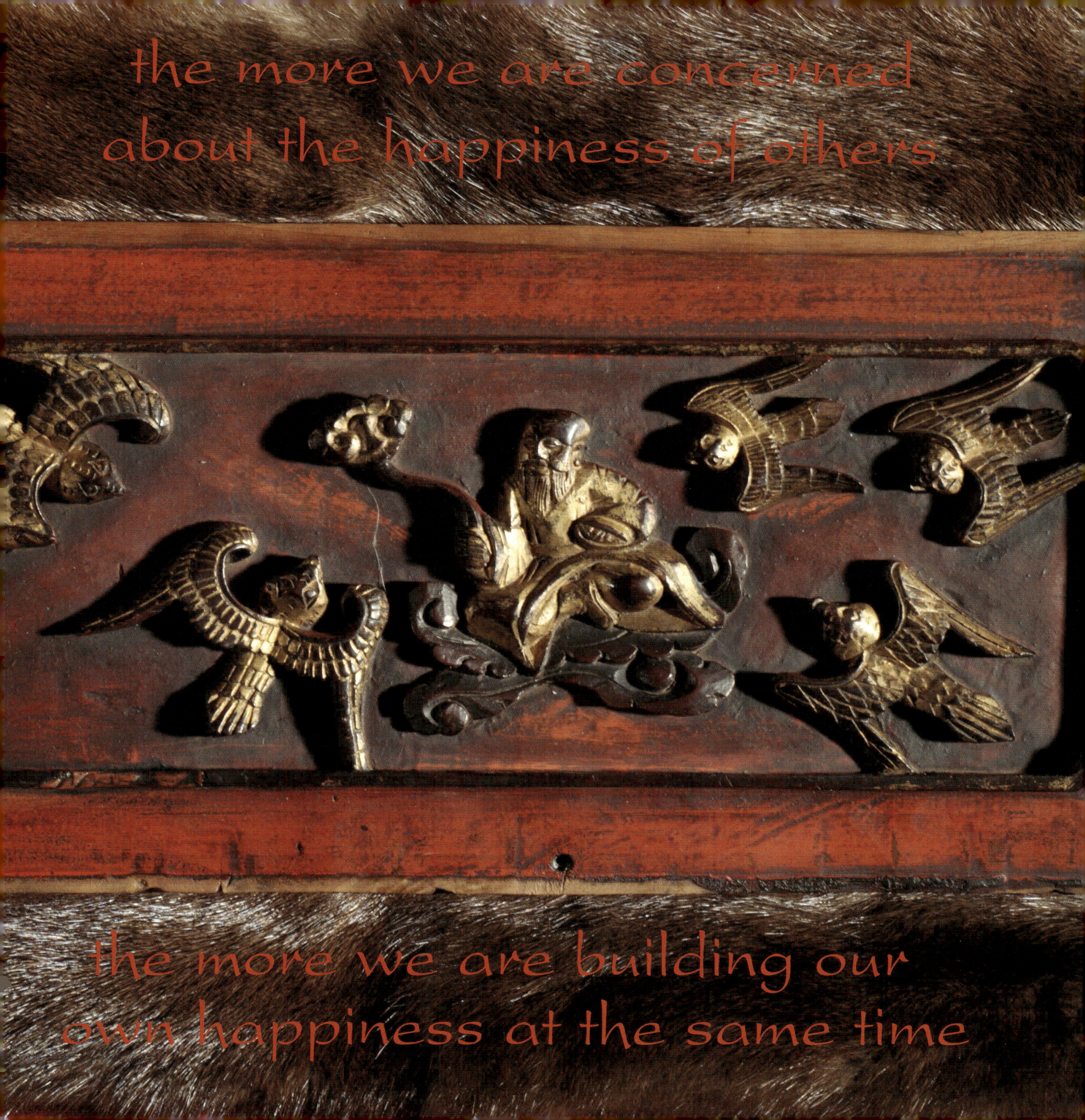
the more we are concerned
about the happiness of others
the more we are building our
own happiness at the same time

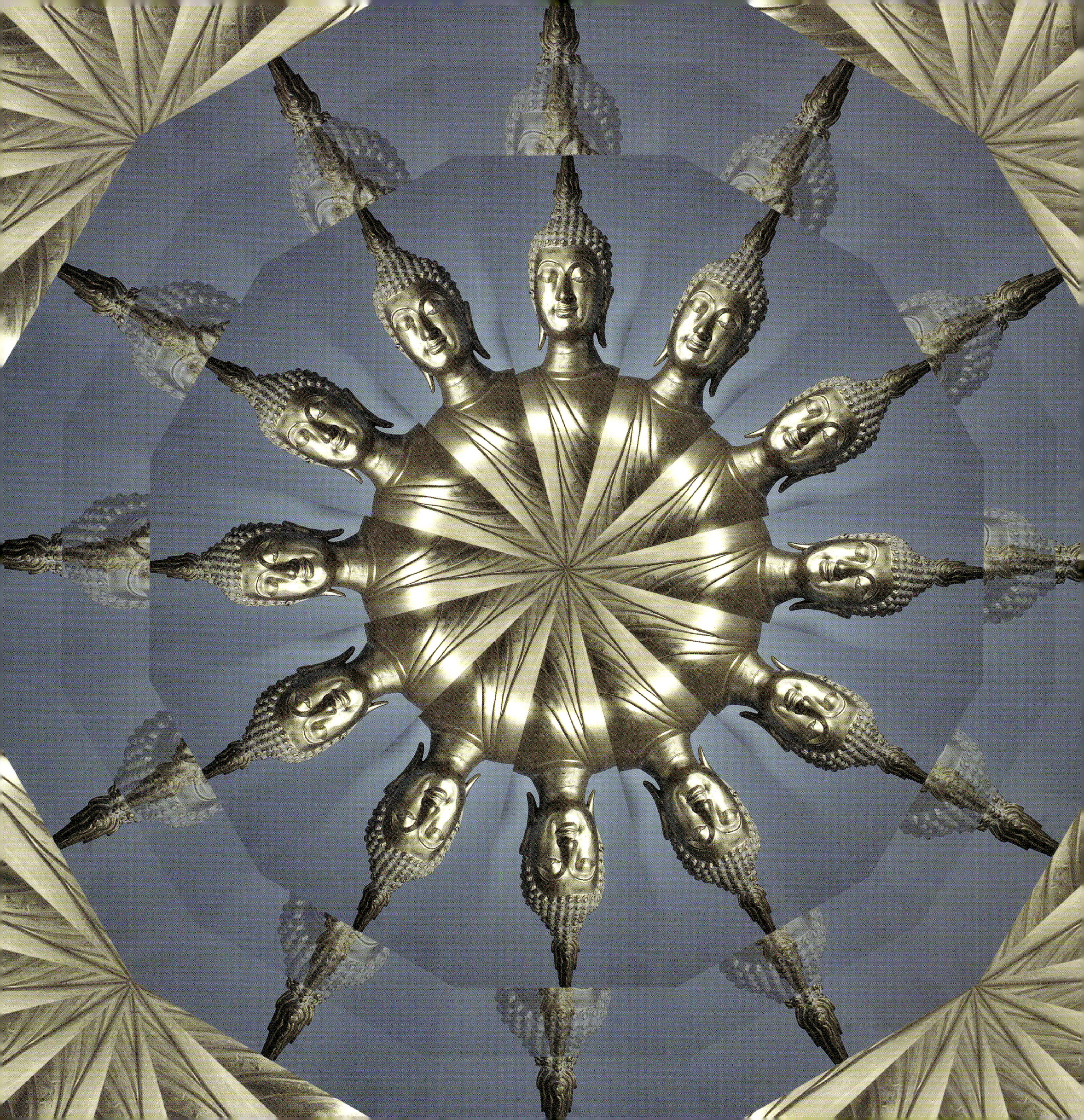

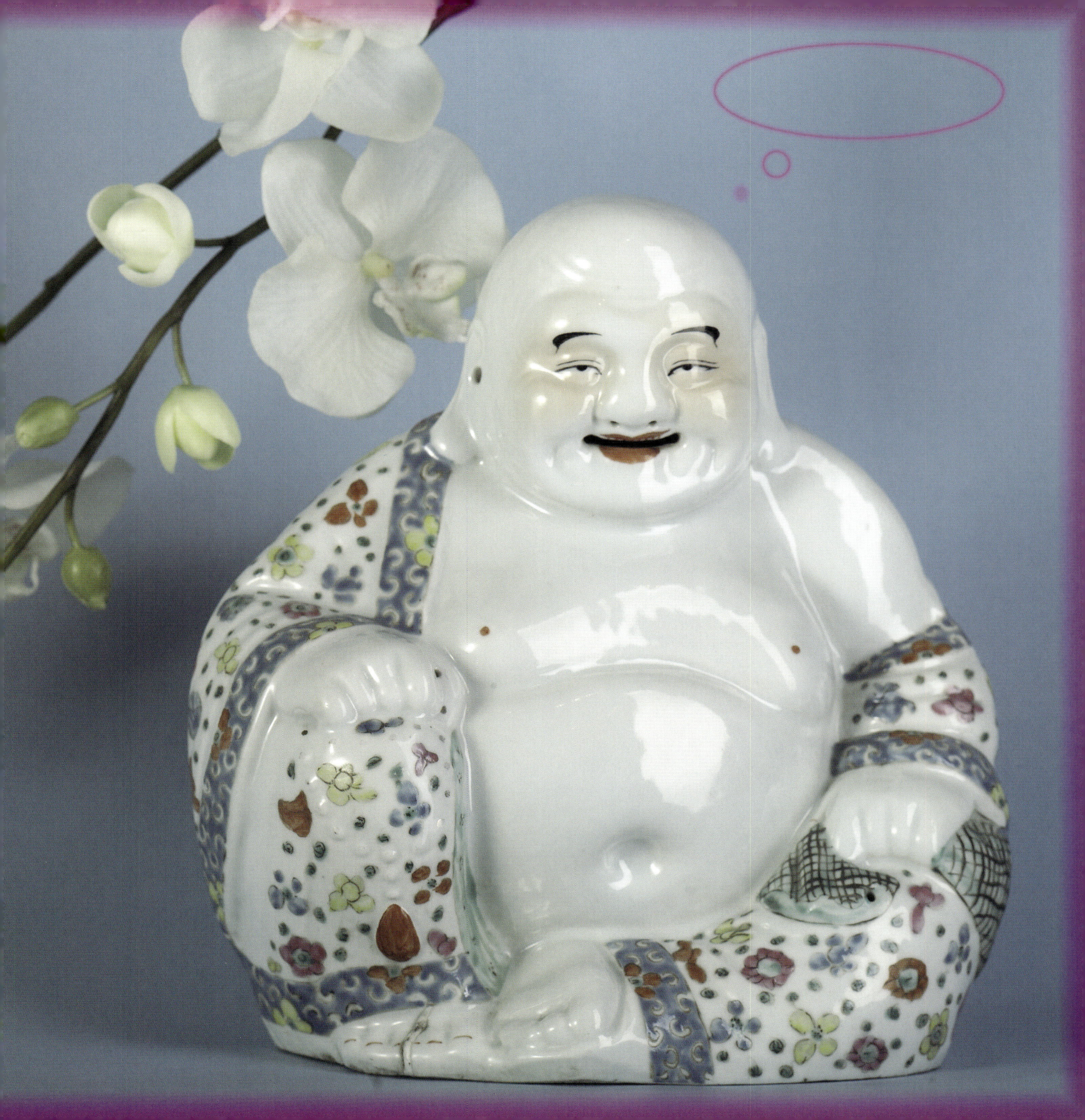

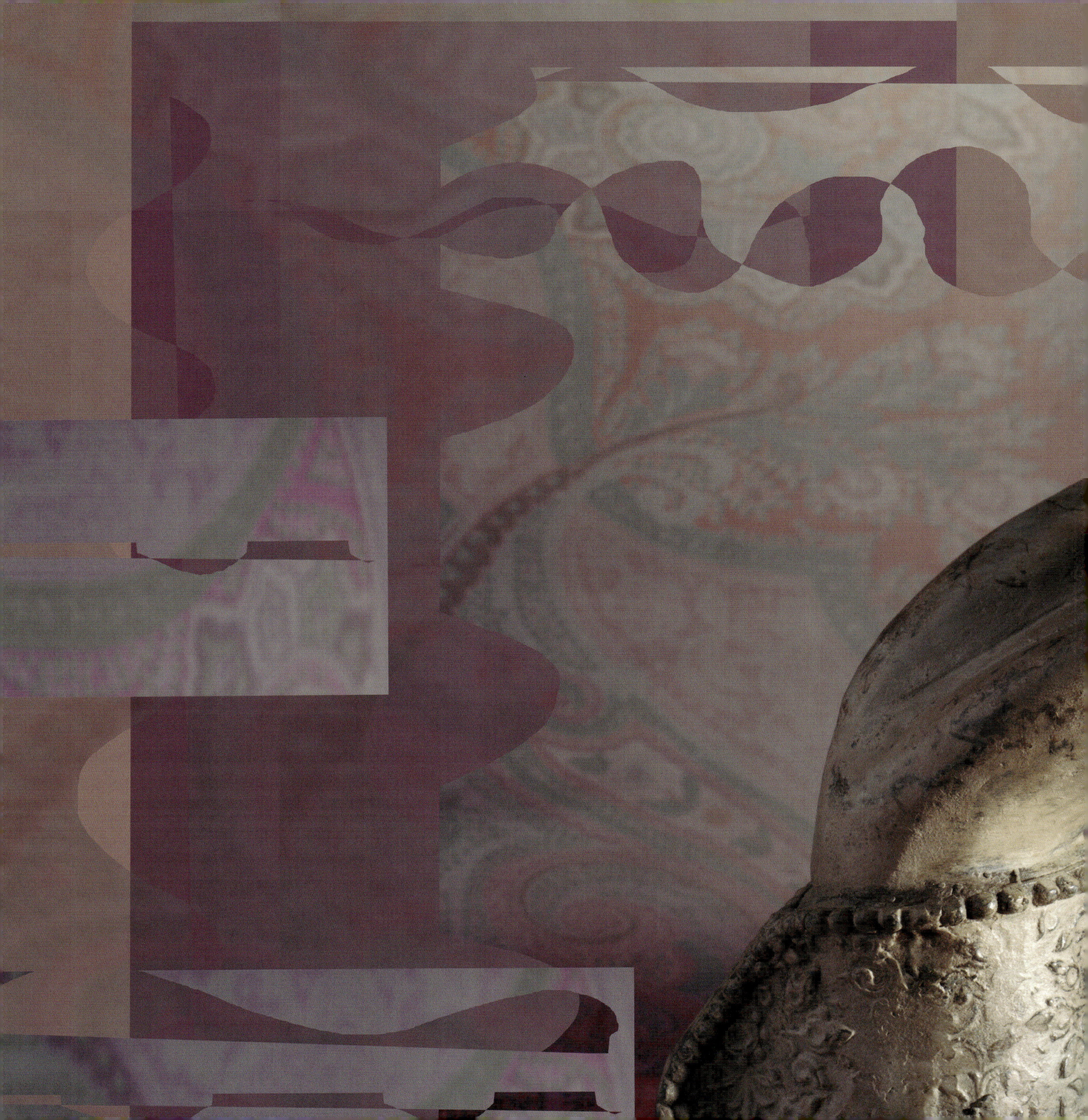

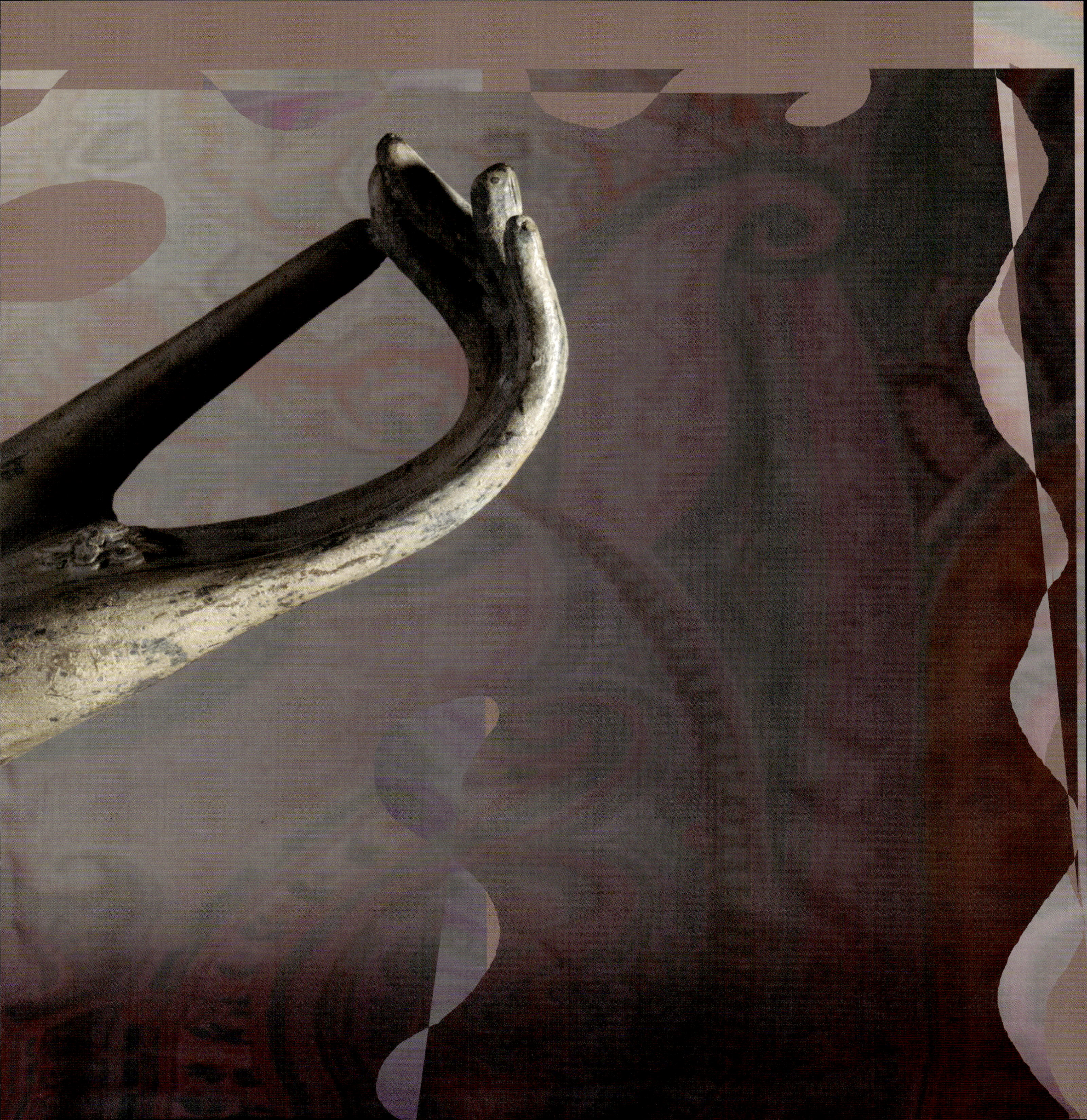

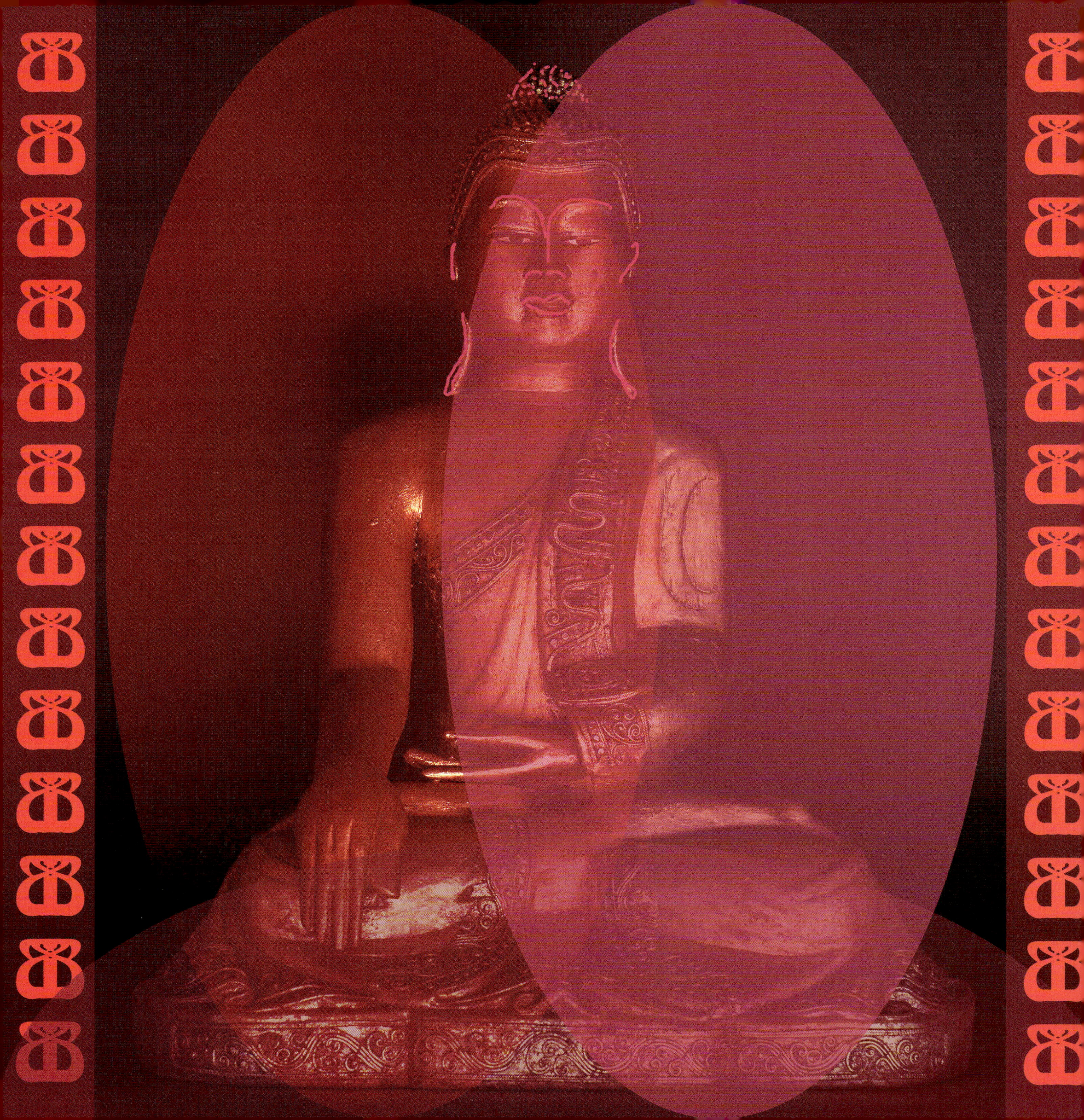

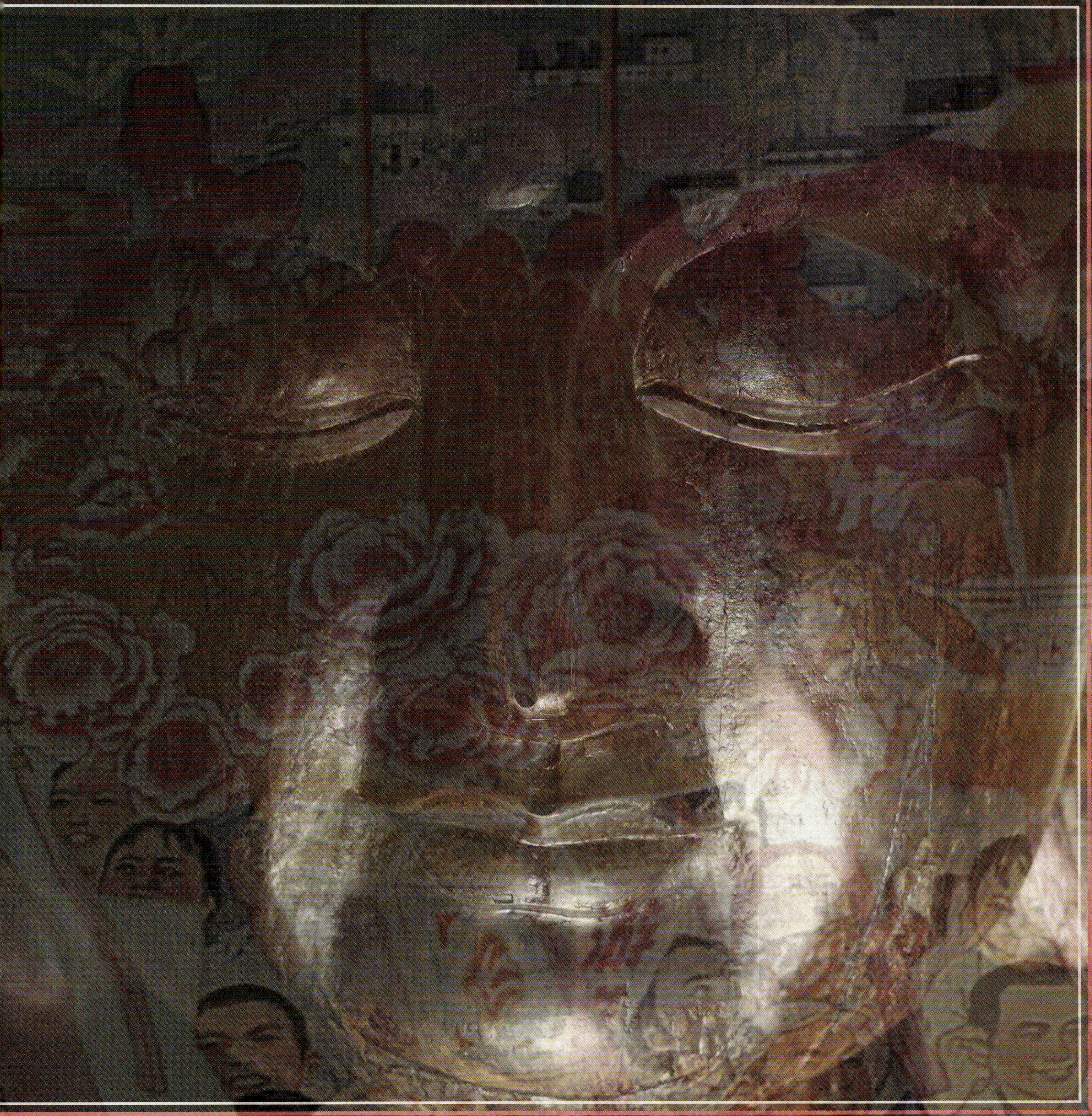

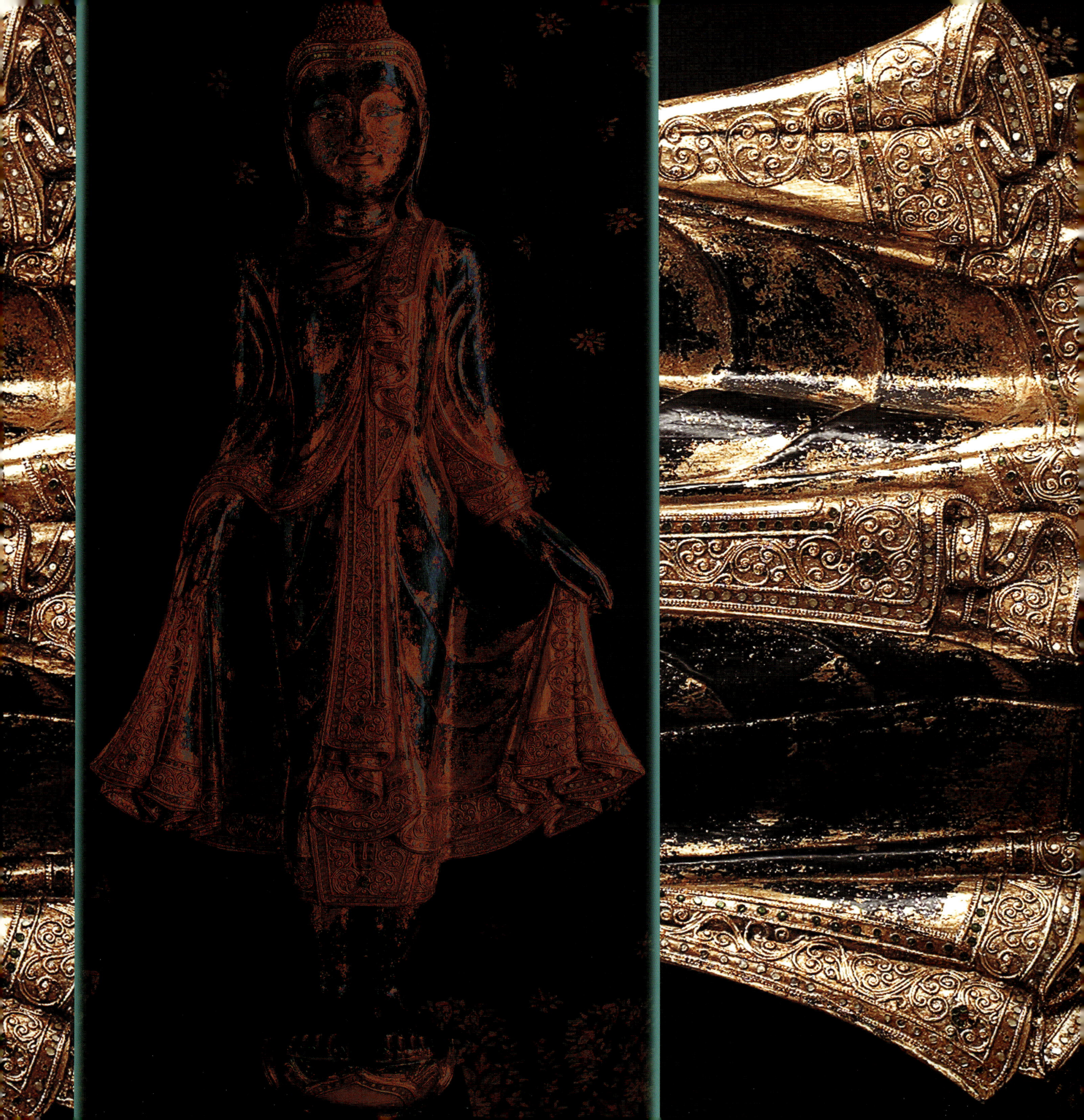

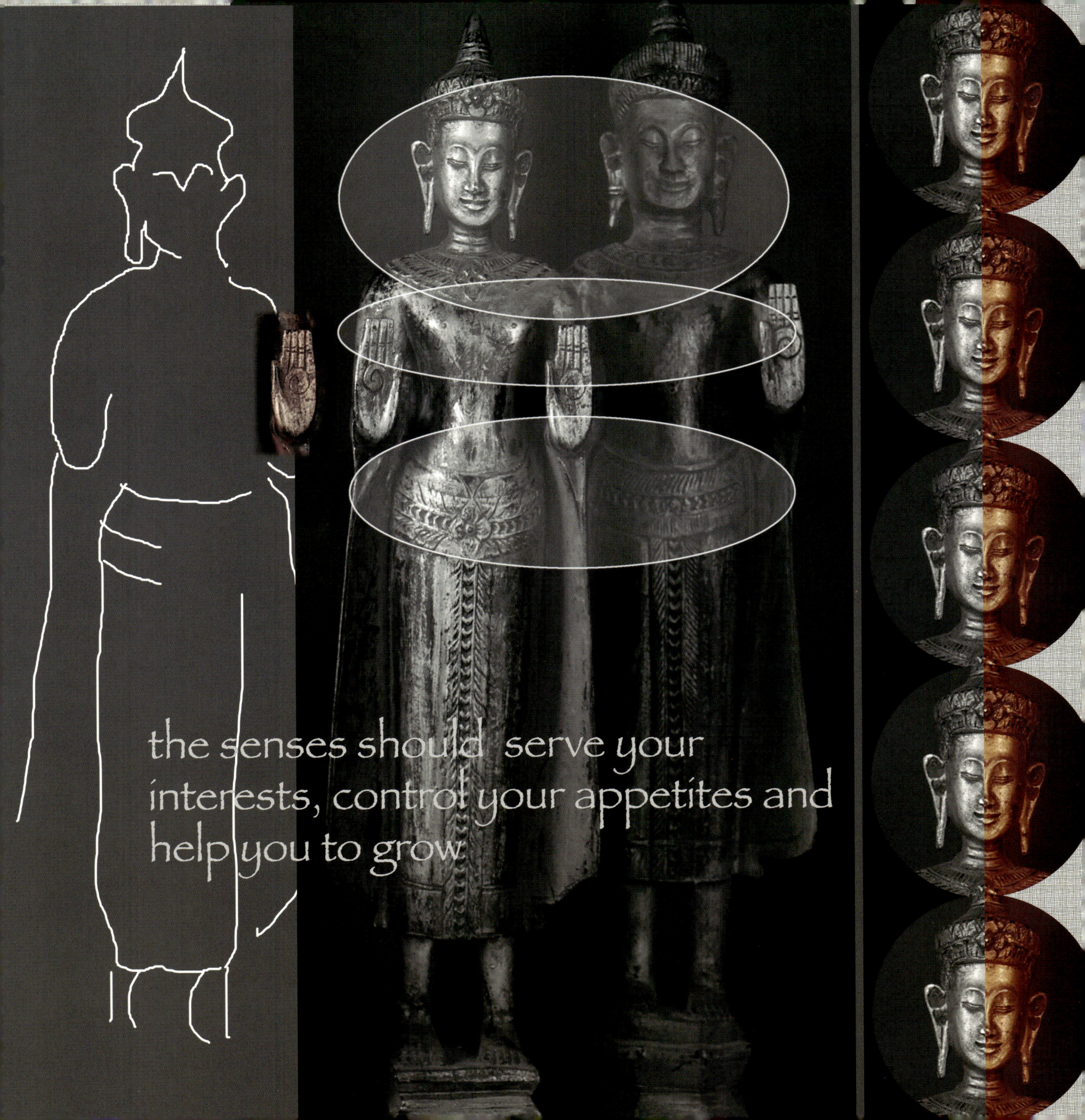
the senses should serve your
interests, control your appetites and
help you to grow

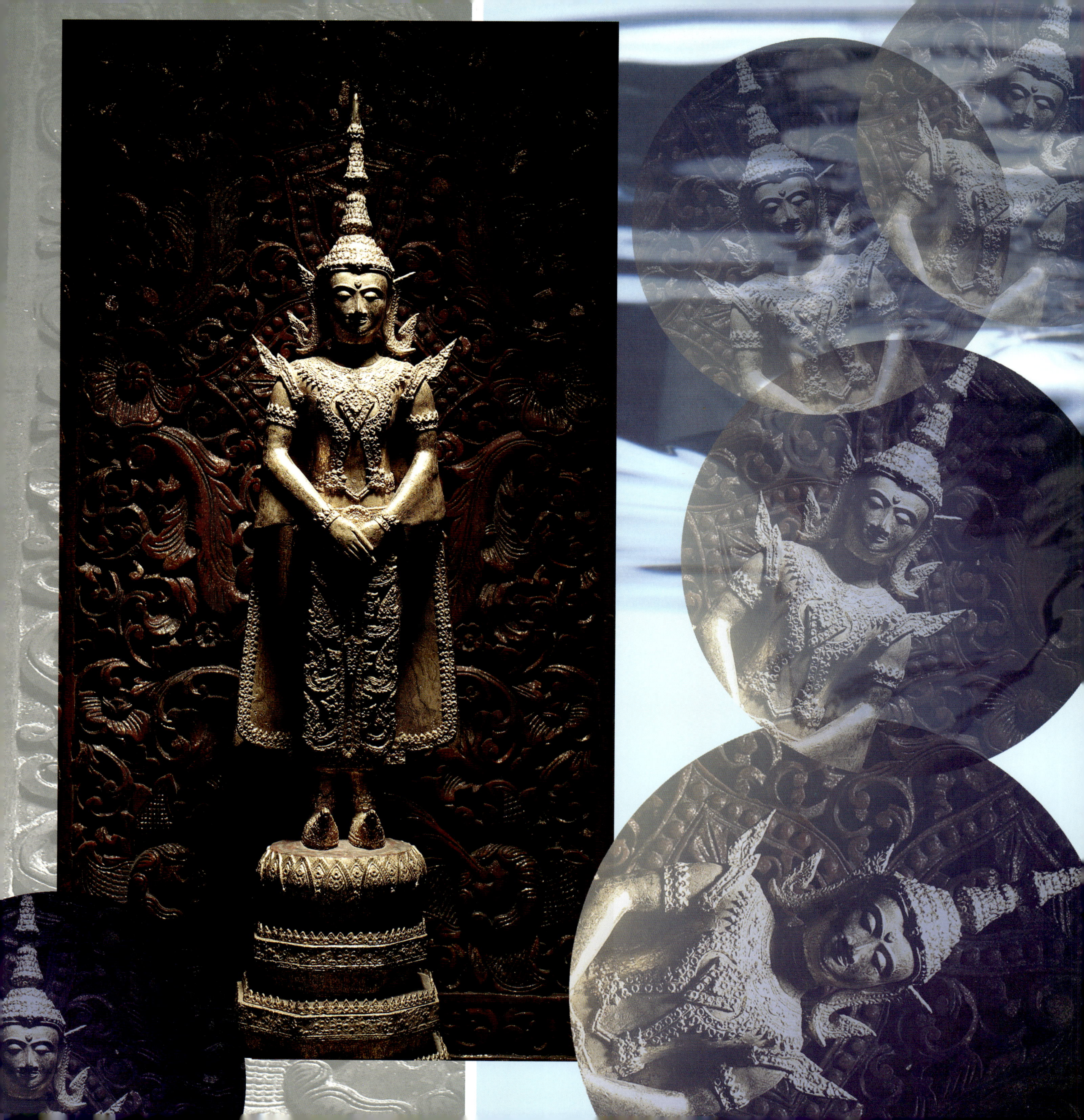

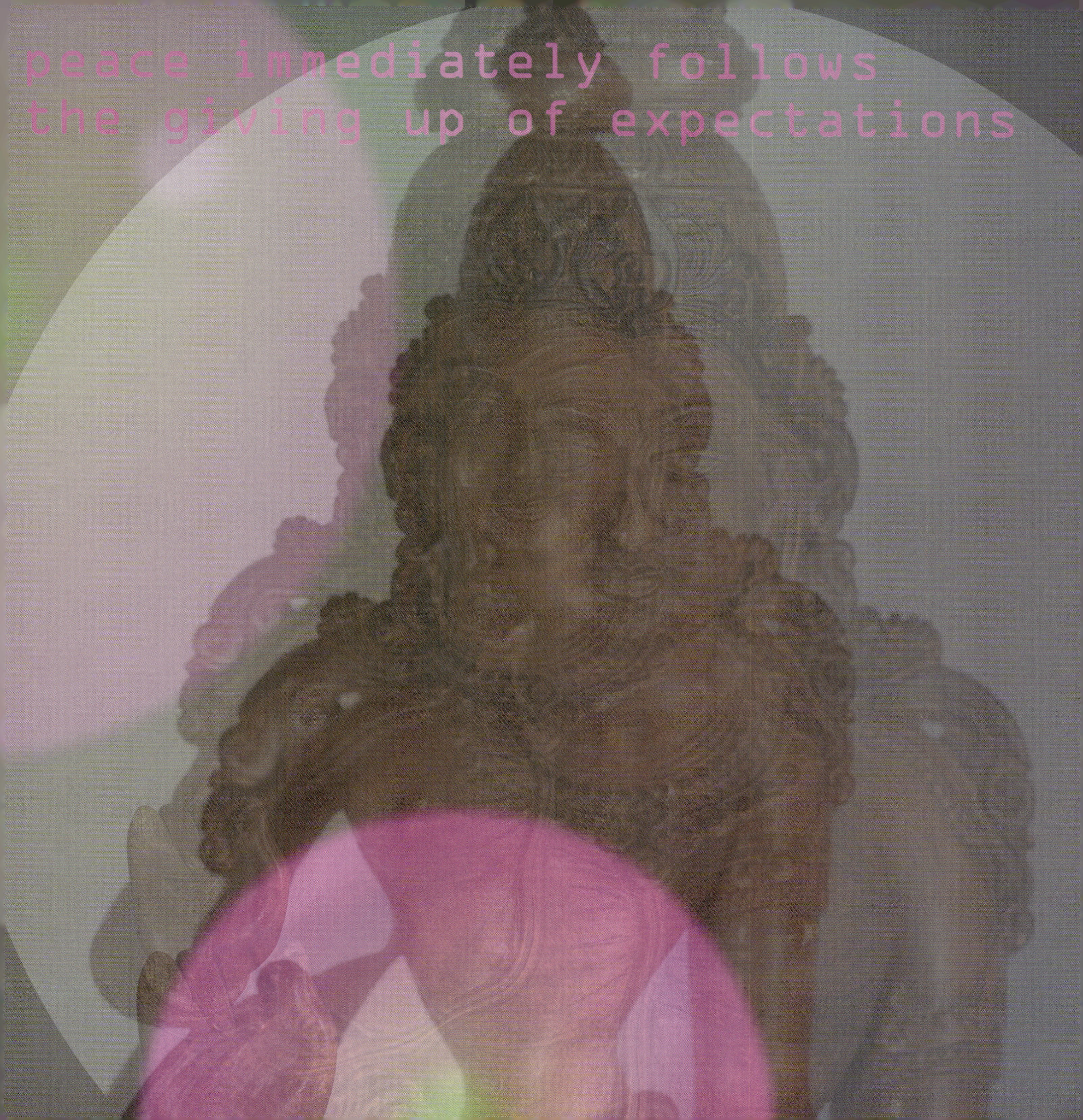
peace immediately follows
the giving up of expectations

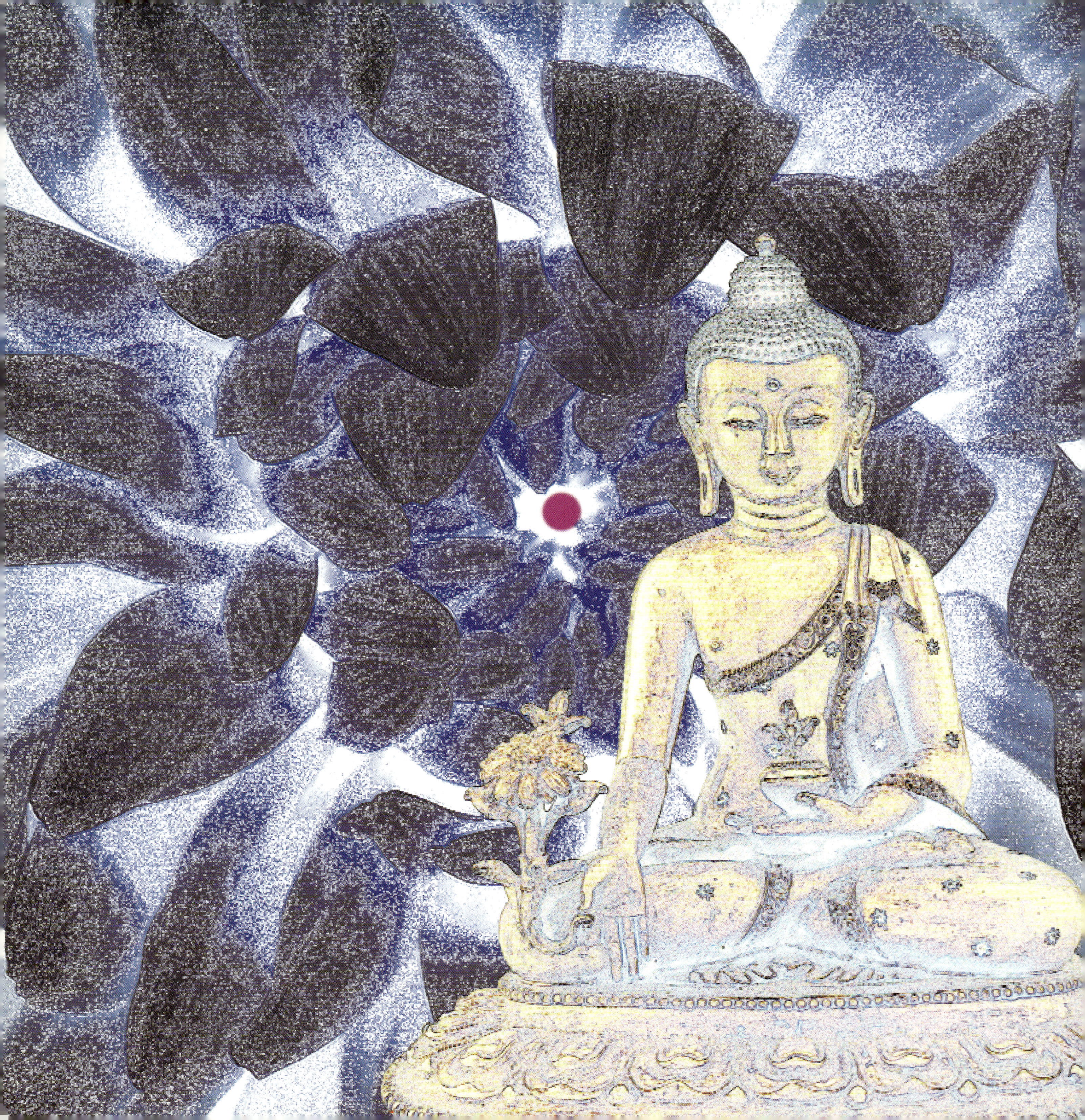

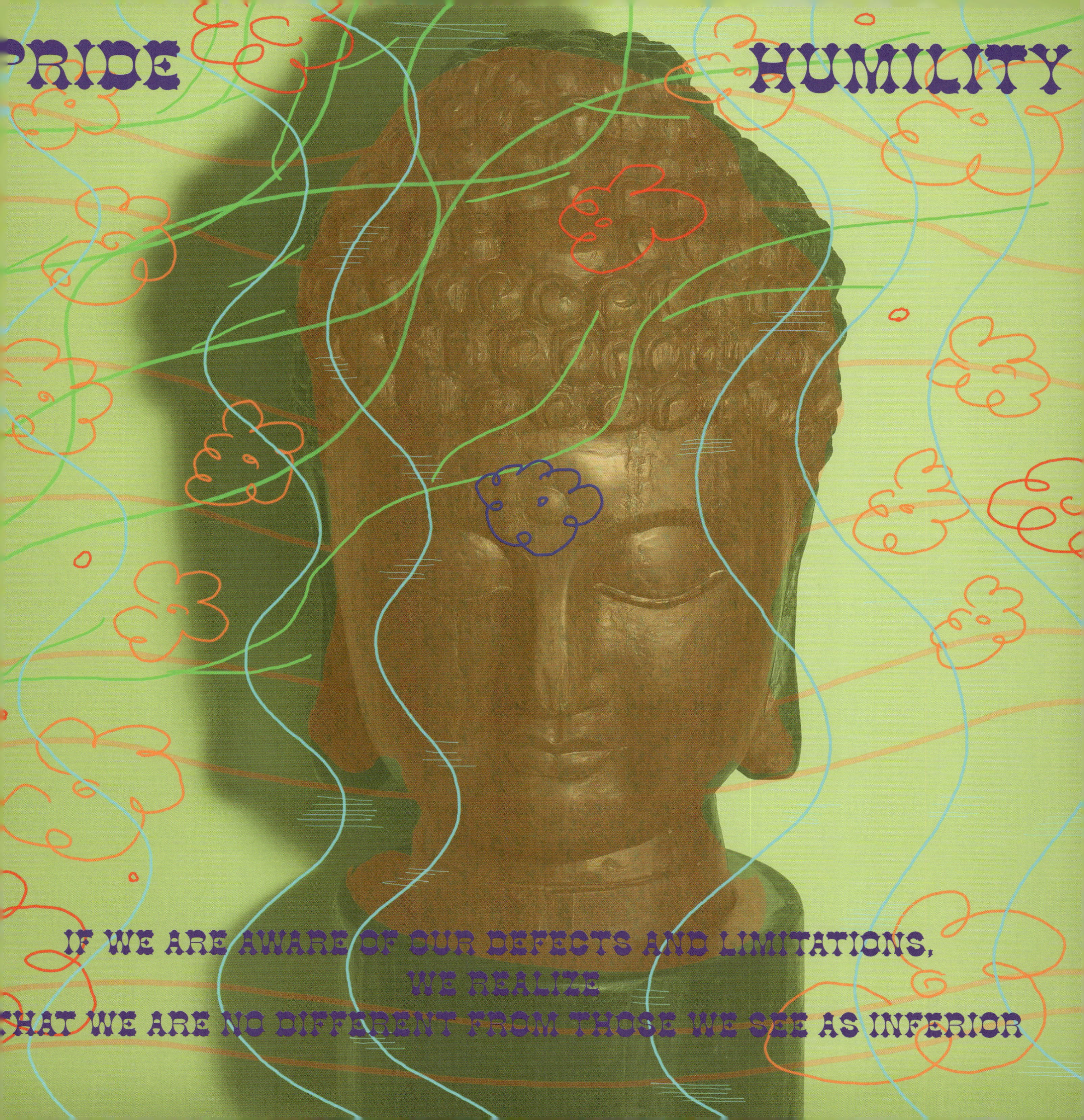
PRIDE
HUMILITY
IF WE ARE AWARE OF OUR DEFECTS AND LIMITATIONS,
WE REALIZE
THAT WE ARE NO DIFFERENT FROM THOSE WE SEE AS INFERIOR

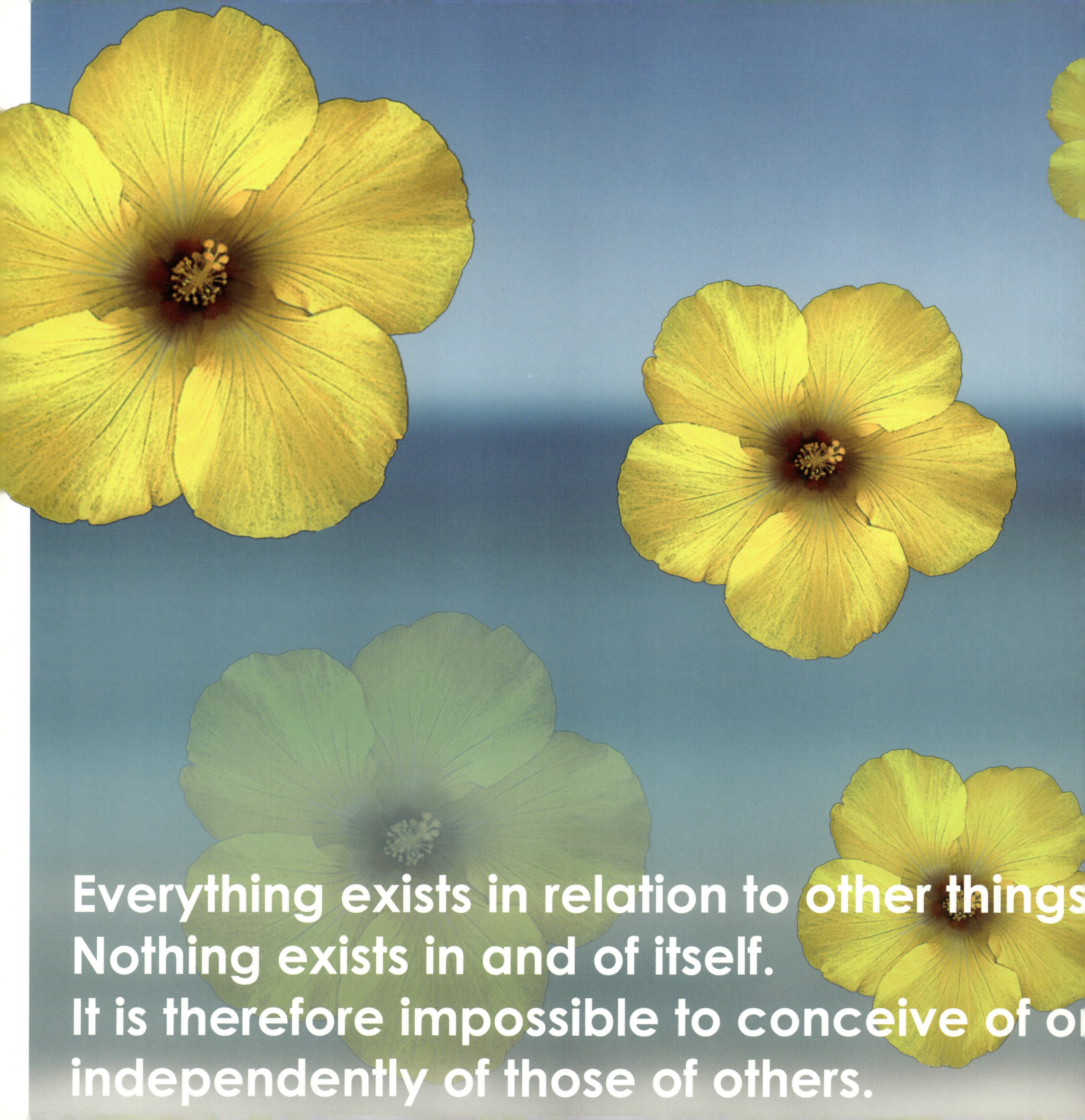
Everything exists in relation to other things
Nothing exists in and of itself.
It is therefore impossible to conceive of
independently of those of others.

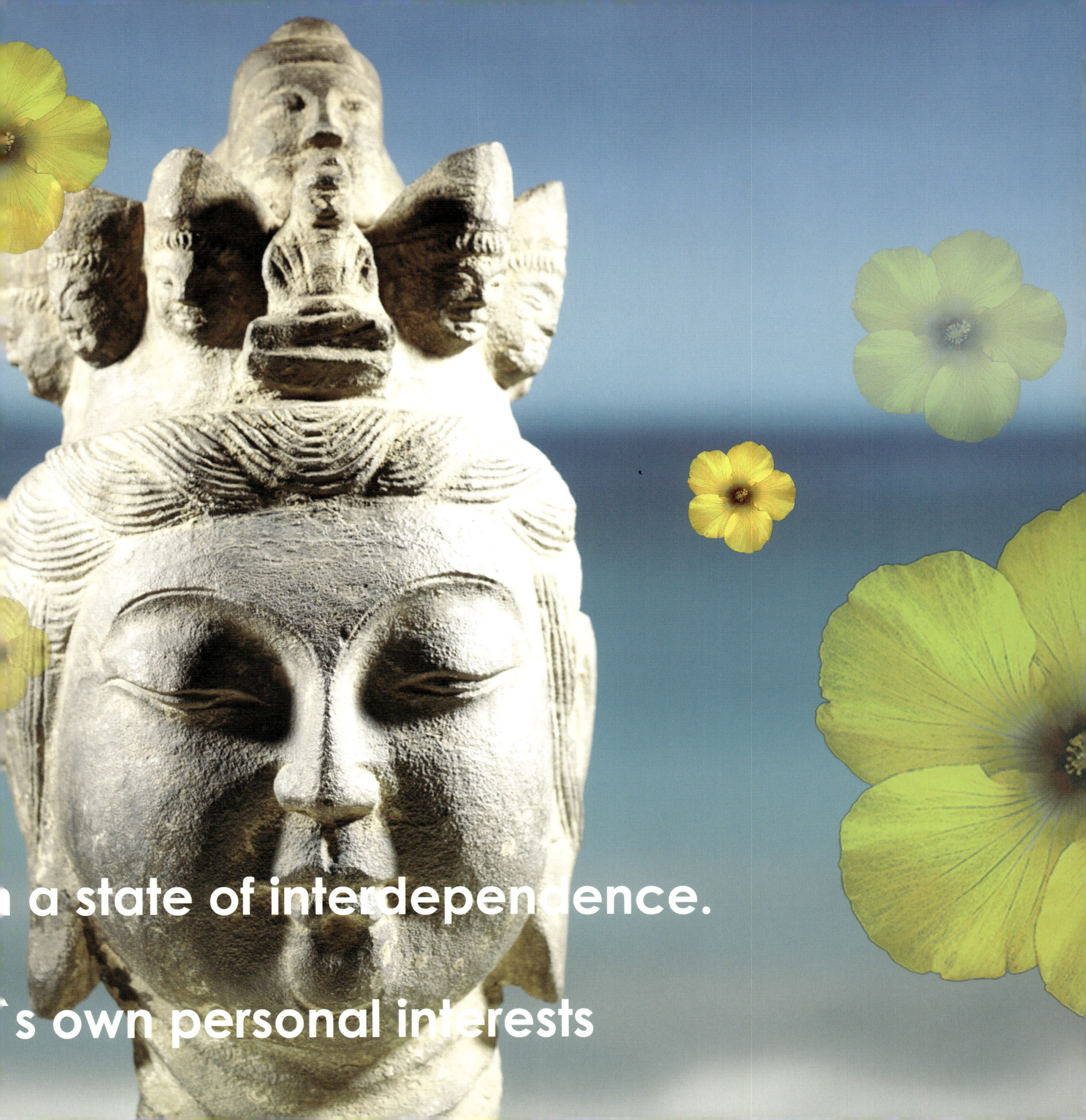

a state of interdependence.

’s own personal interests

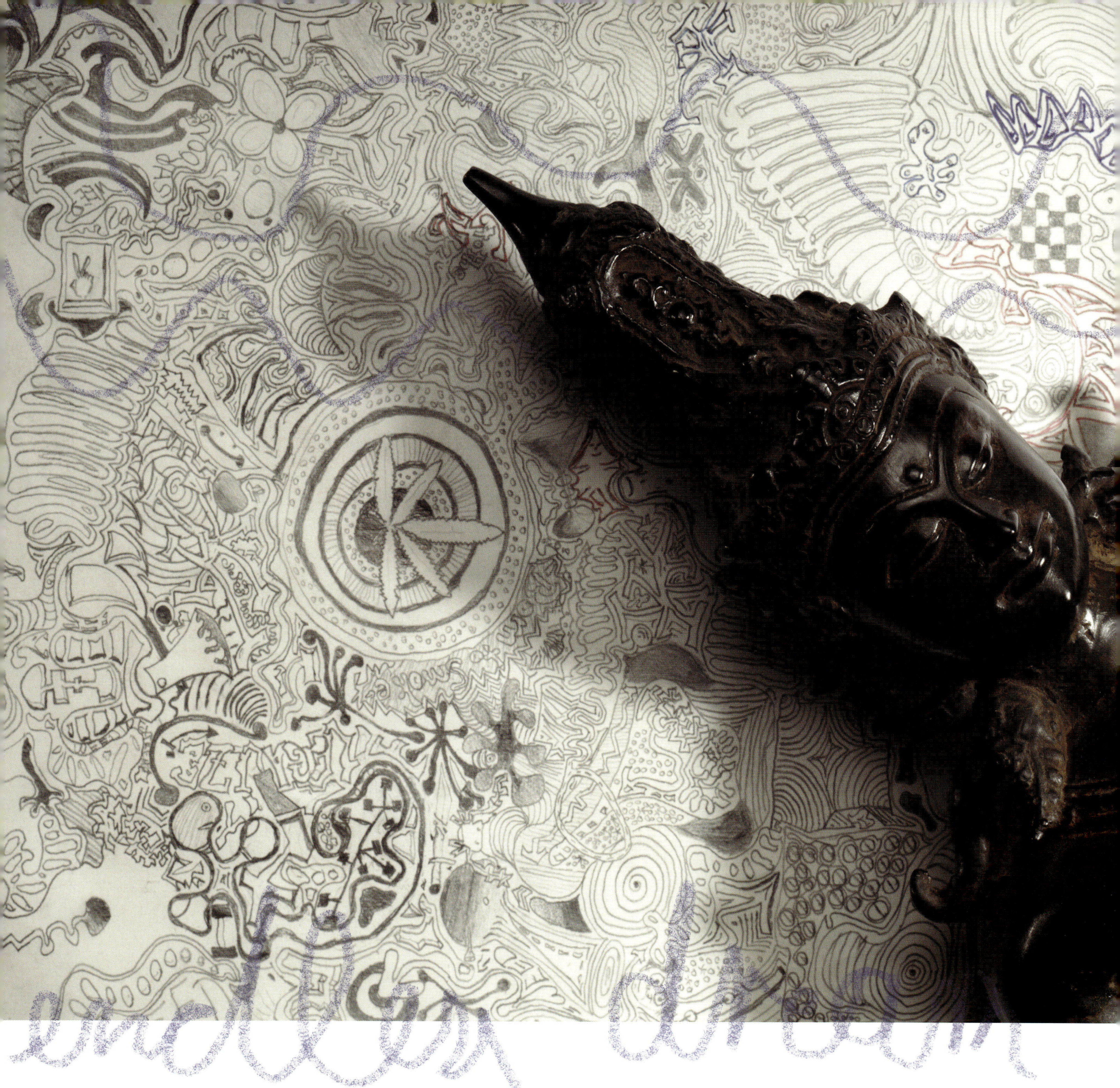

endless dream

takes you through worlds pictures and stories

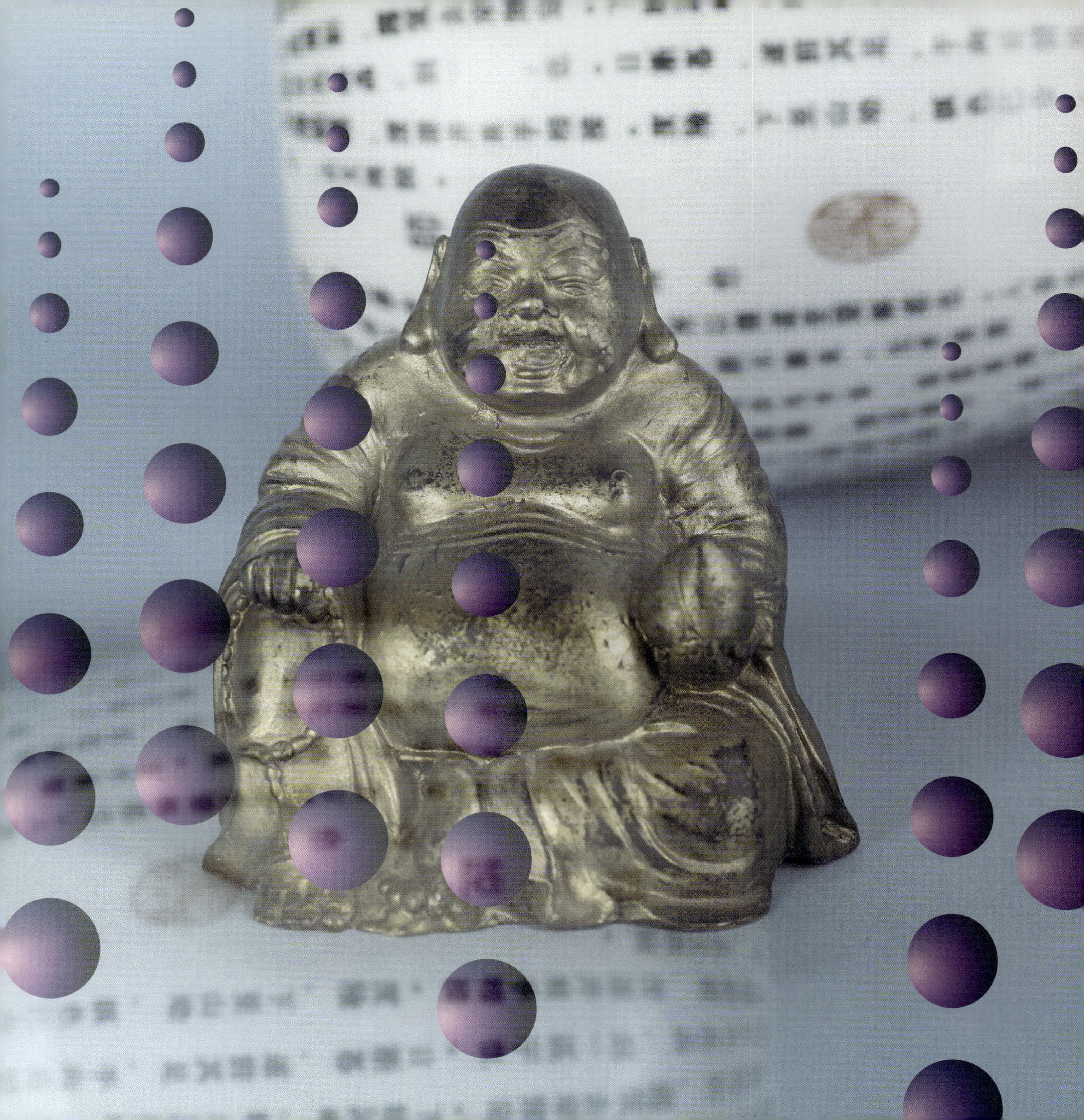

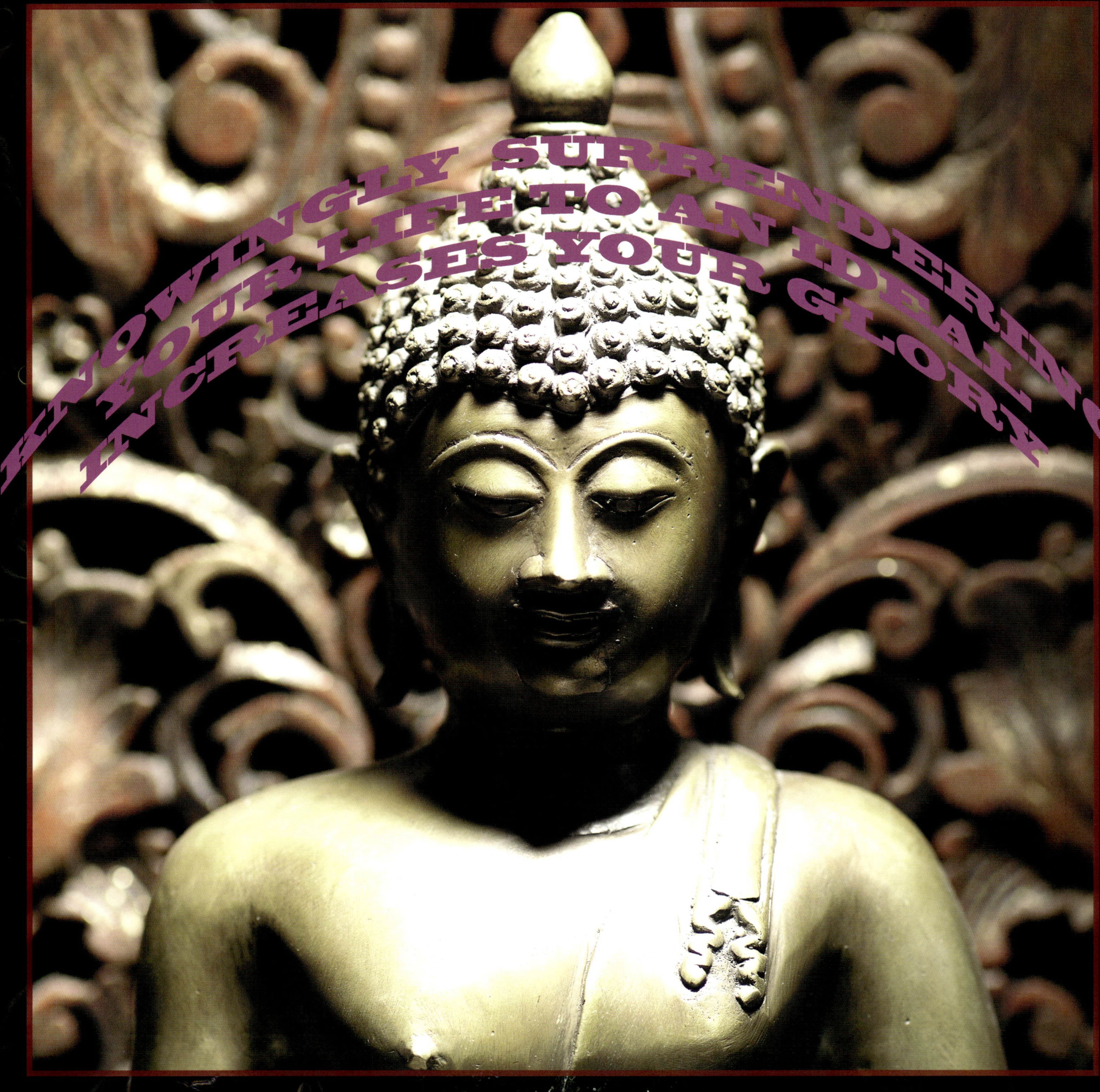
KNOWINGLY SURRENDERIN
YOUR LIFE TO AN IDEAL
INCREASES YOUR GLORY

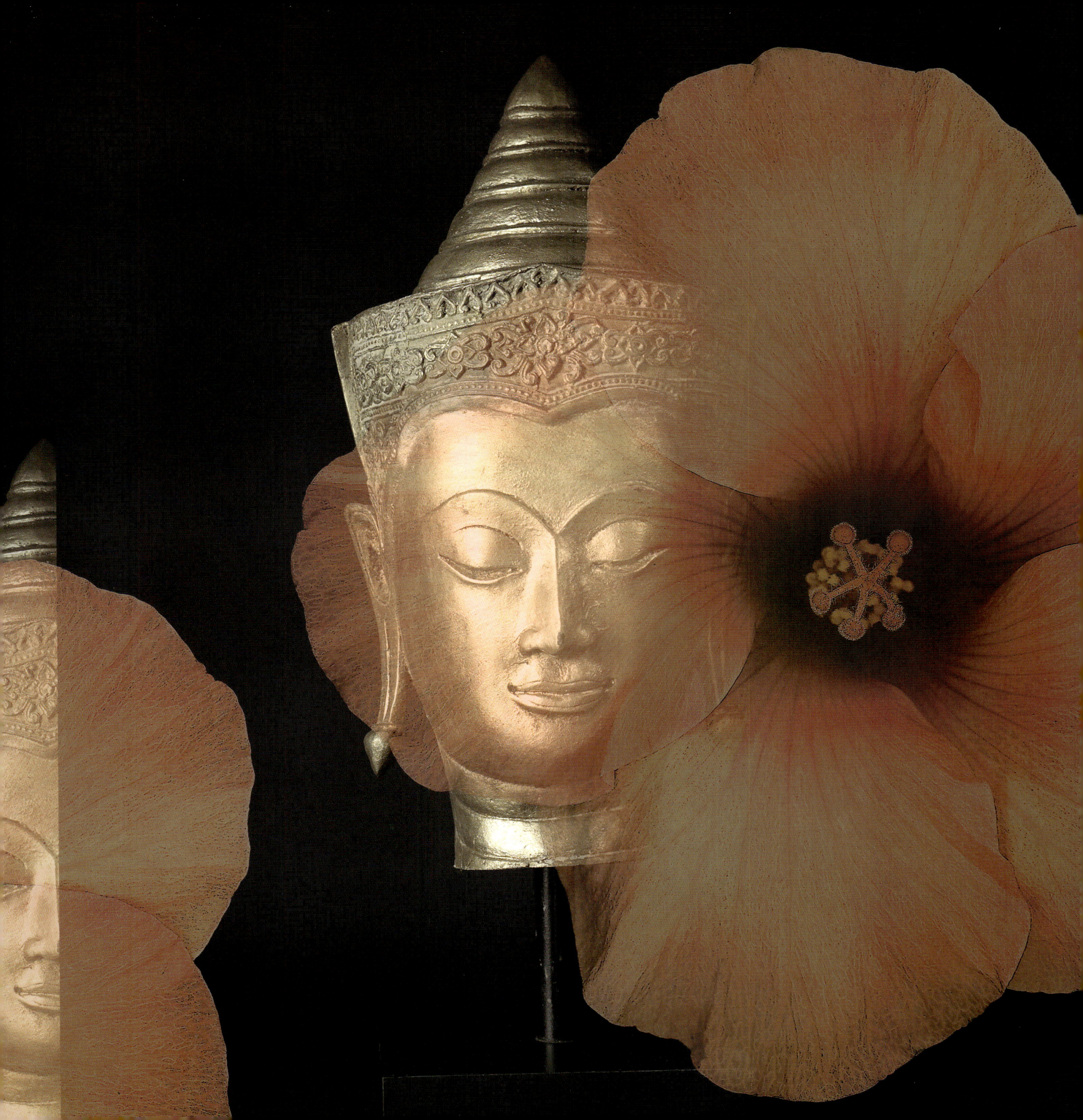

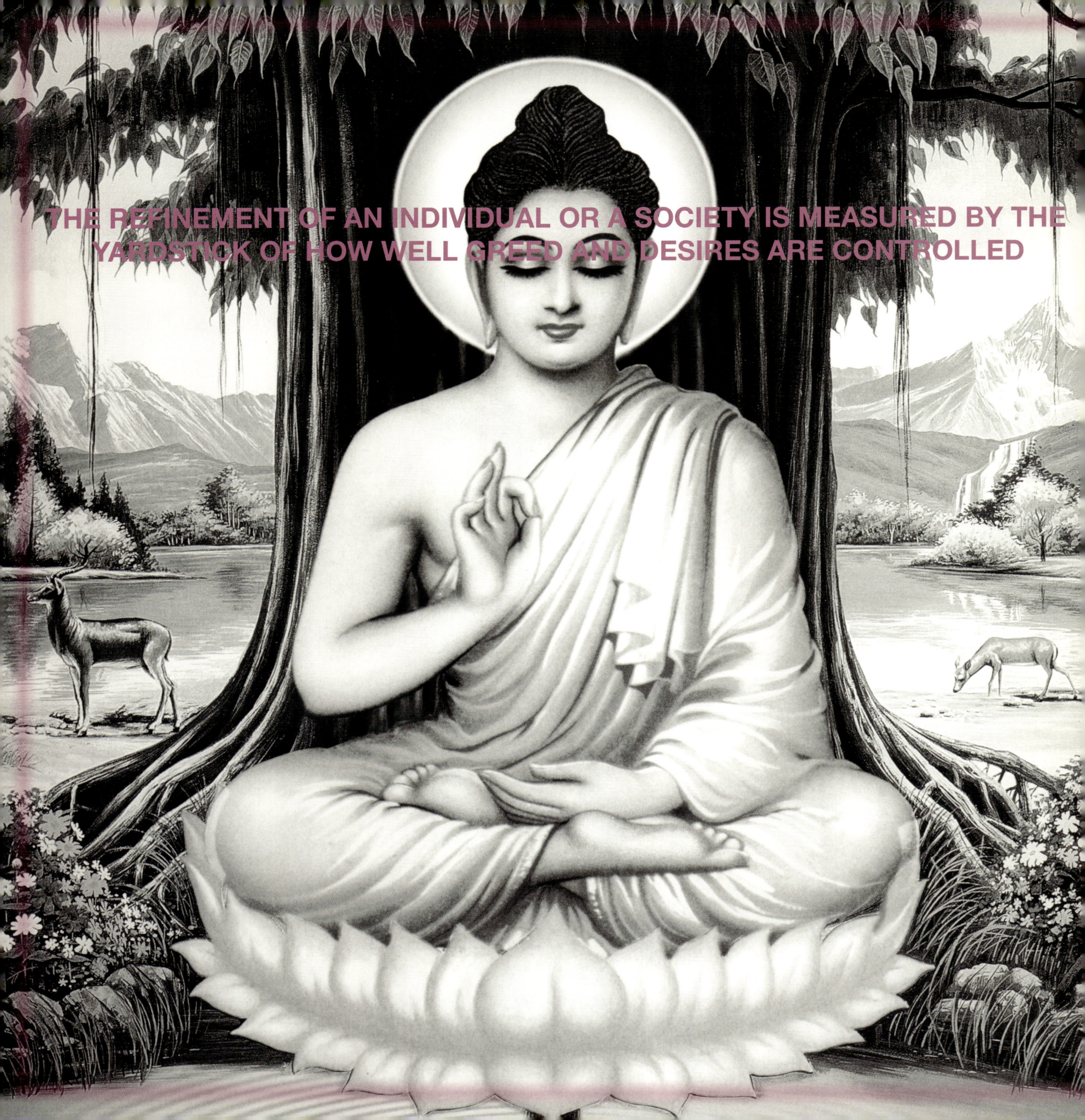
THE REFINEMENT OF AN INDIVIDUAL OR A SOCIETY IS MEASURED BY THE
YARDSTICK OF HOW WELL GREED AND DESIRES ARE CONTROLLED

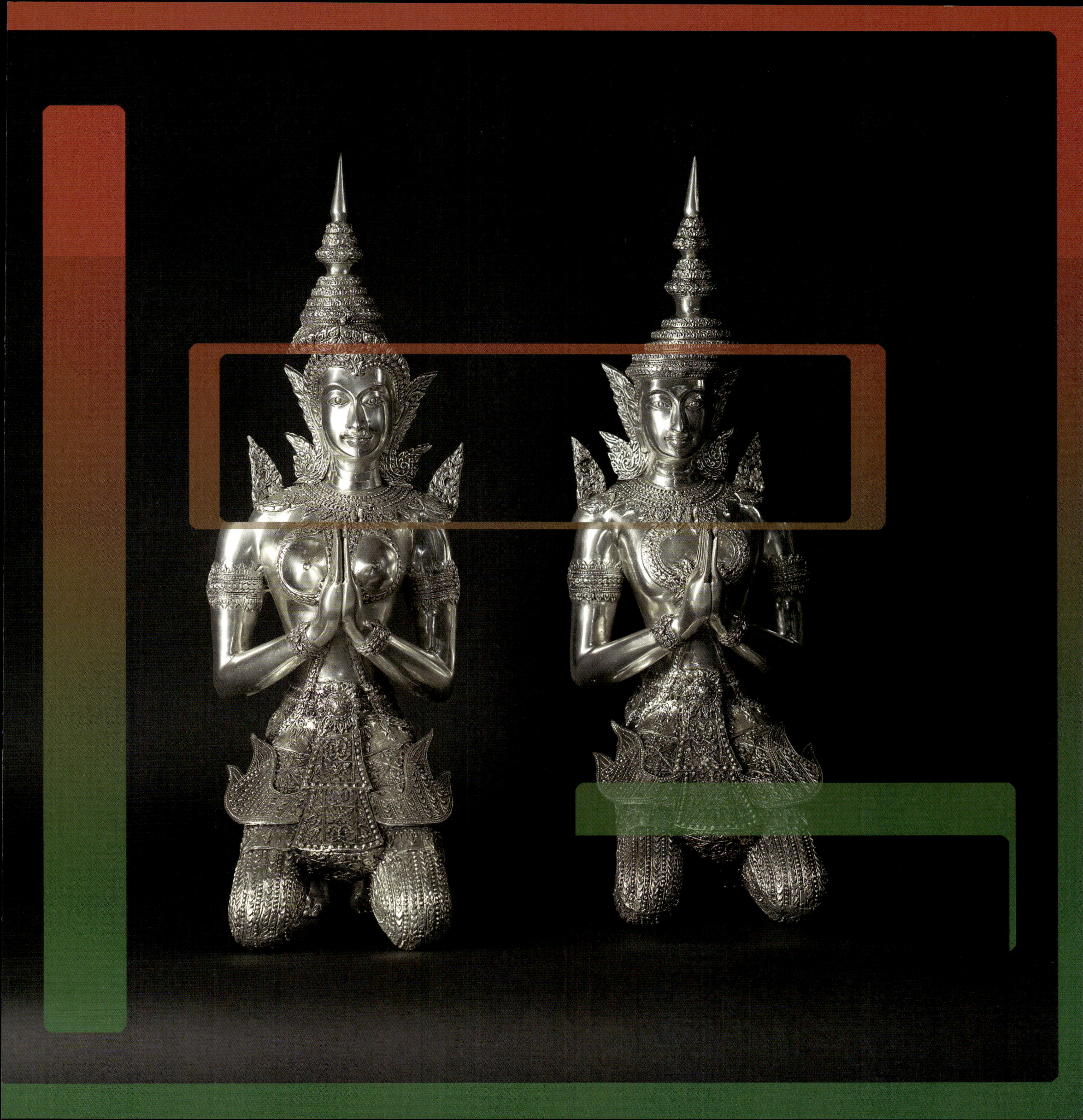

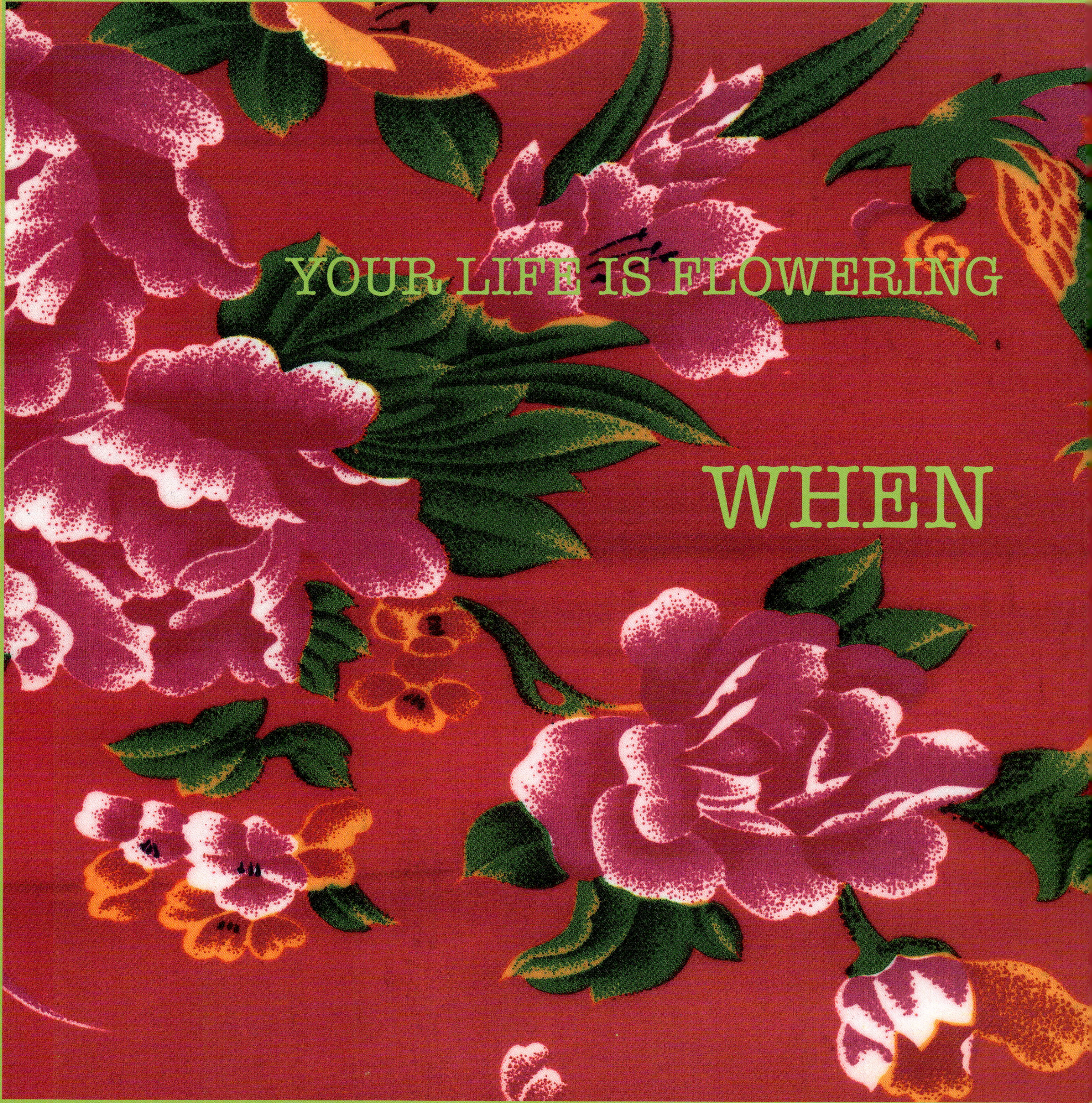

YOUR LIFE IS FLOWERING

WHEN

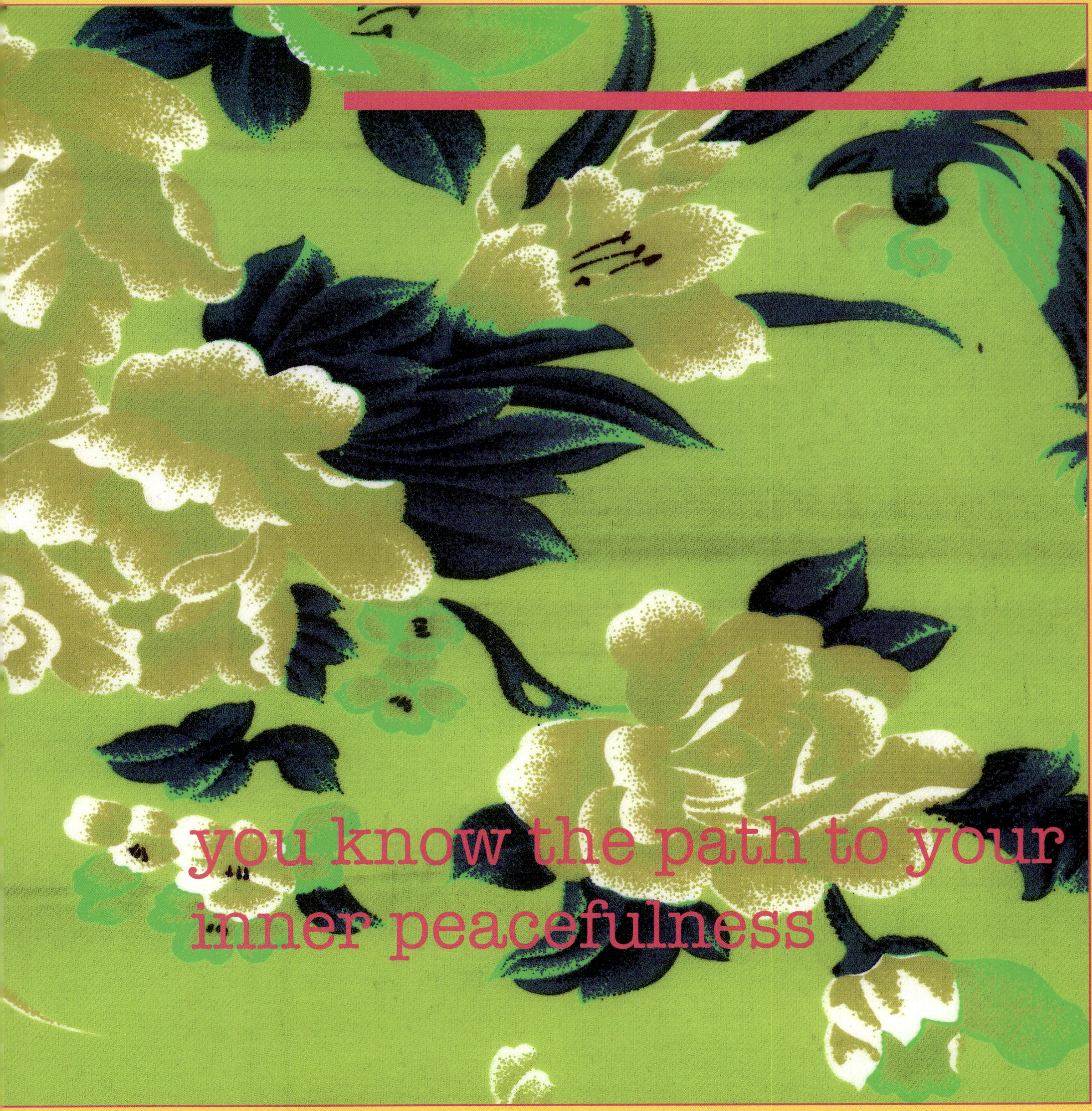

you know the path to your inner peacefulness

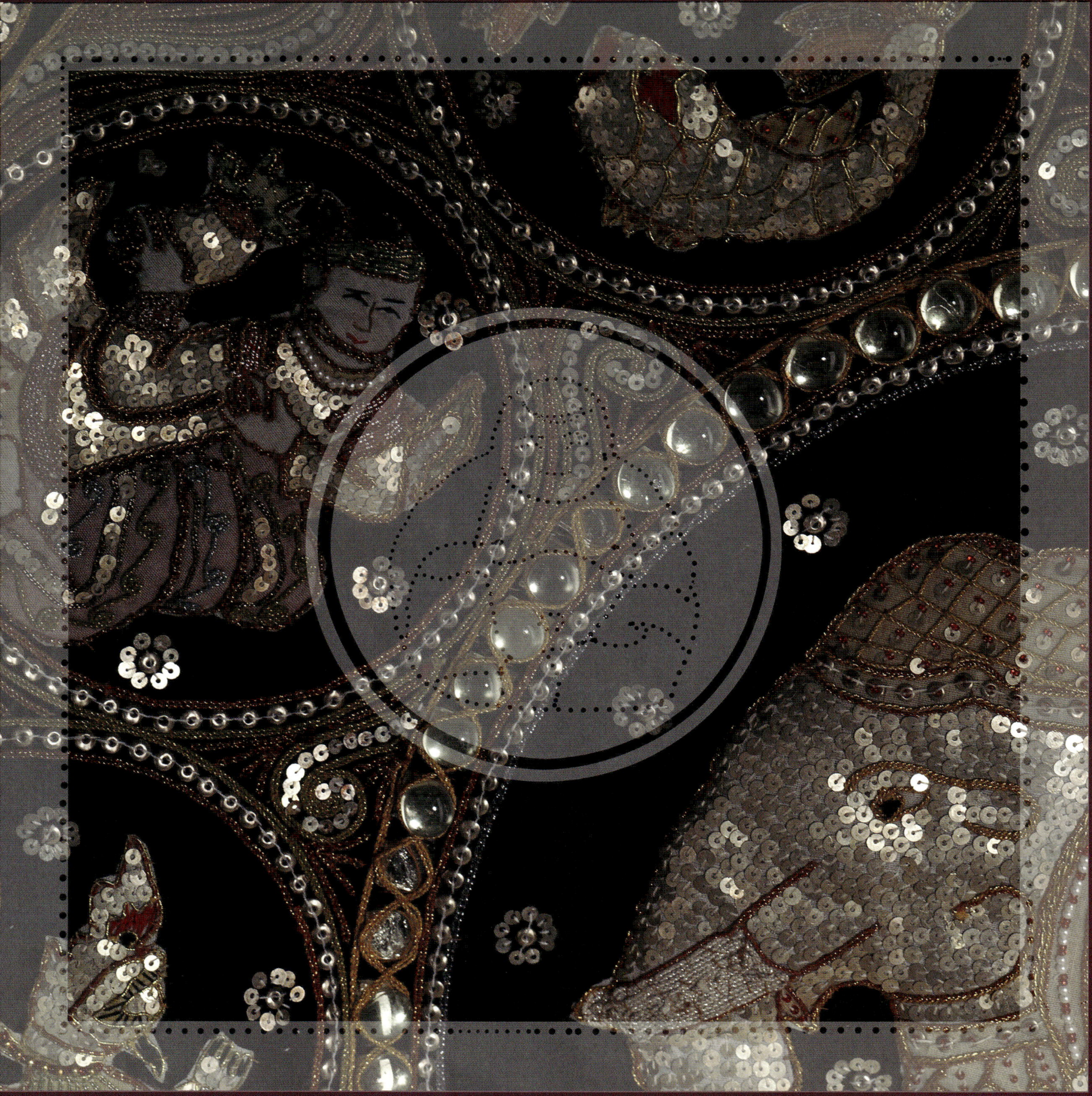

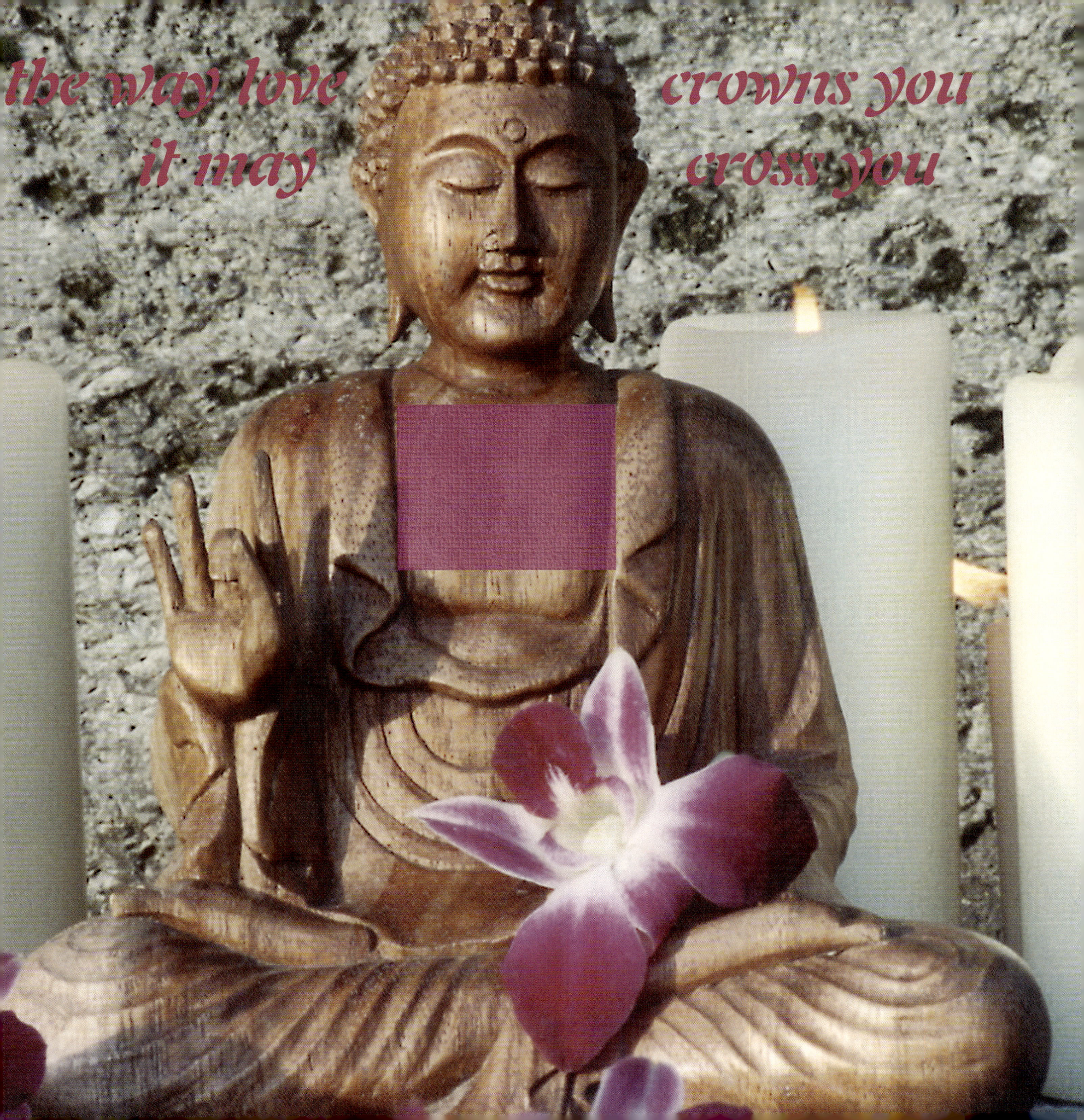
the way love
it may
crowns you
cross you

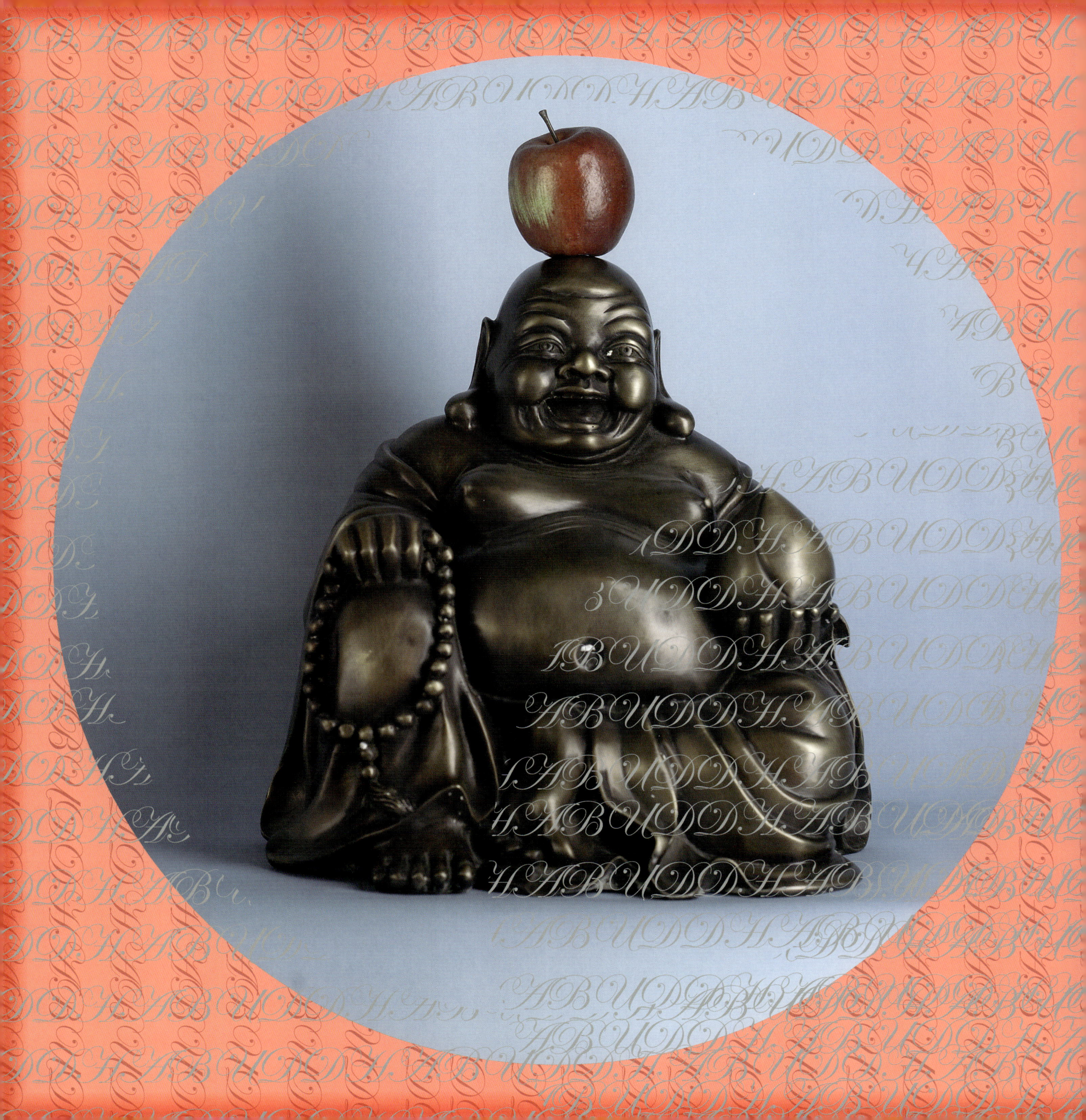

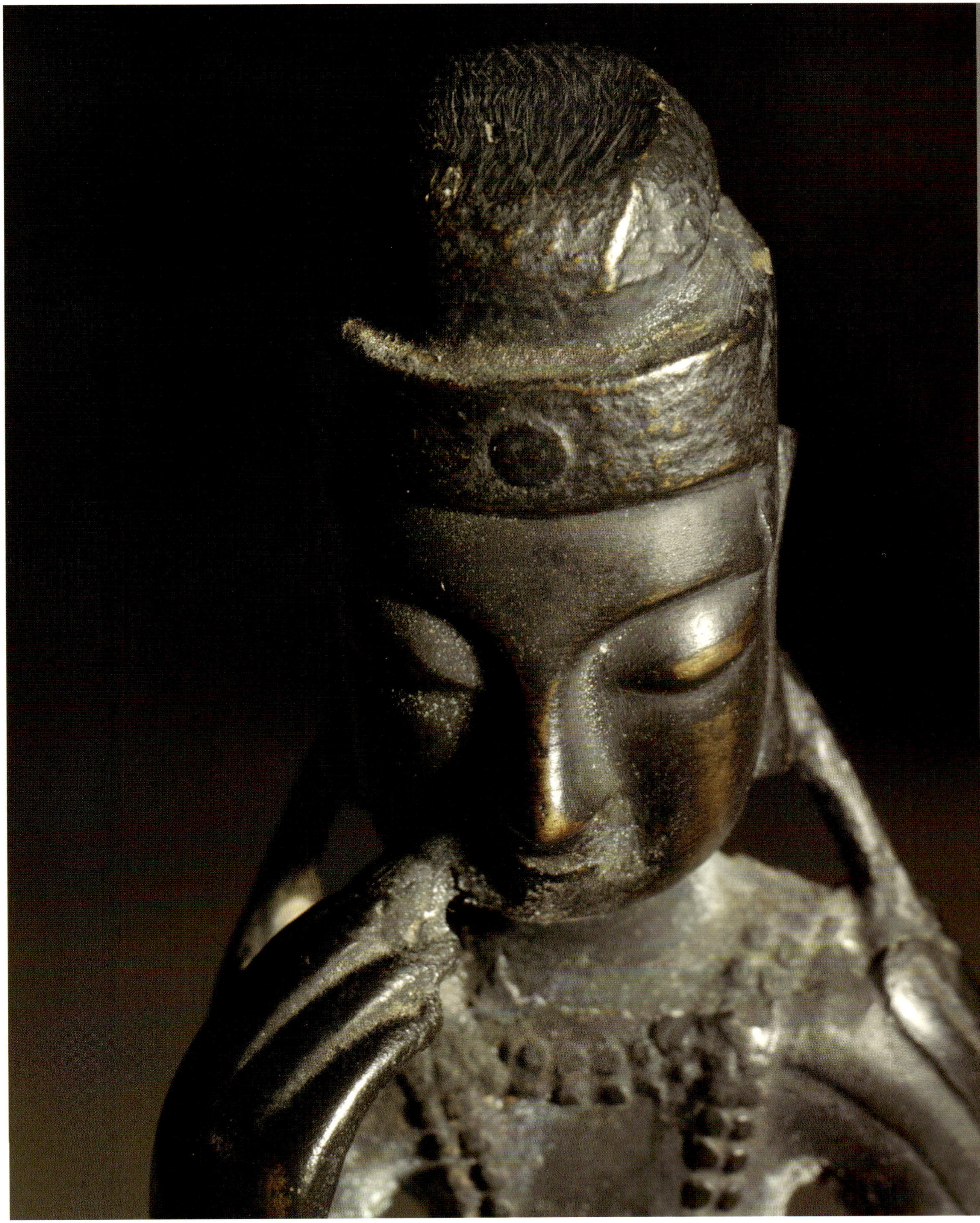

ACCEPT THE
KNOCKS
OF LIFE
AS
BLESSINGS
IN DISGUISE

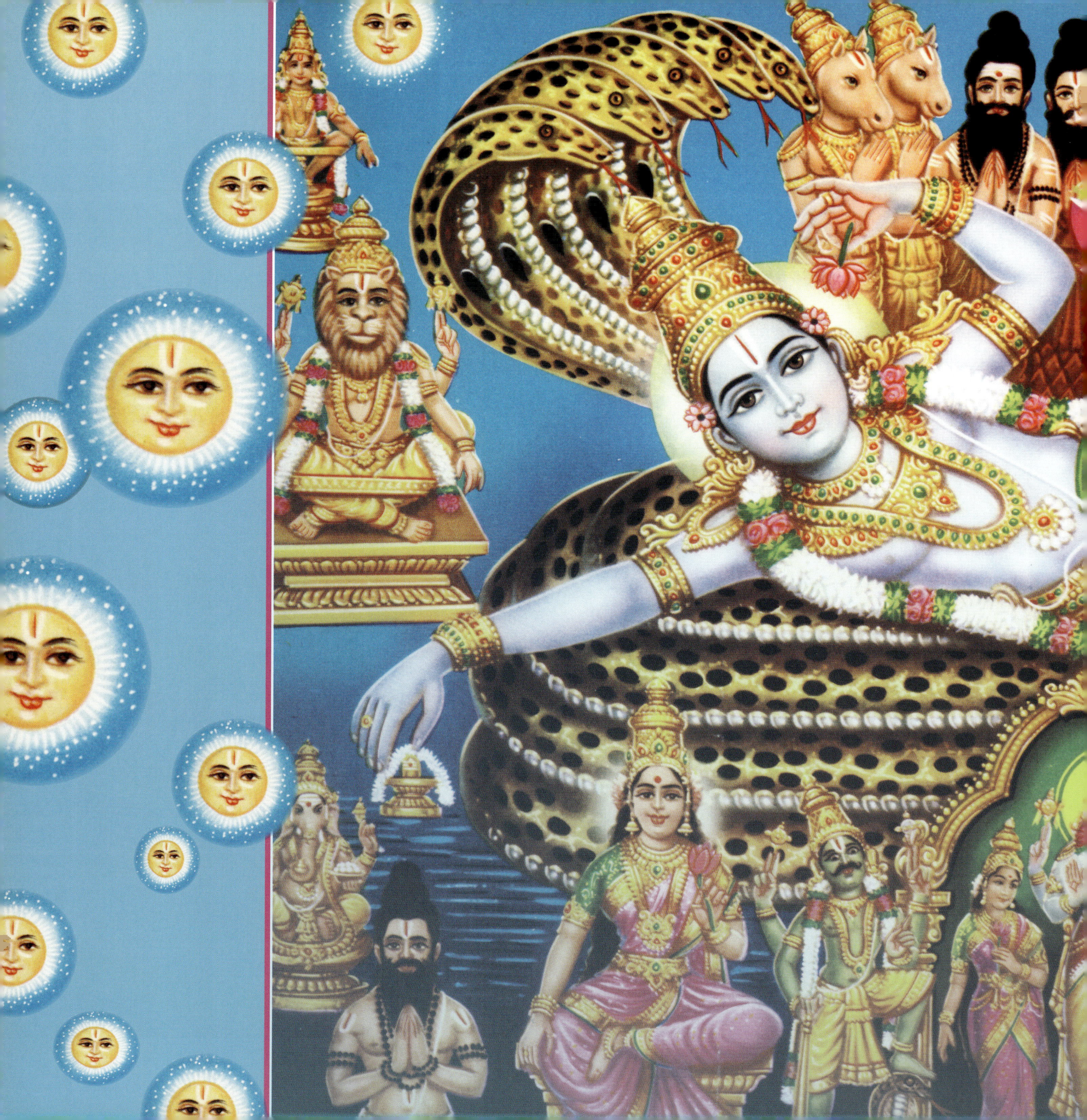

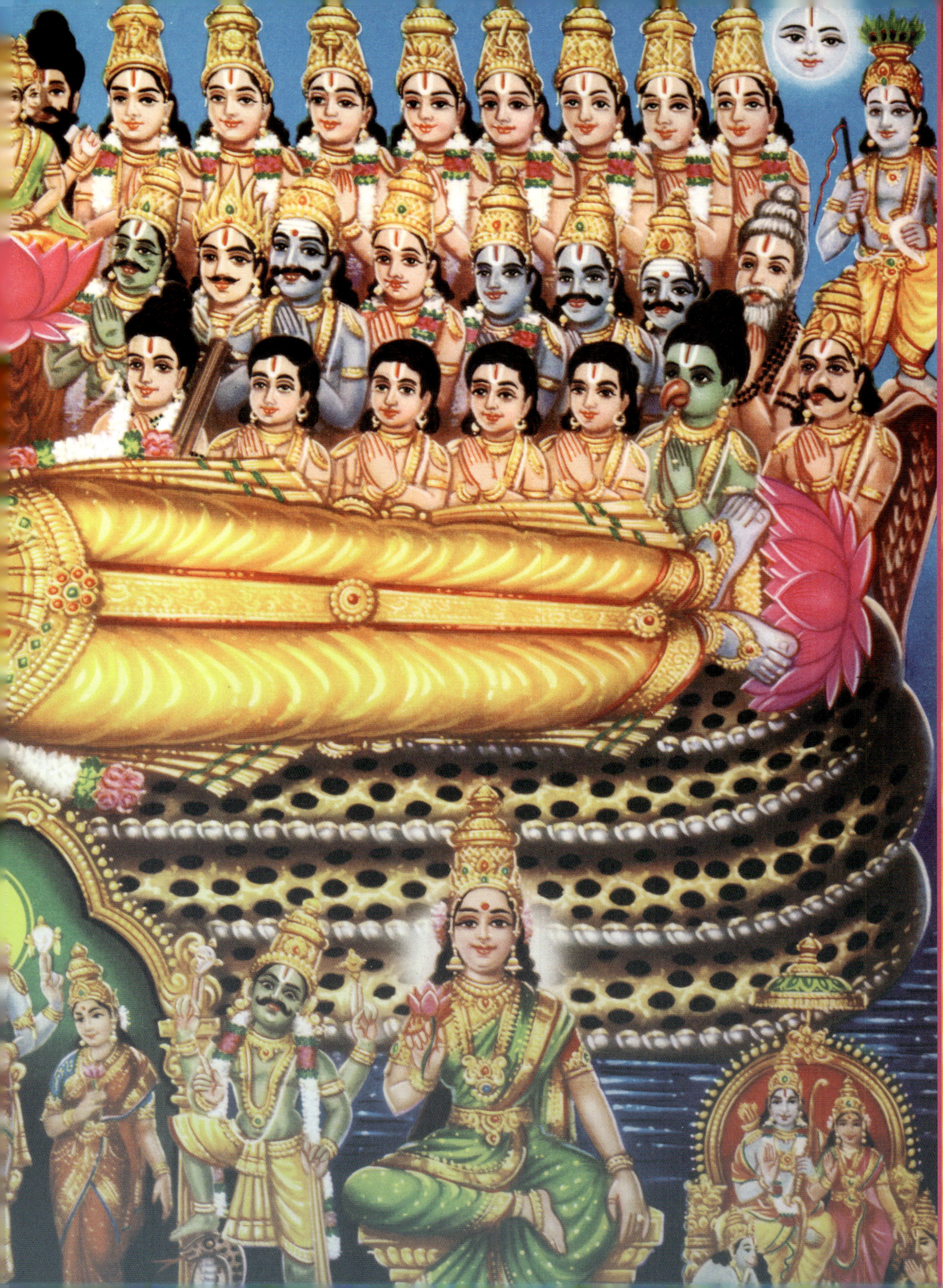

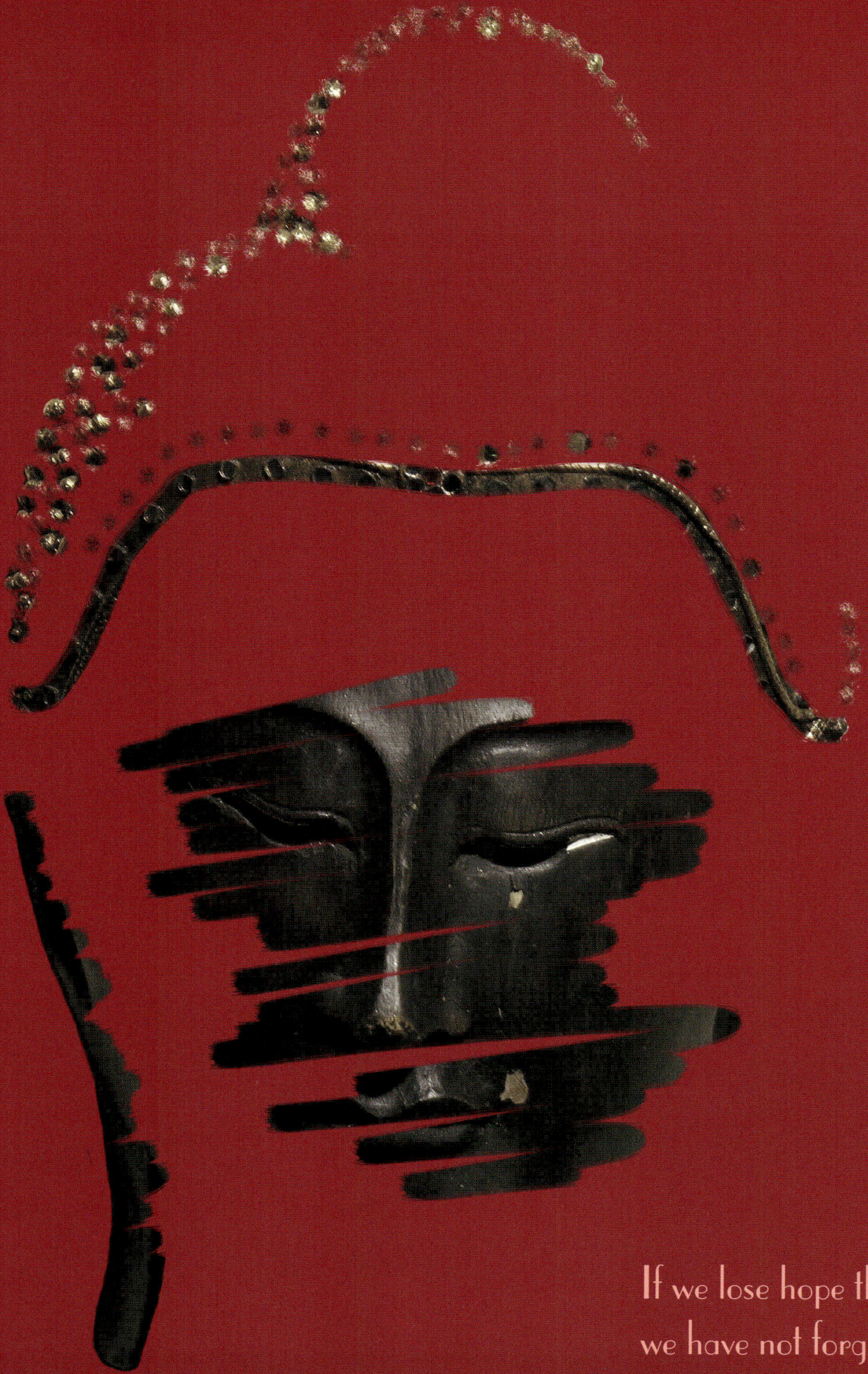

If we lose hope that means
we have not forgiven ourselves

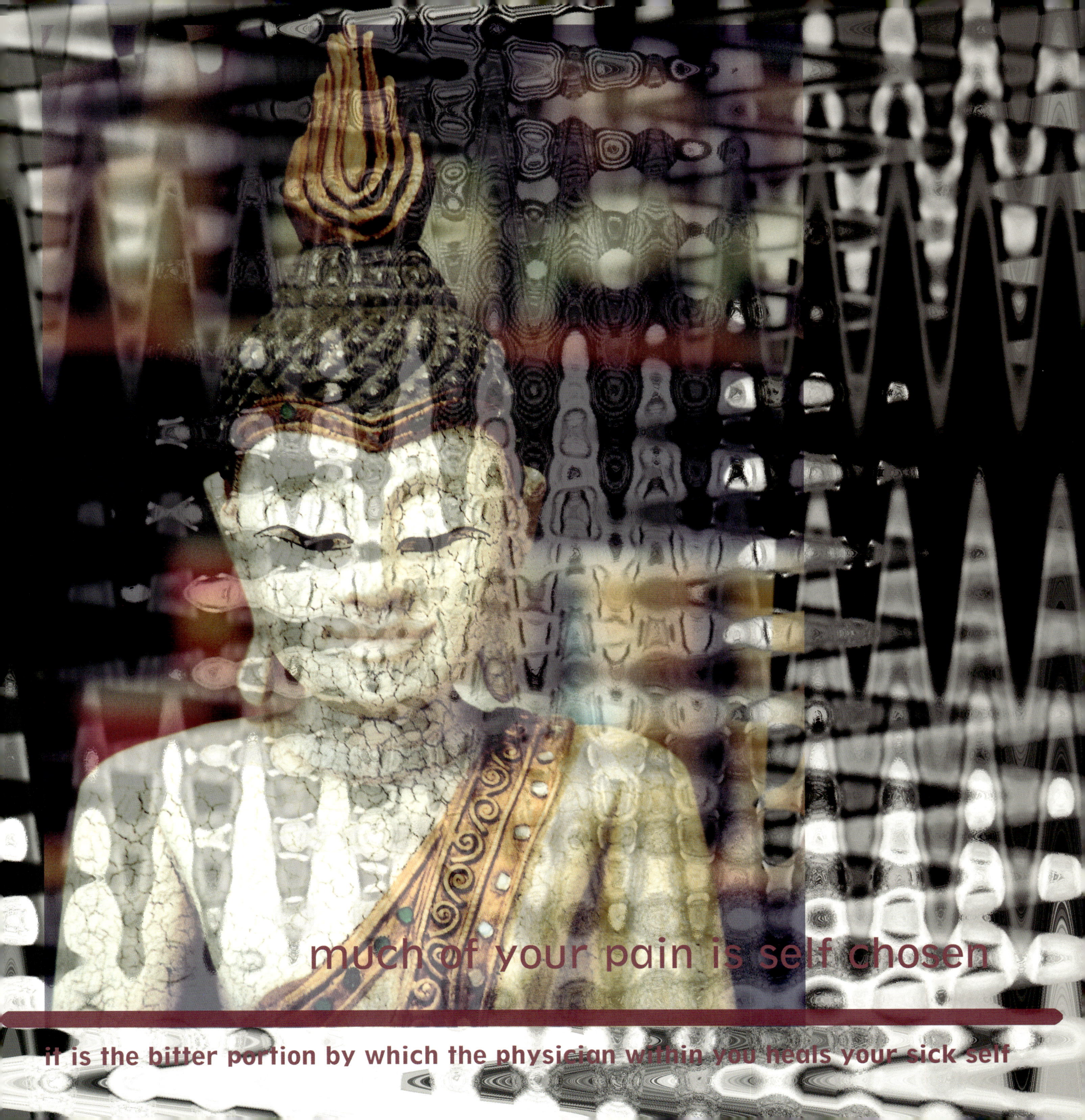
much of your pain is self chosen
it is the bitter portion by which the physician within you heals your sick self

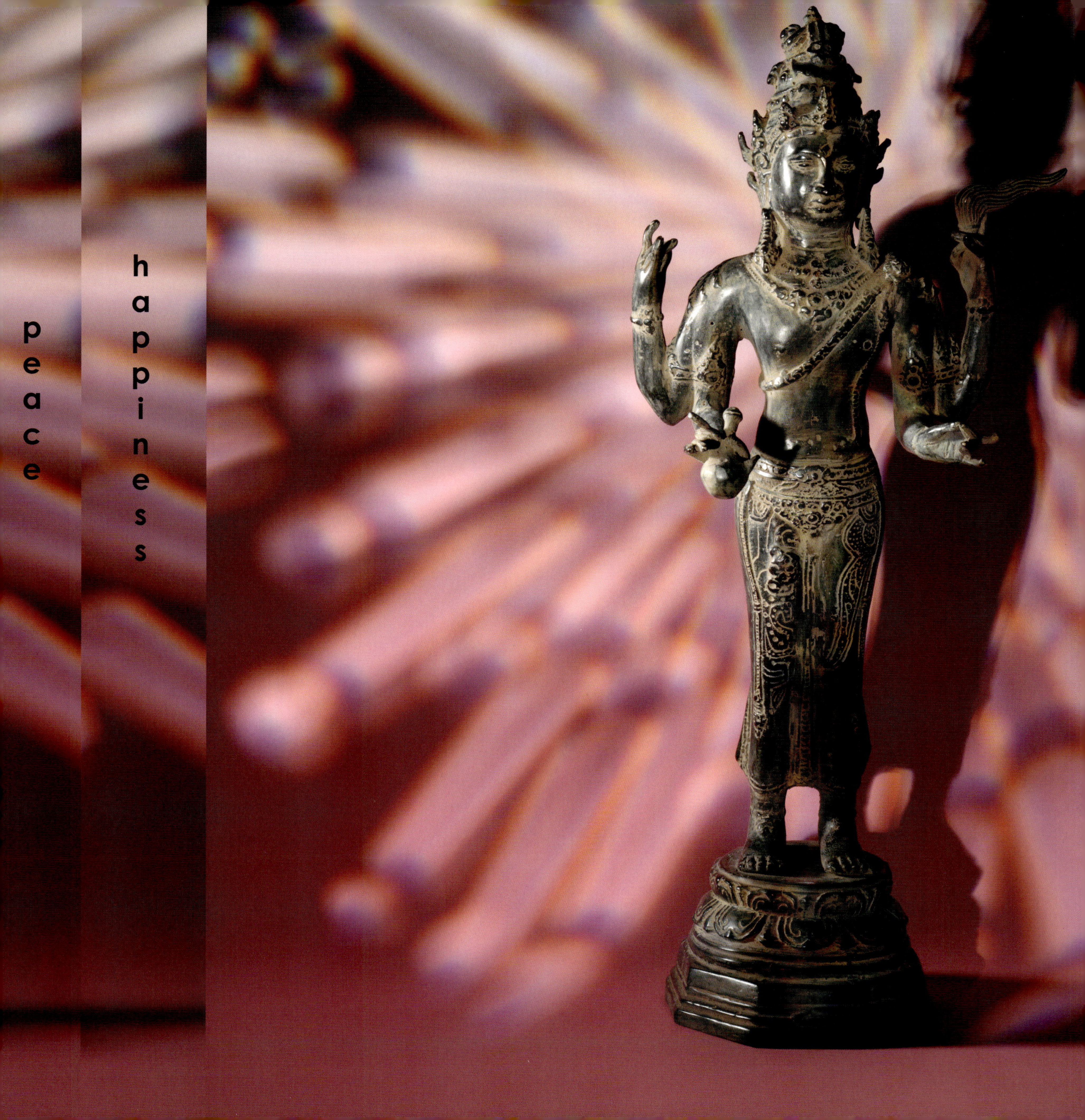
peace
happiness

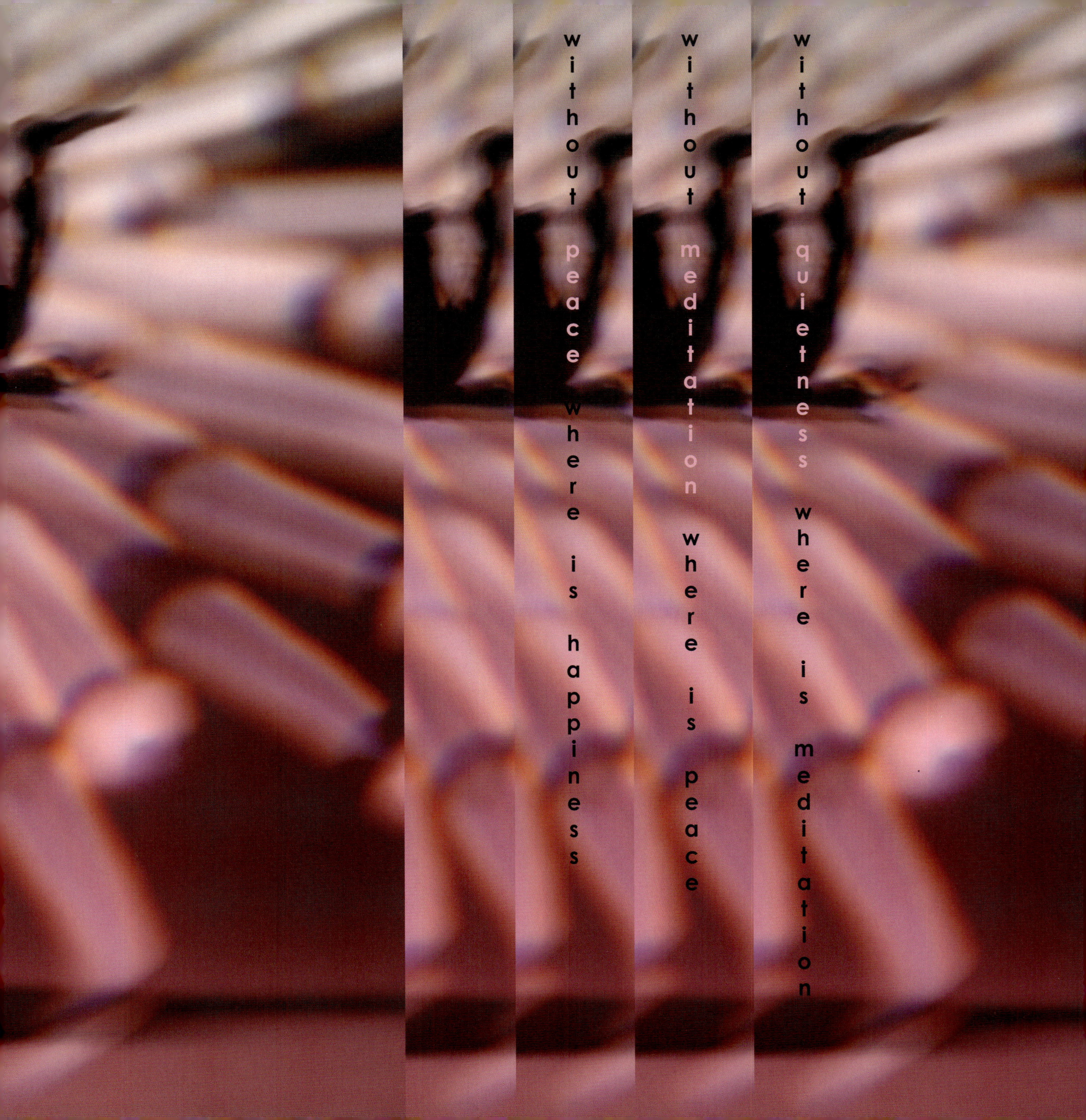
without peace where is happiness
without meditation where is peace
without quietness where is meditation

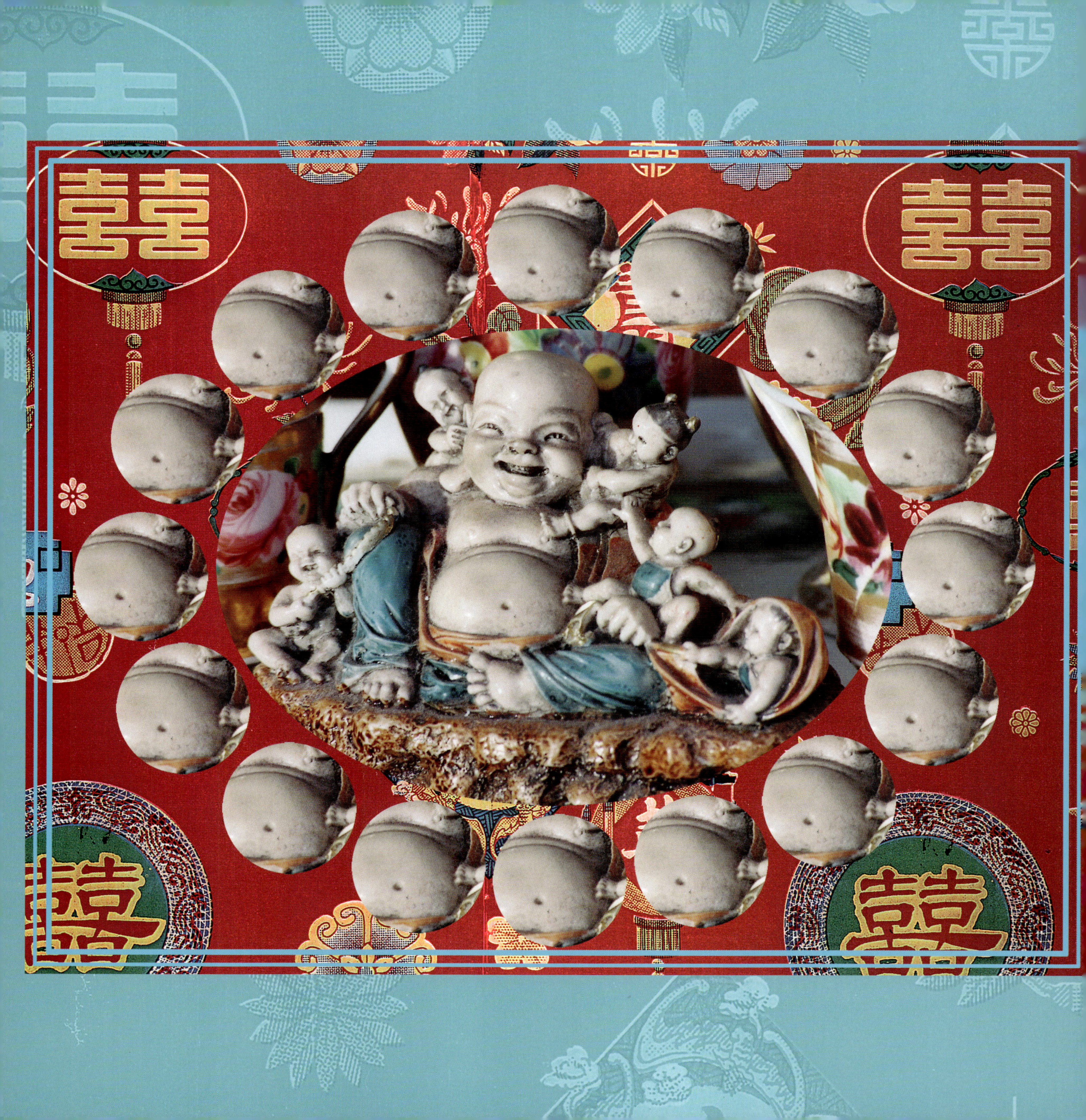

The wise man does not invite you into his house of wisdom
but leads you to the threshold of your own mind

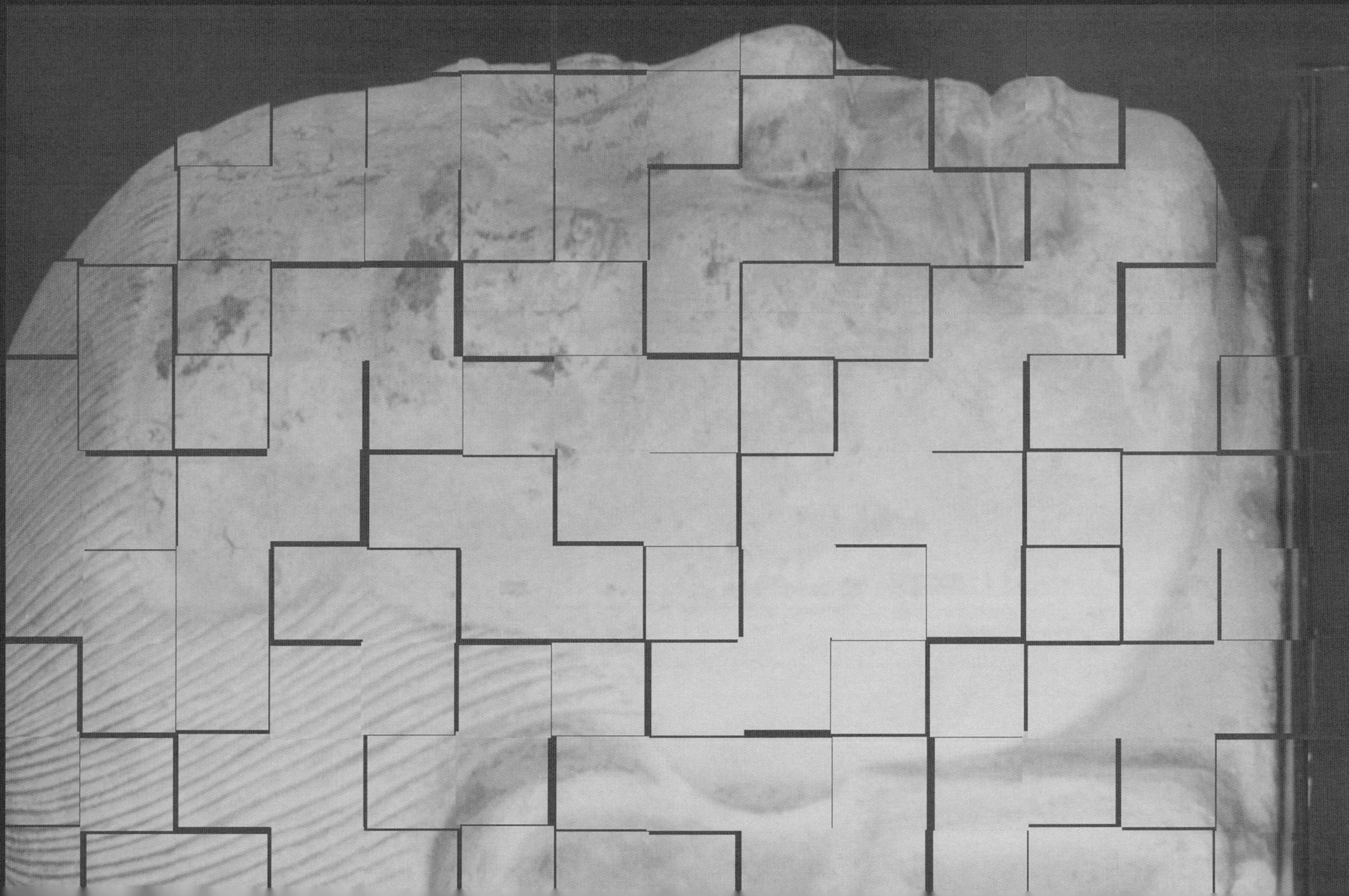

THE FRUIT OF YOUR EFFORTS LEAVE TO GOD

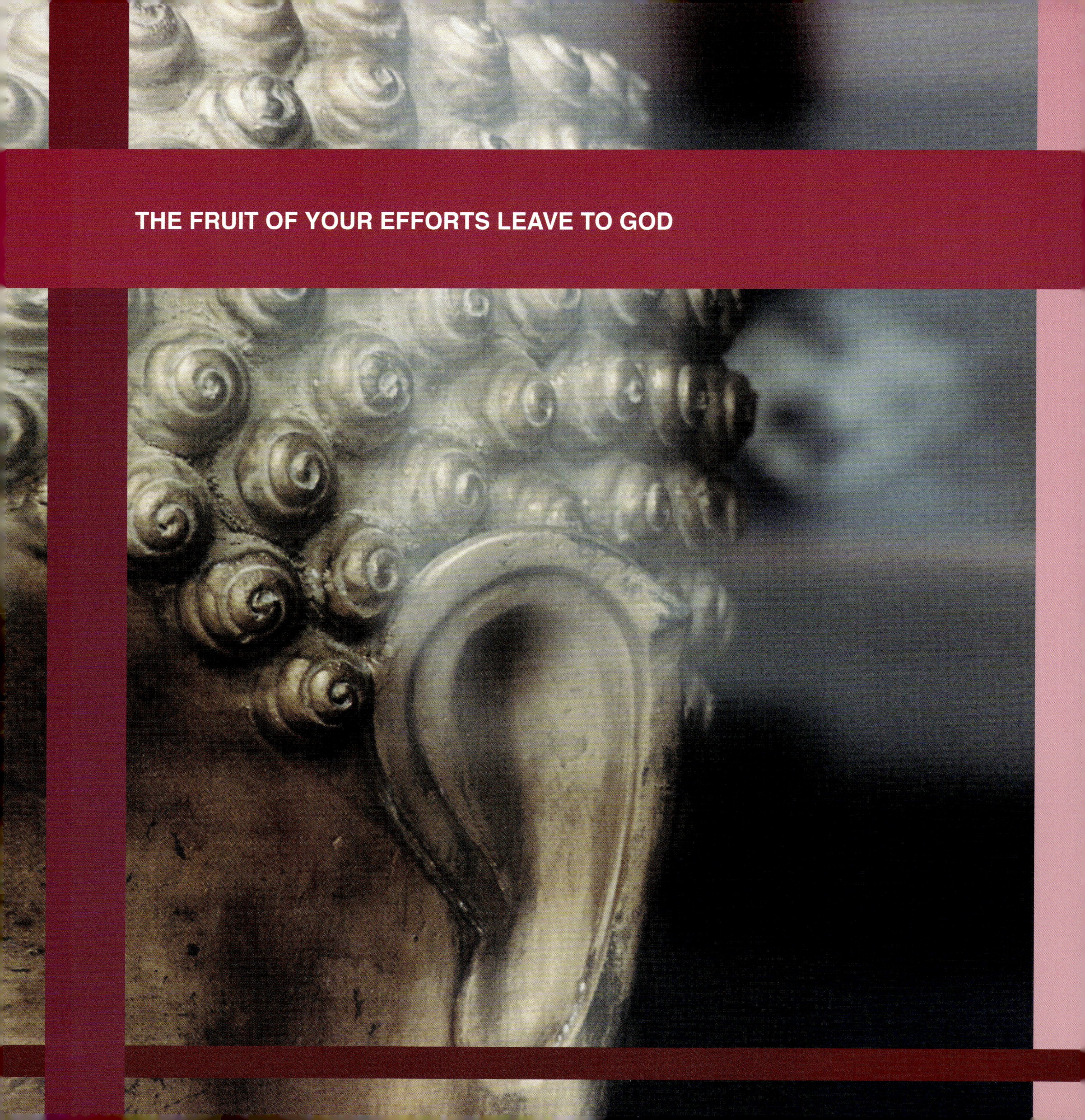

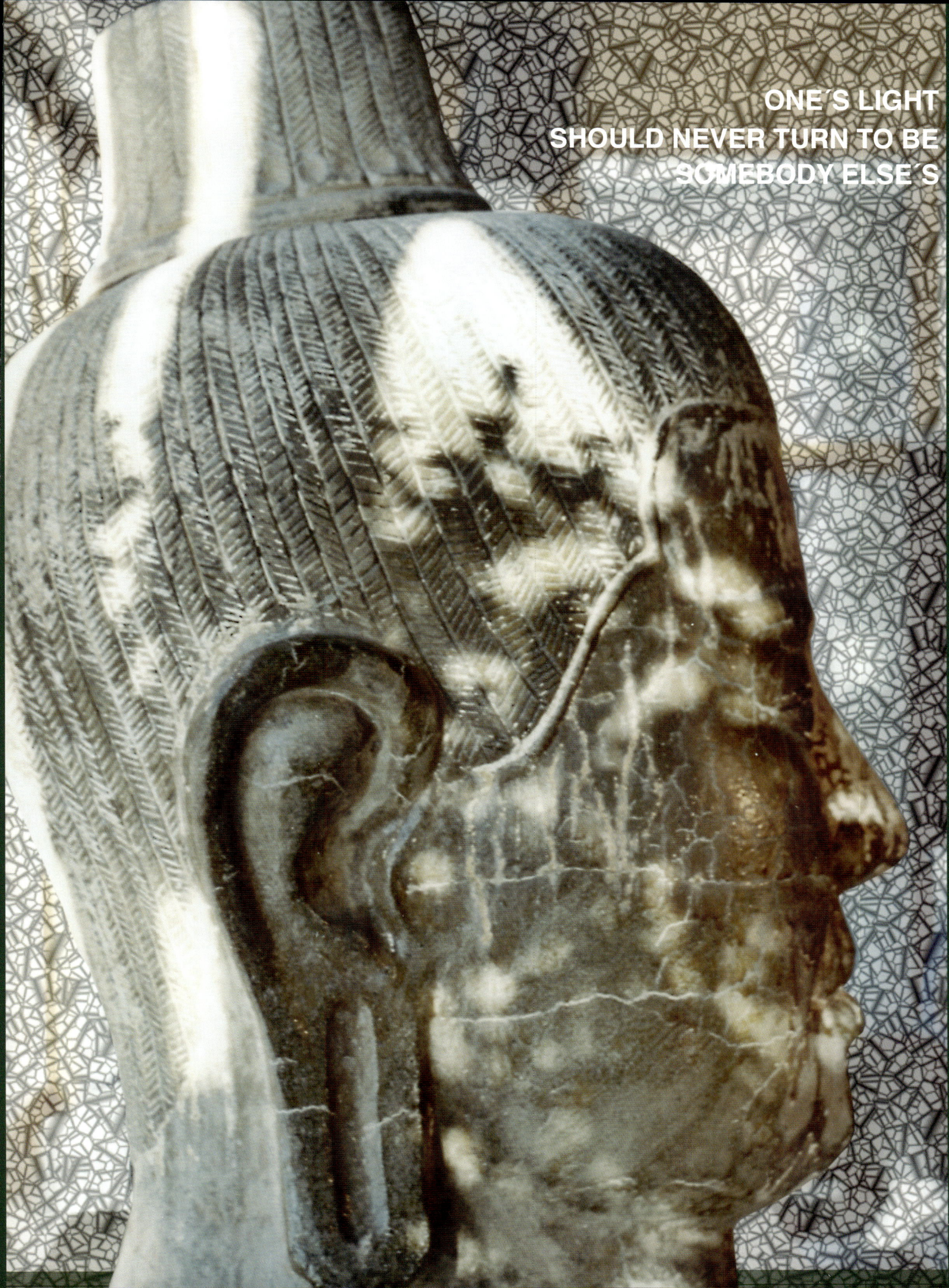

ONE´S LIGHT
SHOULD NEVER TURN TO BE
SOMEBODY ELSE´S SHADOW

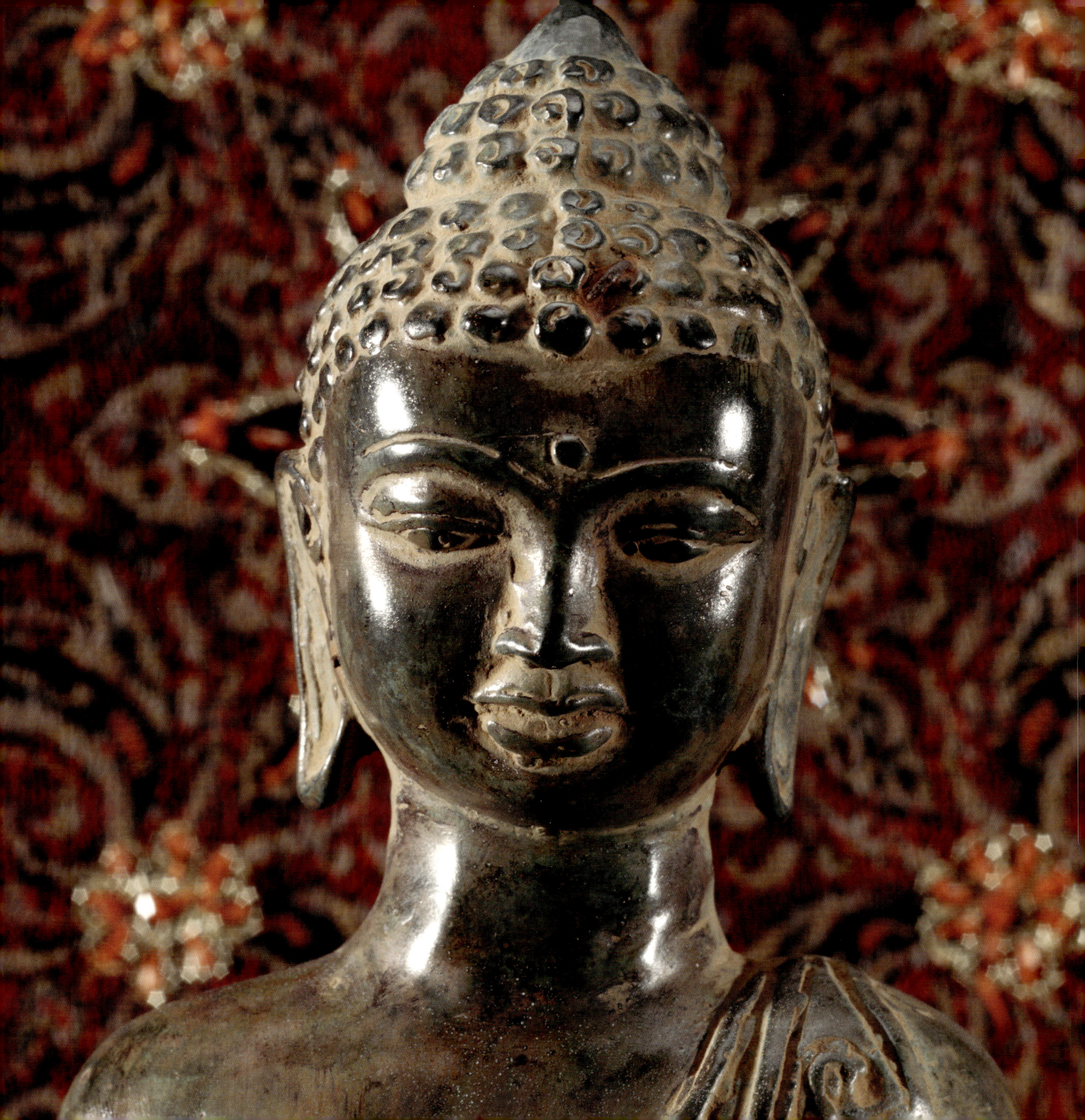

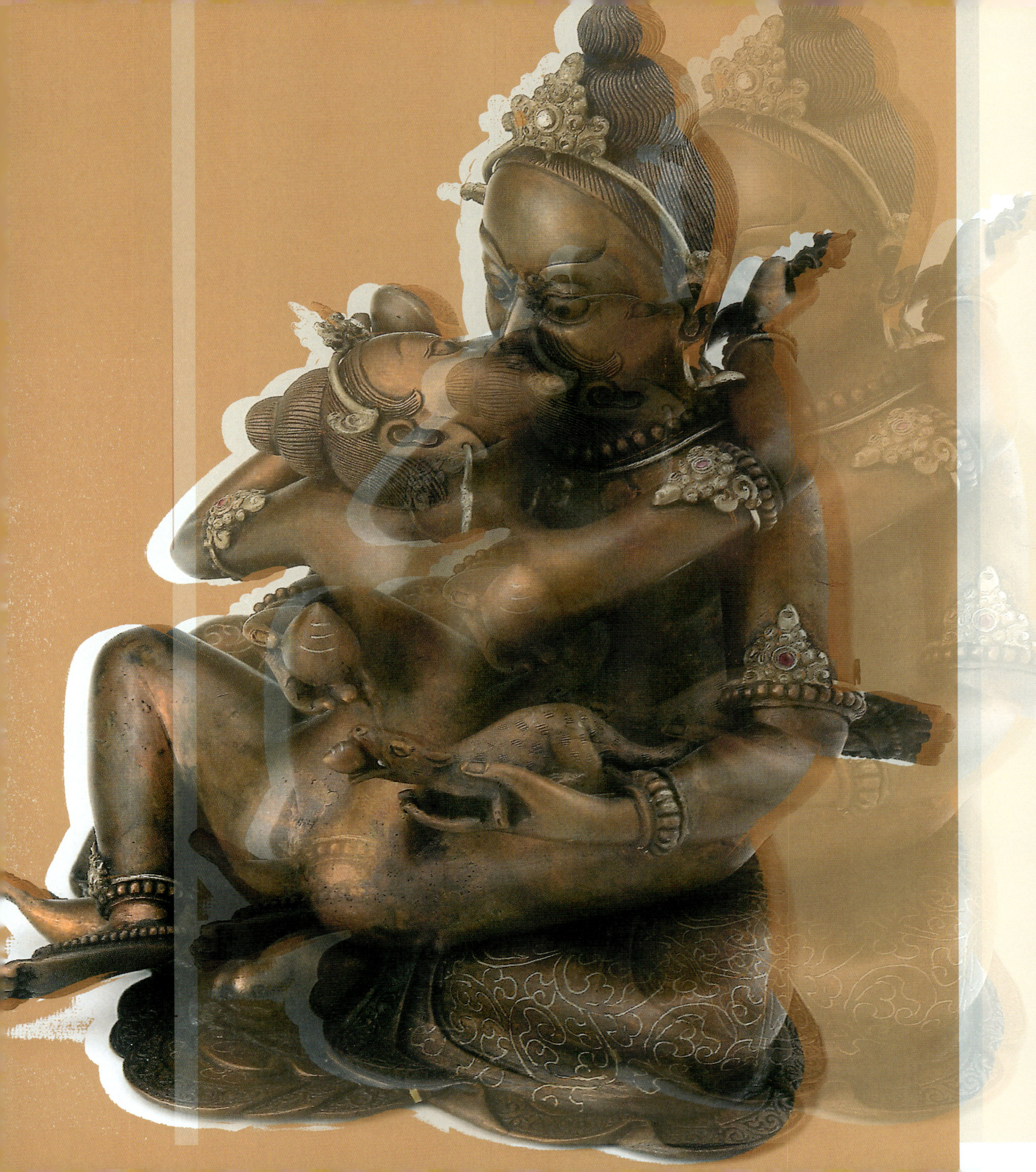

to really love is to know

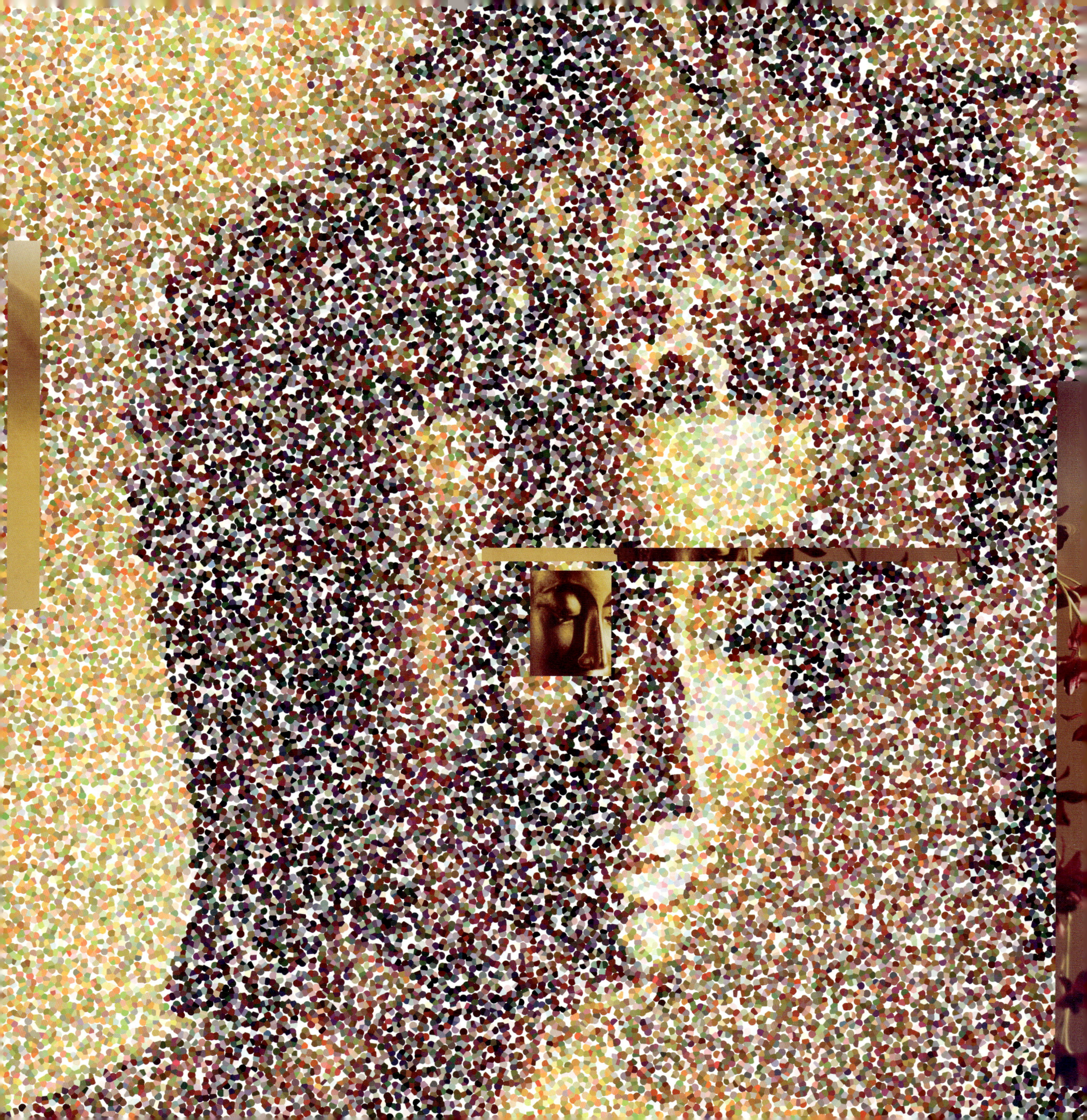

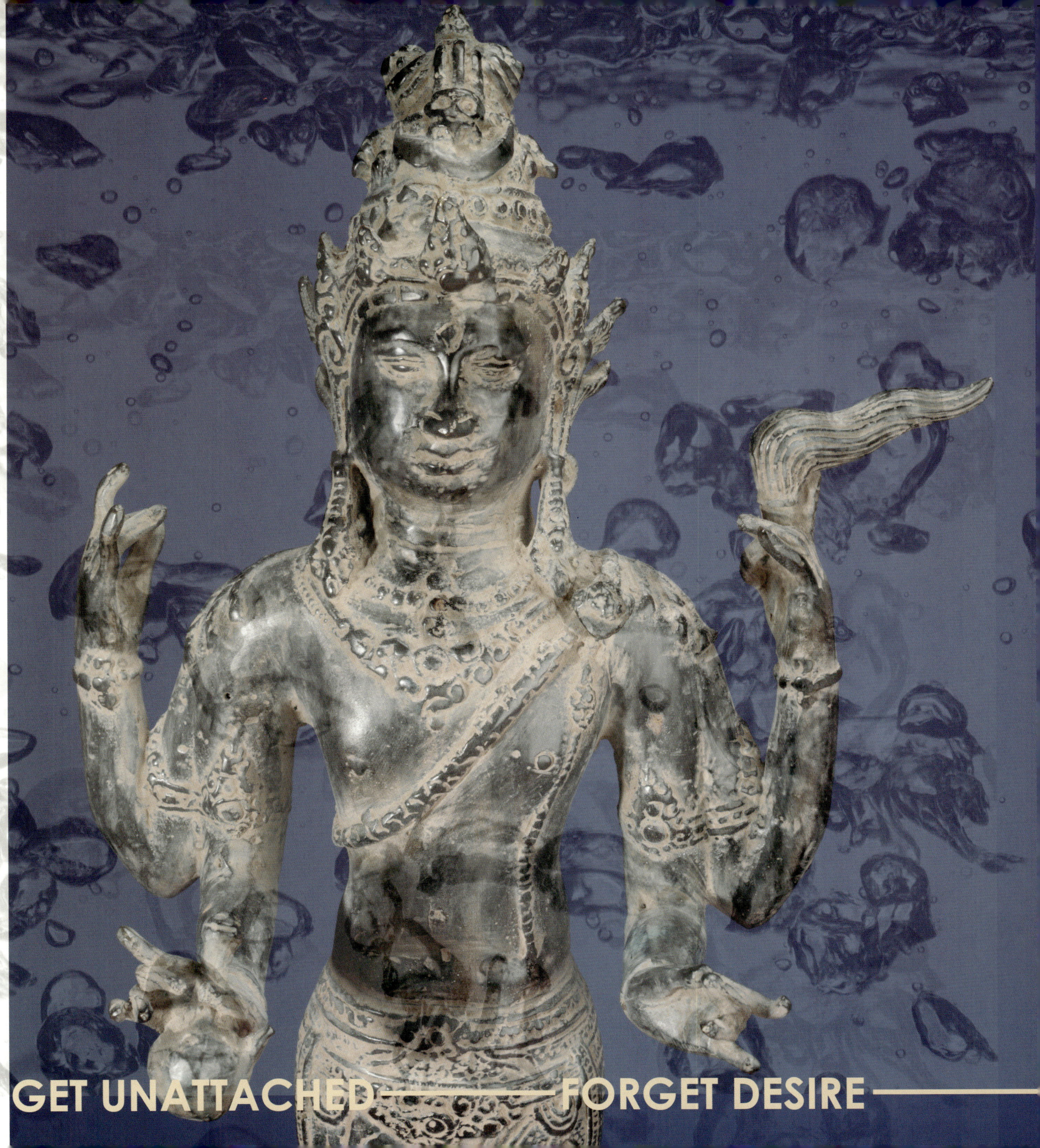
GET UNATTACHED
FORGET DESIRE

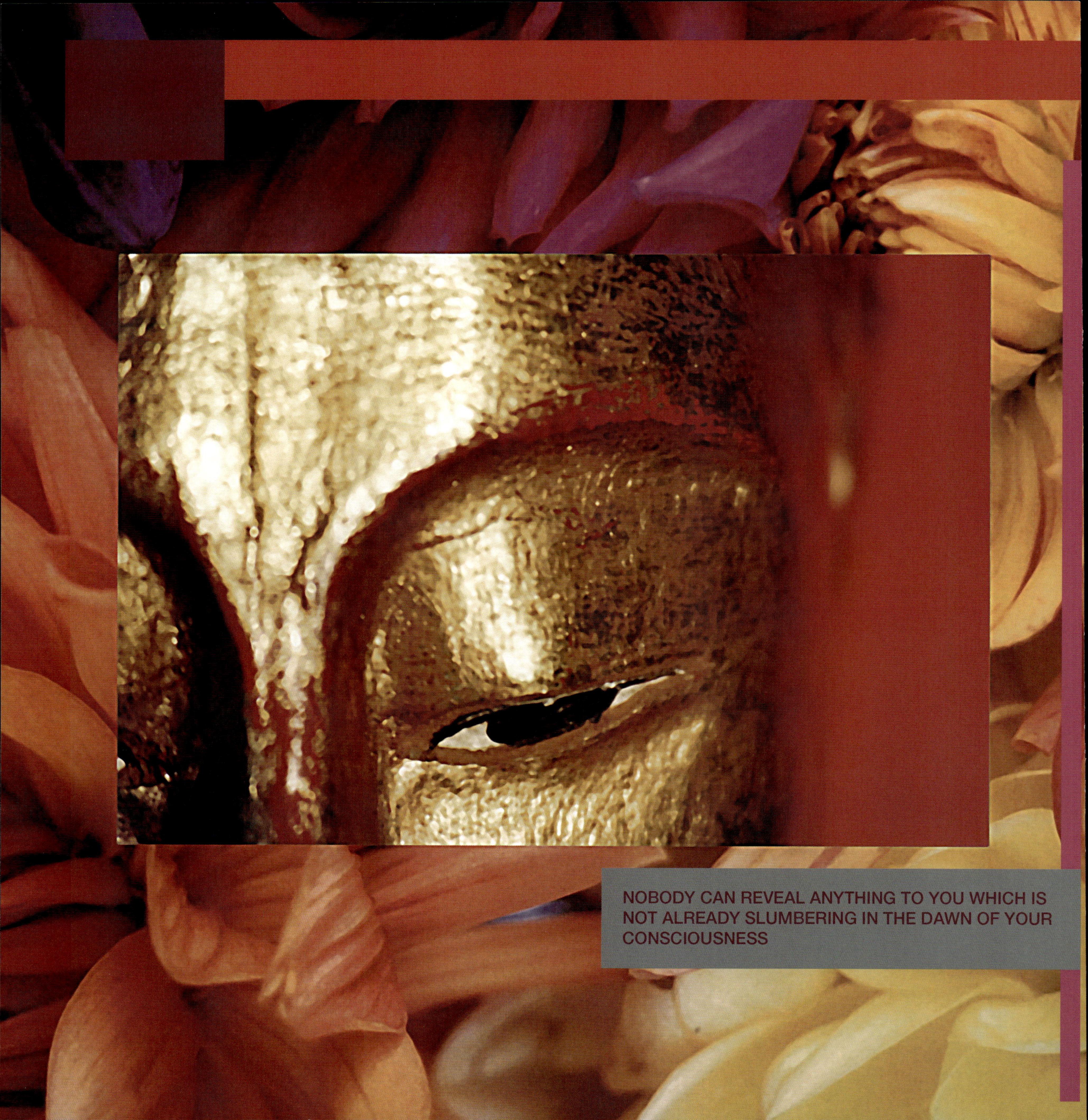

NOBODY CAN REVEAL ANYTHING TO YOU WHICH IS NOT ALREADY SLUMBERING IN THE DAWN OF YOUR CONSCIOUSNESS

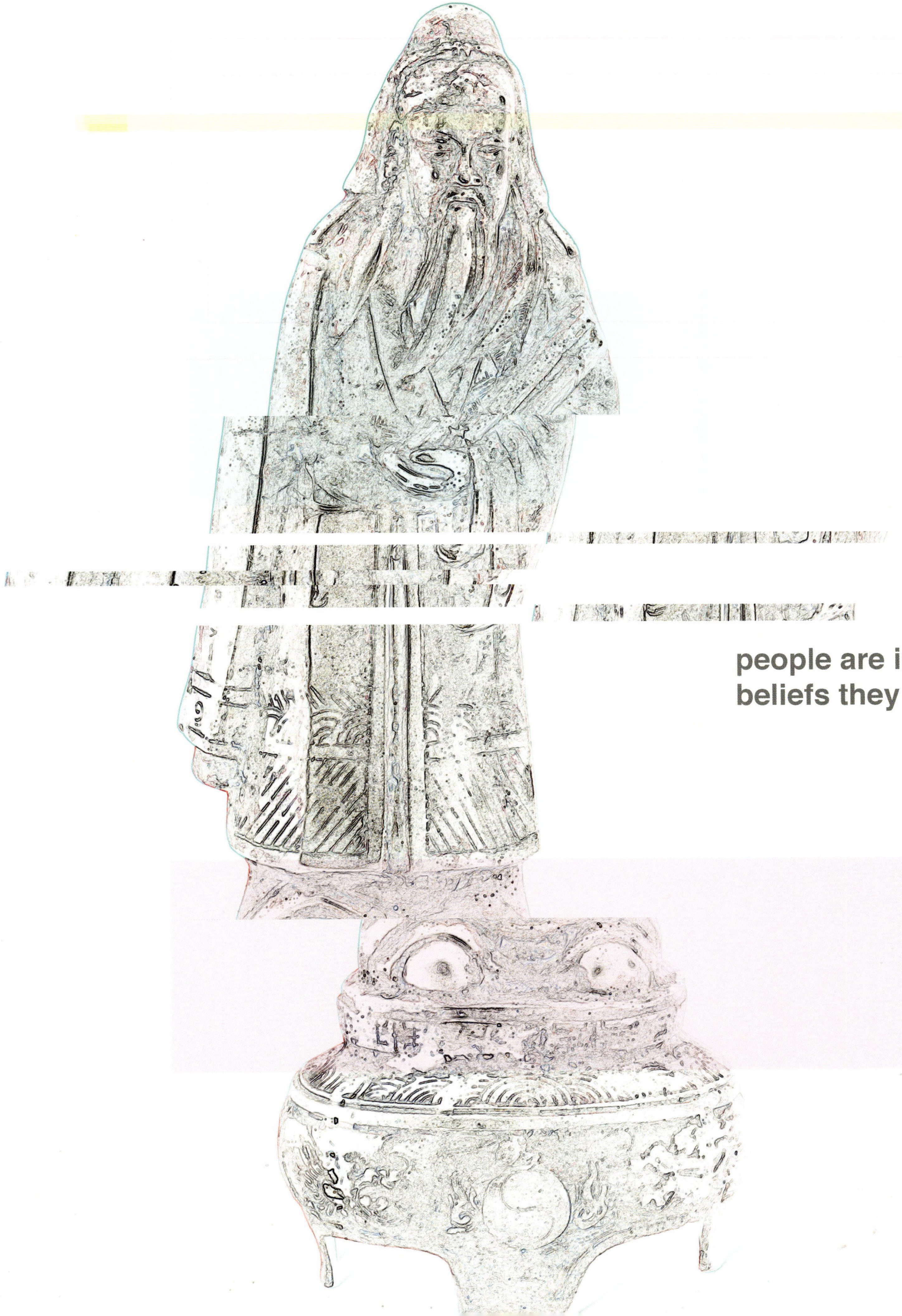

people are in face the total sum of
beliefs they carry in their heart

CD 1

Ray of Gold

Sharion

1 Ray of Gold
2 Ceremony
3 Eclipse
4 Whales
5 The Delta Process
6 Hologram
7 Alpha Wave
8 K2
9 Levitation
10 Timeless
11 The Garden

ISBN 3-937406-14-X

CD 2

Flying Buddha

Akmusique vs Elephant Castle

1 Open Eyes
2 Marmor
3 Red Stone
4 Lunamare
5 Endless Heaven
6 Sand Moon
7 My Makimono
8 Seven Buddhas
9 A Daily Lama
10 Blue Flying Buddha

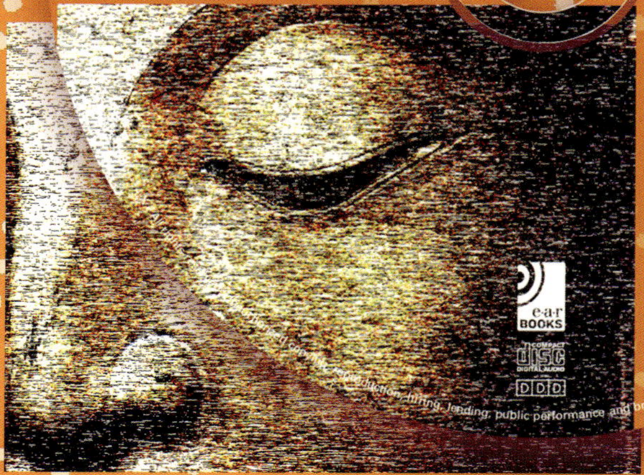

CD1

RAY OF GOLD
SHARION

1	Ray of Gold	5:34
2	Ceremony	4:47
3	Eclipse	6:06
4	Whales	5:50
5	The Delta Process	5:51
6	Hologram	4:51
7	Alpha Wave	7:01
8	K2	4:46
9	Levitation	5:40
10	Timeless	5:21
11	The Garden	6:03

All titles composed by Kels/Schaub
All instruments by Reinhard Schaub

CD2

FLYING BUDDHA
AKMUSIQUE VS ELEPHANT CASTLE

1	Open Eyes	4:25
2	Marmor	4:31
3	Red Stone	5:36
4	Lunamare	4:44
5	Endless Heaven	4:29
6	Sand Moon	5:11
7	My Makimono	5:45
8	Seven Buddhas	8:08
9	A Daily Lama	6:57
10	Blue Flying Buddha	7:27

1-6 composed by Heinrich/Kels · 7-10 composed by Kels/Kolinski
1-6 Keyboards and programming: Tim Heinrich
7-10 Keyboards and programming: Andreas Kolinski
1 voc: Alexandra Schacht
2 voc: Susann Teutenberg
4 voc: Sandra Batkowski
2+4+6 git: Martin Gorenz
8-10 git: Markus Segschneider

For all 4 CDs: All titles published by REVILO MV - (P) 2004 edel CLASSICS GmbH - With kind permission of Olli Kels Music

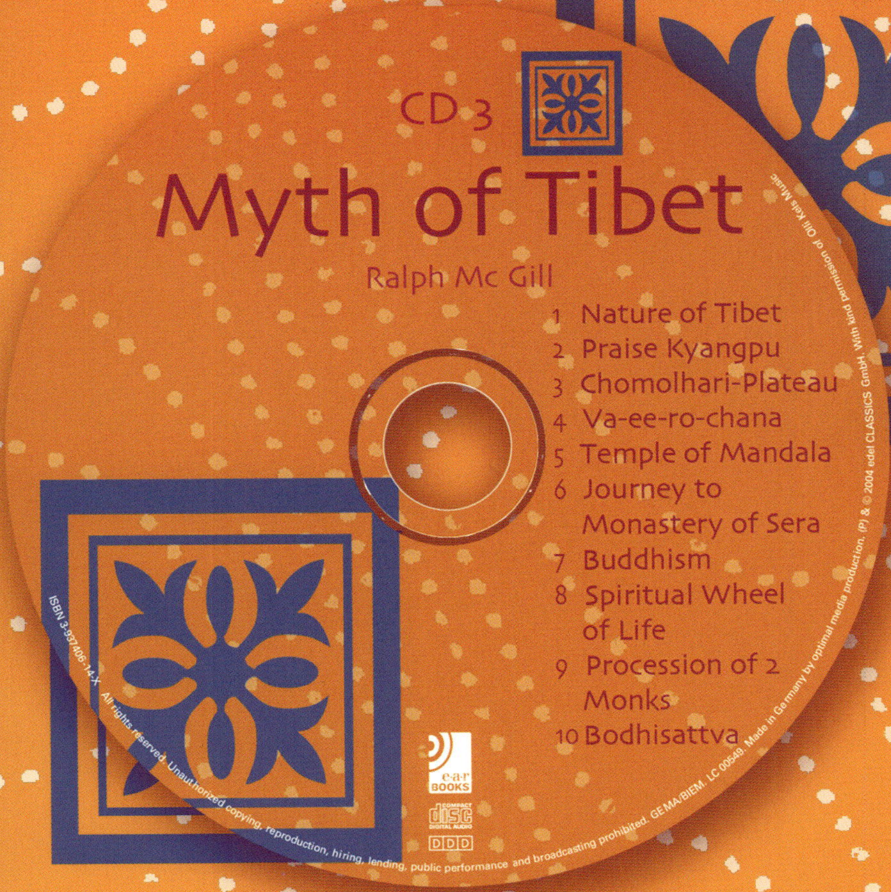

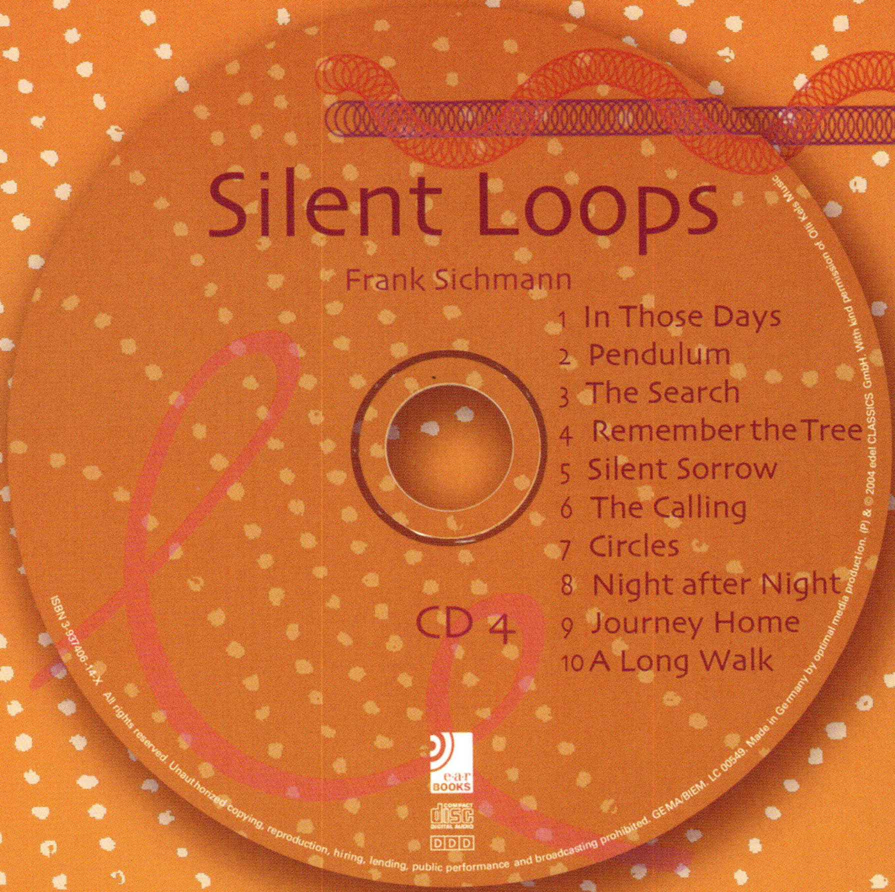

CD3

MYTH OF TIBET
RALV McGILL

1	Nature of Tibet	6:44
2	Praise Kyangpu	5:32
3	Chomolhari-Plateau	6:08
4	Va-ee-ro-chana	6:31
5	Temple of Mandala	5:21
6	Journey to Monastery of Sera	6:20
7	Buddhism	6:33
8	Spiritual Wheel of Life	5:30
9	Procession of 2 Monks	3:52
10	Bodhisattva	7:24

All titles composed by Kels/McGill
All instruments by Ralv McGill

CD4

SILENT LOOPS
FRANK SICHMANN

1	In Those Days	6:15
2	Pendulum	5:02
3	The Search	3:30
4	Remember the Tree	6:26
5	Silent Sorrow	5:49
6	The Calling	8:33
7	Circles	11:28
8	Night After Night	3:43
9	Journey Home	4:30
10	A Long Walk	10:12

All titles composed by Kels/Sichmann
All instruments by Frank Sichmann

Thanks to everybody who encouraged, enabled and supported me in this project

Nils, Felix, Justus, Benjamin, Thomas
Barbara, Christian, Judica, Kamilla

Special thanks to Michael who made this possible

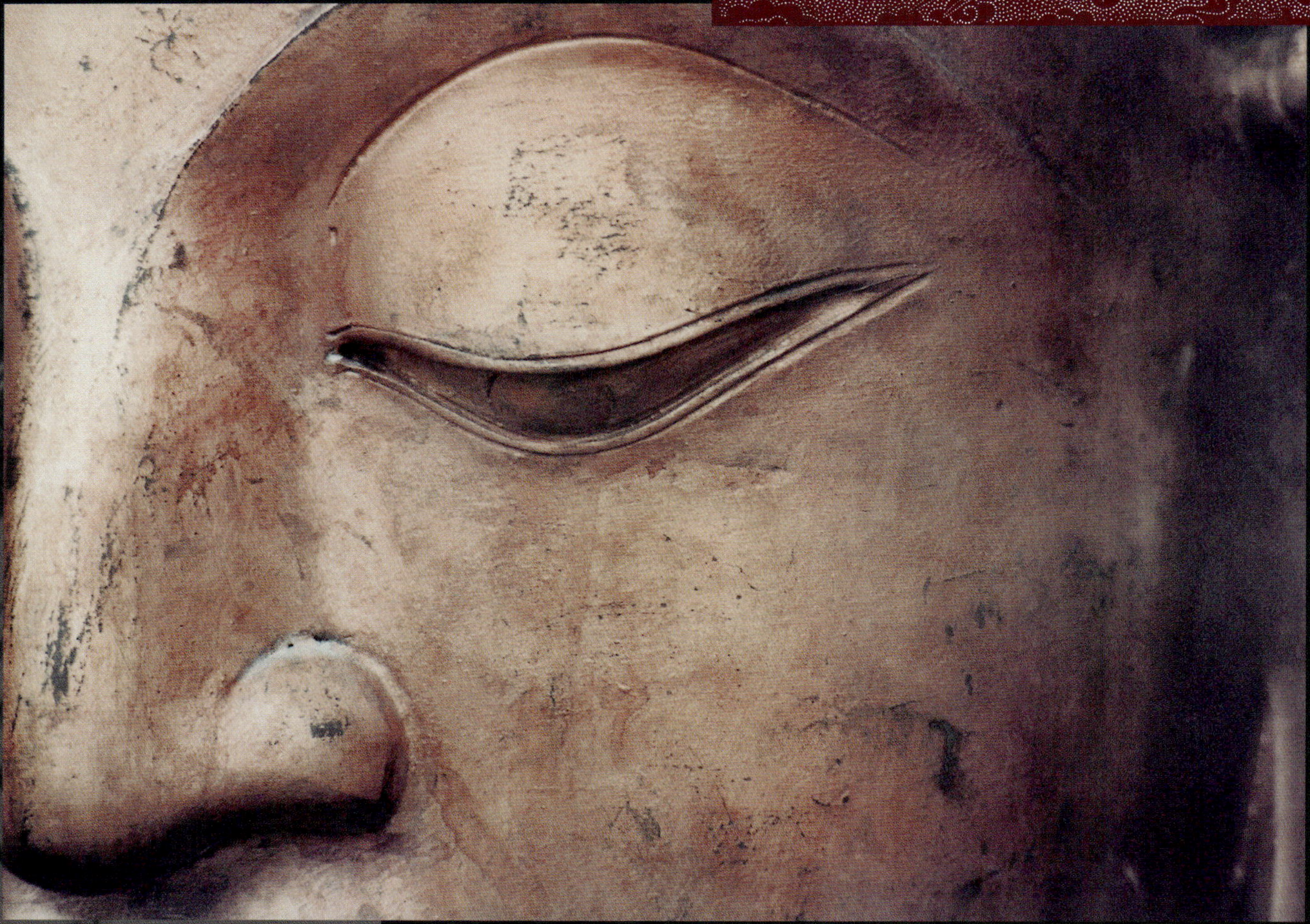

Thanks to the INDOCHINE RESTAURANT, Hamburg